# Luther's Last Battles

*Politics and Polemics, 1531–46*

Mark U. Edwards, Jr.

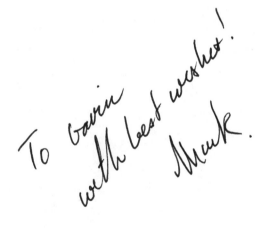

## CORNELL UNIVERSITY PRESS

ITHACA AND LONDON

First published 1983 by Cornell University Press.
Second printing, 1986.
First printing, Cornell Paperbacks, 1986.

International Standard Book Number 0-8014-1564-0 (cloth)
International Standard Book Number 0-8014-9393-5 (paper)
Library of Congress Catalog Card Number 82-72363
Printed in the United States of America
*Librarians: Library of Congress cataloging information appears
on the last page of the book.*

*The paper in this book is acid-free and meets the guidelines for permanence
and durability of the Committee on Production Guidelines for
Book Longevity of the Council on Library Resources.*

# LUTHER'S LAST BATTLES

*To Mom and Dad, Muetti and Pappi,*
*and in memory of Hans Richner*

# Contents

# Illustrations

# Preface

Showing great fortitude and generosity, a number of friends and colleagues have suffered through some very rough drafts of this book and assisted me greatly with their comments. I especially thank John Contreni, Scott Hendrix, Robert Kolb, Steven Ozment, Paul Santmire, Ian Siggins, Lewis Spitz, and David Steinmetz. Steven Rowan kindly directed me to some of the material discussed in chapter six. I also thank the members of the Greater Boston Area Reformation Colloquium, who helped me with their comments at a very early stage of my research when I particularly needed advice. My former colleagues in the history department at Wellesley College urged me to write for a audience wider than Luther specialists. I thank them for the moral suasion they exerted, and apologize if their efforts were only partially successful. I also thank a number of my colleagues at Purdue, all stalwart members of Gibbon, for their constructive criticism: Lester Cohen, Charles Ingrao, James Oakes, Linda Peck, William Stueck, Philip VanderMeer, Regina Wolkoff, and Lamont Yeakey. Lester Cohen, John Contreni, and Linda Peck offered invaluable help during the final stages of revision. Wellesley College assisted me with various grants and with a year's leave under its enlightened "Early Leave" policy for junior faculty. Purdue University, and especially Don Berthrong and Joyce Good, provided the time and support necessary to complete the manuscript and prepare it for publication. Without such assistance this book would have been much delayed.

Scholarship in the sixteenth century was greatly aided by the printing press. Today it is the computer that is changing the way scholars work. This book was composed on a computer, edited on a computer, and typeset by a computer. For their assistance I owe thanks to the computer staffs at Wellesley and Purdue, and particularly to Gene Ott, Lorraine Keating, Bill Bormann, George Goble, Andy Hughes, Steve Mahler, Tom Putnam, and George Wyncott. With great cheerfulness Laurette Hupman did the final editing under an unbelievably tight schedule. The staff at Cornell University Press, and especially Lawrence Malley, were remarkably supportive of this venture. They have made it possible for me to boast that *all* errors in this book, even typesetting errors, are my own.

Elizabeth Spilman Rosenfield made helpful editorial suggestions at several stages in the writing of this book. I owe to her the love of good writing. I only wish I could meet her high standards!

I dedicate this book to my parents both here and in Switzerland. In 1963 my father, Mark U. Edwards, and my mother, Margaret Newsom Edwards, sent, with some trepidation, their seventeen-year-old eldest son to spend a year in Switzerland as an American Field Service exchange student. To their relief they soon realized that Hermann and Annalis Richner, my Swiss exchange parents, had their youngster well in hand. Without the love, support, and encouragement of both sets of parents, I would never have become a historian of the German Reformation.

While I was still working on this book, both my families suffered a staggering blow. My Swiss brother, Hans Richner, had been studying to become a historian of Latin America, when he was stricken with leukemia. With his tragic death in 1979 I lost a brother and the world lost a scholar of great promise. I also wish with this book to honor his memory.

Unless otherwise indicated, all translations are my own.

M.U.E.

*June, 1982*
*West Lafayette, Indiana*

# LUTHER'S LAST BATTLES

# Introduction

Martin Luther was thirty-four years old when his Ninety-Five Theses swept the German Nation. He was thirty-seven when he was excommunicated by the Roman Catholic church, forty-one when he married the former nun Katharina von Bora, and forty-six when the Augsburg Confession was read to the Imperial Diet. On 10 November 1530 he turned forty-seven, and already behind him were his "breakthrough" to Reformation theology, his rejection of the Roman Catholic church, the Peasants' War, the major battles of the Sacramentarian controversy, and the submission of the Augsburg Confession. Although the vast majority of historical studies of Luther deal exclusively with the events through 1530, Luther did not die at the closing of the Imperial Diet of Augsburg. On the contrary, after living another fifteen years—a period longer than the hectic span from 1517 to 1530—he died of heart failure on 18 February 1546, sixty-two years old.

There are reasons for the relative neglect of the older Luther. Since World War One, when the revolution in theology was brought on by Karl Barth, among many others, most research on Luther has been done by theologians, who often seek in him insights to enrich contemporary theology. In this quest their most fruitful source has been the young Luther, who gradually broke away from medieval Catholicism and who, in a struggle easily seen as heroic, hammered out a new understanding of the Christian faith. In contrast, the older Luther's theology is thought to differ little from that of the younger and, in its lack of development and perhaps in its greater dogmatic rigidity, to be less interesting and suggestive.[1]

Among biographers and historians the neglect of the older Luther is more difficult to explain. Of course there is something intrinsically fascinating about the younger Luther. Here was a monk and university professor who on the basis of conviction and conscience successfully defied two of the great institutions of his age: the Roman Catholic Church and the Holy Roman Empire. If modern scholars shy away from the simplistic picture of the "heroic Luther" found in earlier Protestant hagiography, they still find much to admire in the anxious professor and unwilling heretic. In contrast, the older Luther appears to be something of a problem.

The problem is not that the older Reformer was inactive.[2] Despite ill health, Luther was involved in many activities during these last fifteen years. In his home in the Wittenberg Black Cloister he was the center of attention and was surrounded by wife, children, students, friends, and guests. Three of his six children were born during these later years: Martin in 1531, Paul in 1533, and Margarete in 1534. They joined Hans, born in 1526, and Magdalene, born in 1529. The Luthers' sixth child, Elizabeth, had died in 1527, when less than a year old. Living with Luther, his wife Kathie, and their children were several orphaned relatives, a varying crew of student boarders, and frequent long- and short-term guests. At meals, various students and guests assiduously copied down all Luther's utterances, preserving a vast wealth of obiter dicta for posterity. From these remarks, and from his voluminous correspondence and the observations of friends and guests, there emerges a picture of Luther as a devoted, often tender-hearted father, a loving, teasing, and sometimes irritable husband, a man of strong friendships, and a compassionate pastor and counselor.

Luther also continued his labors at the University of Wittenberg. In 1531 he presented a series of lectures on Galatians. Then from time to time he lectured on selected Psalms. Beginning in 1535, he undertook to expound the book of Genesis, a labor that occupied him until 1545. He also participated in the reform of the theological faculty in 1533 and in the reorganization of the university curriculum in 1536. He frequently took part in disputations, which were reinstituted during this period after a hiatus of over ten years. In 1535 he became dean of the university, a position he held for the rest of his life. Many hours were spent in training students for the ministry and placing them in parishes. He also served his university and community as pastor and preacher. For extended periods he substituted in the pulpit for Johann Bugenhagen, who was away helping introduce the Reformation into various North German cities and territories.

For years Luther and his coworkers had labored on a German translation of the Old Testament, publishing their efforts a part at a time. In 1531 they completed a revision of the Psalms, in 1532 a

German edition of all the Prophets, in 1533 various other books. Finally, in 1534, the full German Bible appeared. Beginning in 1539, they undertook a revision of the whole translation, which was published in 1541. In 1544 they began to revise the Pauline letters, a revision that first appeared in 1546, after Luther's death.

Clearly, the older Luther remained intensely involved in academic, pastoral, and familial activities. But Luther was also very much concerned in these later years with affairs beyond Wittenberg. Through written opinions and published treatises he participated fully in several bitter controversies. It is this activity, and especially his published polemics, that historians find most difficult to explain and integrate into their overall view of Luther. In some of the treatises Luther apparently retreated from positions of principle established earlier in his career. In others he contributed to disputes that seem so petty or mundane as to be unworthy of a man of his religious stature. And some of the later polemics were so violent and vulgar that they offended contemporaries and remain offensive to this day.

In the last five or six years of his life, for example, Luther published violent attacks on Catholics, Turks, Jews, and other Protestants. By far the most notorious of these polemics are his attacks on the Jews, especially his *On the Jews and Their Lies* and his *On the Ineffable Name and on Christ's Lineage,* both of 1543. These treatises contain considerable exegesis of the Old Testament, but exegetical passages are overshadowed by the pervasive vulgarity of Luther's language and by the incredibly harsh recommendations he offered for the treatment of contemporary Jews. Their synagogues and schools should be burned, their homes destroyed, their books seized, their rabbis forbidden to teach, their money taken away from them. They should be put to work in the fields or, better yet, expelled from Germany. Even contemporary Protestants were shocked by these writings. Rivaling his anti-Jewish treatises for vulgarity and violence of expression is *Against Hanswurst* of 1541, Luther's contribution to a gutter fight between the Catholic Duke Heinrich of Braunschweig-Wolfenbüttel on the one side and the Protestant Landgrave Philipp of Hesse and Elector Johann Friedrich of Saxony on the other. Luther outdid even the violence and vulgarity of *Against Hanswurst* in his 1545 *Against the Papacy at Rome, Founded by the Devil.* On the heels of these treatises he published a series of scatological and violent woodcuts that, in most graphic terms, suggested how good Christians should treat the papacy. In these and other treatises Luther bestialized his opponents, most frequently likening them to pigs or asses, or called them liars, murderers, and hypocrites. They were all minions of the devil. He directed the devil to his ass, he renamed the papal decretals "decraptals" [*Drecketalen*], and the Farnese pope "Fart-ass" [*fartz Esel*] and "Her Sodomitical Hellishness Paula III," and he threw around words for excrement with great abandon. And in the woodcuts by Lucas Cranach commissioned by Luther near the end of his life, he had the papal church depicted as being expelled from the anus of an enormous she-devil and suggested, once again in picture, that the pope, cardinals, and bishops should be hung from gallows with their tongues nailed alongside.

Not all of his later polemics were vulgar, but many had strong political overtones, and so raise the question whether religious principle was occasionally being subordinated to politics. By the late 1520s most of the leaders of the Protestant estates were prepared to use armed force to defend their faith even against an imperially led attack. In *Warning to His Dear German People* (1531) and *Concerning the Three Hierarchies* (1539) Luther appeared to sustain the ruler's decision, even though in earlier years he had most adamantly rejected armed resistance to the emperor in defense of faith. In the 1530s the Protestant rulers also decided to reject out of hand a papal invitation to a general council of the church, although for years they and Luther had called for a council. Although Luther disagreed with their decision, he was given the task of discrediting the council called by the pope and justifying the Protestant refusal to participate in it. He was also given the task of justifying in print the seizure of the bishopric of Naumburg by Elector Johann Friedrich, and he defended and applauded the two offensives of the League of Schmalkalden against Braunschweig-Wolfenbüttel. He also, albeit under the seal of the confessional and while being much misled by Landgrave Philipp, advised the landgrave to commit bigamy, and, when rumors of the second marriage began circulating, Luther urged the landgrave to reply to inquiries with "a big, fat lie." He was much criticized at the time for many of these activities and publications, which have cast a shadow over the older Luther's reputation to this day.

Scholars have tended to look for the explanation of these polemics within Luther himself: in his theology, in his apocalyptic world view, or in his ill health and age.[3] And because he seldom acted without a theological rationale, scholars have tended also to explore the theological content of his polemics and evaluate his theology chiefly in terms of its consistency with earlier thought and its cogency within his overall theology. Excesses of language and argument that cannot be explained by his theology or by his apocalyptic world view are generally attributed to ill health and the effects of aging.

For all its cogency and usefulness, however, this approach to Luther's polemics is not without its shortcomings. First, it tends to overestimate Luther's independence and underestimate the extent to which he was constrained by forces beyond his control. He did not always initiate his own polemics. The stance he took, the issues he discussed, indeed the very tenor of the disputes were frequently set by others before he ever picked up his pen. Second, the conventional approach tends to highlight the theological component of the polemics and underestimate the secular aspects, as well as the rhetorical effect on readers of Luther's forceful language and arguments. Finally, traditional analyses fail to consider the varying meanings a polemic may have had for different readers, such as Protestant rulers, Protestant laity, and opponents. Instead it is mistakenly assumed that the meaning of a polemic is determined by Luther's explicit intentions and theological arguments.

At the heart of this book rests the conviction that much modern scholarship on Luther effectively diminishes both his humanity and the context in which he wrote. It is only as we enlarge our view to consider the changed character of the Reformation movement by the late 1520s, the new pressures impinging on Luther, and the severely limited alternatives that he faced, that we can fairly judge the polemics of his later years. To view Luther entangled within his net of time and circumstance is to transcend the need to accuse or to excuse. It is enough to approach a firmer understanding.

## CHAPTER ONE

# Anger and Illness

The harshness of Luther's later polemics was not a new element in his work and thought. His polemics were angry and abusive from the beginning. By his own admission, he was an angry man. Anger was his special sin.[1] But anger could also be necessary and proper— and useful.[2] It helped him, he said, to write well, to pray, and to preach. "Anger refreshes all my blood, sharpens my mind, and drives away temptations," he once commented.[3]

But Luther's anger and his abuse of opponents could also spark criticism, and did so from the very beginning of the Reformation. In August 1520, for example, Luther acknowledged that "nearly every-one condemns my mordancy."[4] And in his famous appearance before the Diet of Worms in 1521 he admitted that in some of his writings he had been sharper than befitted a monk and professor.[5] In later years he often acknowledged that some were offended by his harsh-ness and anger.[6] But he had an explanation: "I was born to war with fanatics and devils," he wrote in 1529. "Thus my books are very stormy and bellicose. I must root out the stumps and trunks, hew away the thorns and briar, fill in the puddles. I am the coarse woodsman, who must pioneer and hew a path."[7]

This explanation is, of course, self-serving, but there is also much truth in it. Luther was a pioneer who used his angry pen to blaze a way and open a path for others. A man of equal theological genius but of another temperament might have broken with the Roman Catholic church with less violence and name-calling. It should be pointed out, however, that Luther's colleague, Philip Melanchthon, a man of such temperament, although not as profound a theologian, believed that the times had required a man of Luther's harshness.[8] In any case, Luther's polemical skills from the beginning played a vital role in mobilizing support for his Reformation insights and program.

A reading of Luther's polemical corpus does leave the distinct impression that in his later years his anger became more shrill, and less leavened by compassion, humor, or even theological reflection. Moreover, his always pungent language became more coarse and scatological. The targets of his ire become under his pen the vilest of hypocrites, totally wicked and insincere, willing minions of the devil, deserving the most horrible fate.

The trend toward greater harshness was relatively gradual and extended over a number of years (see Figure 1).[9] The issue, really, is not Luther's anger *per se* but, first, whether illness and old age exacerbated this characteristic of his personality to the point that they can be said to account for the polemical excesses of the later years, and, second, whether such a judgment exhausts the historic significance of the polemics. The rest of this chapter will explore this question. This coverage should clear the way for other considerations regarding Luther's polemics, considerations of political pressure, available alternatives, contemporary context, and the power of apocalyptic.

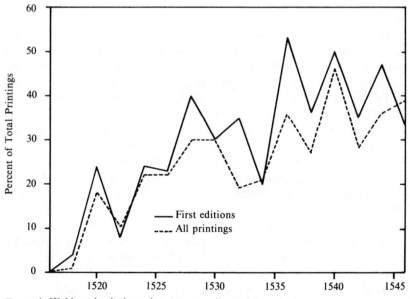

*Figure 1.* Highly polemical treatises (two-year intervals)

When the issue is dealt with at all, scholars have not hesitated to attribute the polemical excesses of the older Luther to ill health and aging. The older Luther is seen as overly coarse, abusive, and verbose because he was a sick, depressed, and perhaps even slightly senile old man.[10] For some this is an attractive interpretation. One tends to be more tolerant of the foibles of the sick and the old, attributing normally unacceptable behavior to the effects of illness or of age, rather than to the individual himself. In Luther's particular case, his later ill health and its disconcerting effects can be attributed to the austerities he practiced while a monk. Even the often astonishing anger and vulgarity of his later years can be seen as a regrettable but quite understandable product of his attempt as a monk to merit his salvation. In other words, this interpretation may serve to exculpate from responsibility for later excesses the "real" (that is, the younger) Luther, his theology, and the Reformation movement he initiated.

For some, then, the excesses and distortions caused by ill health and aging appear late in Luther's career to pervert or distort the often admirable qualities of the younger theological genius. A few investigators, however, see the perverse qualities as being *always* present. These qualities, they suggest, may even lie at the heart of Luther's original break with Rome. For writers such as Hartmann Grisar, Paul Reiter, and, following them with some modification, Erik Erikson, the Reformation from its beginning was the product of a psychologically as well as physically sick man.[11]

It is obvious to anyone familiar with the younger Luther and his accomplishments that the diagnosis of mental illness does little if anything to advance historical understanding. Few would deny that the younger Luther's psyche was unusual. On the contrary, it would be difficult indeed to account for his struggle for the right understanding of justification or for his steadfast defense of his insight in the face of papal and imperial disapproval without acknowledging that Luther was scrupulous and tenacious to a highly unusual, even abnormal degree. But could it be otherwise? A "normal" man would likely have accepted the assurances of such a gifted confessor as Johann Staupitz and not have continued to bang his head against the words "the righteous of God." A "normal" man would likely have compromised at some point when the powers of church and state were arrayed against him. A "normal" man, in other words, would perhaps have initiated a reform, but would not have unleashed the Reformation.

Most scholars freely concede the unusual and perhaps even abnormal aspects of Luther's personality, without, of course, accepting the diagnosis that attributes these traits to an underlying psychosis. By most standards, the younger Luther *was* a neurotic man. Given all the evidence of productivity, clarity of thought, and ability to work with others, however, it is highly doubtful that he can be properly diagnosed as psychotic.[12]

## Luther's Physical Health

Throughout his career as a reformer Luther often was not well. He was sick during his appearance before the Diet of Worms in 1521, and he complained of severe constipation during his stay on the Wartburg. In subsequent years he suffered from frequent headaches and dizziness. In 1525 he complained of hemorrhoids, and in 1527 of heart congestion, which, he claimed, nearly killed him. 1527 also saw several fainting spells. In 1529 he labored under spells of dizziness and roaring in the ears. It was also during the second half of the decade that one first hears of an open, flowing ulcer on his leg, which his doctors made strenuous efforts to keep open, believing that this allowed the noxious humors to drain off.

The years 1531 to 1546 saw more frequent and more serious illness. In January 1532 he took to bed with a ringing in his ears followed by "weakness of his heart." About this same time he suffered the first symptoms of his uric acid stones, which were to cause him agony during much of the rest of his life. In the spring of 1536 he suffered from the "stone," and in February and March 1537, while at the meeting of the League of Schmalkalden, he experienced the most severe stone attack of his life, an attack that included vomiting and diarrhea, the passing of numerous calculi, and eight days of complete inability to urinate. He barely survived. In November 1537 stone attacks recurred, as they did again in the summer of 1538, in April 1539, July 1541, August 1543, October 1544, and June 1545.

Also in 1538 he suffered from diarrhea and from pain in his joints, probably arthritis. In early 1540 he complained of excruciating pain in his arm. 1541 was a particularly bad year with a reopening of the ulcer on his leg, an abcess in his throat, an acute middle ear infection, and a spontaneous perforation of his ear drum. In December 1544 he suffered from severe angina. It was a heart attack in February 1546, that ended his life.

A confident diagnosis is difficult over so many centuries, although there have been many recent attempts. The most plausible hypothesis is that Luther suffered from an abnormally high concentration of uric acid in his system which would account for his uric acid stones and probably exacerbate his arthritis. His frequent spells of dizziness, fainting, and roaring in the ears suggest Meniere's syndrome, which is often caused by a severe middle ear infection that impairs the sense of balance. It is known that he suffered an acute ear infection in 1541 and may have had a similar illness in his adolescence. The evidence, however, is far from conclusive.

What might reasonably be concluded from this catalogue of ailments? Spasms caused by stone attacks are among the most painful experiences that one can have. It seems likely that this intense pain together with headaches, dizziness, and probable arthritis aggravated his tendency to give way to anger. His generally poor health, and especially probable arteriosclerosis, with its usual circulation impairment, raises the question of possible senility or at least of reduced intellectual acuity in his later years. High concentration of uric acid in his body may have caused painful gout. Renal damage, with its devastating results, may have been caused by extended retention of urine during the acute stone attack of 1537.[13] Each condition may have exacerbated the other conditions. But how might any of this be verified?

Luther's repeated complaint that his illnesses kept him from his work suggests at least one way to test for the effects of illness and age: how productive was Luther during these later years? This is not, actually, an easy question to answer as there are many confounding factors. But statistics on publications are suggestive.[14]

To begin with, it must be remembered that by almost any standard Luther was enormously productive throughout his life. In 1531 he was ill for 6 months and still produced 180 sermons, wrote at least 100 letters and 15 treatises, lectured on Galatians, and worked on his translation of the Old Testament. And in 1537, when he suffered his most severe and debilitating stone attack, he preached some 90 sermons, lectured, wrote at least 55 letters, and produced some 25 treatises. Many of the treatises of this year were written during his convalescence from the stone attack. By themselves these statistics represent truly remarkable productivity. Only when such figures are compared with Luther's earlier years can the effects of illness and age be assessed.

If attention is turned to 1530 as a plausible dividing line between the younger and the older Luther, it is seen that two-thirds of his first editions and nearly three-quarters of the total printings of his works during his lifetime (excluding his translations of the Bible) issued from the press during the period 1516 to 1530 (see Figures 2 through 6). In the remaining fifteen years of his life, the period 1531 to 1546, Luther produced the remaining third of his original works. Reprints of these and earlier works make up the final quarter of the total printing of his

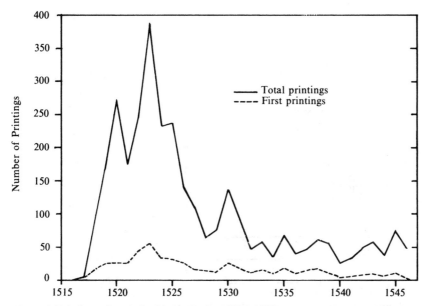

*Figure 2.* Printings of works by Martin Luther, 1516–1546

*Figure 3.* Publication statistics by year

| Year | First editions | Total printings | Year | First editions | Total printings |
|------|------|------|------|------|------|
| 1516 | 1 | 1 | 1531 | 17 | 94 |
| 1517 | 3 | 6 | 1532 | 12 | 46 |
| 1518 | 17 | 87 | 1533 | 16 | 59 |
| 1519 | 25 | 170 | 1534 | 10 | 35 |
| 1520 | 27 | 275 | 1535 | 19 | 68 |
| 1521 | 26 | 174 | 1536 | 10 | 40 |
| 1522 | 45 | 248 | 1537 | 16 | 47 |
| 1523 | 55 | 390 | 1538 | 18 | 62 |
| 1524 | 34 | 232 | 1539 | 12 | 56 |
| 1525 | 32 | 237 | 1540 | 5 | 26 |
| 1526 | 26 | 141 | 1541 | 7 | 34 |
| 1527 | 16 | 110 | 1542 | 9 | 49 |
| 1528 | 15 | 64 | 1543 | 11 | 58 |
| 1529 | 12 | 76 | 1544 | 7 | 38 |
| 1530 | 26 | 138 | 1545 | 12 | 74 |
|  |  |  | 1546 | 3 | 48 |

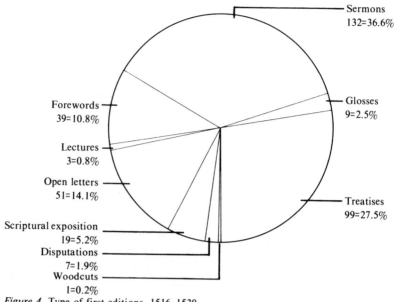

*Figure 4.* Type of first editions, 1516–1530

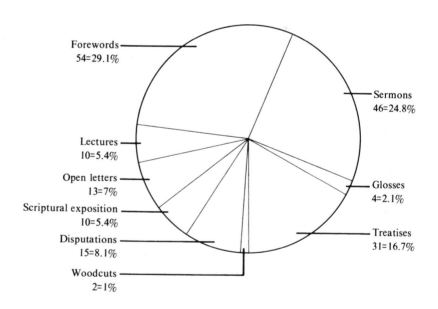

*Figure 5.* Type of first editions, 1531–1546

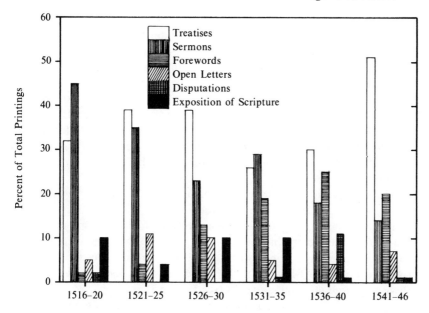

*Figure 6.* Type of publication

works. The decrease in Luther's publishing activity is even more dramatic than these figures suggest since nearly thirty percent of the original publications during the later period are short forewords to the works of others. Only about eleven percent of his original publications in the earlier period are forewords.

As large as this decline was, it must be understood in relation to the prodigious productivity of the earlier period. Excluding Bible translations, some 360 of Luther's original works were printed in the period 1516 to 1530. The latter period saw only 184 original works, a staggering number by any measure.

It must be stressed that the major decline in Luther's productivity came in the late 1520s, years before his most severe illnesses. The year 1523 witnessed the greatest number of first editions of Luther's works (and reprints). The real falloff in publication did not come until after 1525. Note the decline in first editions from the period 1521-1525 to the period 1526-1530: 192 first editions in the earlier period and only 95 first editions in the following period. An examination of the type of work printed in these two crucial periods shows that treatises declined to 56 percent of their previous total, sermons to 30 percent, and open letters to 39 percent. Only forewords grew to 157 percent of their earlier level—a sign, perhaps, that new or younger men were at work in the vineyard. It is also worth noting that almost twice as many sermons as treatises were published in the period 1521-1525 while their numbers were roughly equal in the period 1526-1530. Was the first, major pastoral work accomplished by this time? Were Germans receiving more of their sermonic sustenance from local Protestant pastors? Or had interest simply waned? It seems more likely, in any case, that the sharp decline in the second half of the 1520s may be more plausibly explained by the development of the Reformation beyond Martin Luther, or by effects of the Peasants' War, or by changes in the printing industry rather than by changes in Luther's health.[15]

The decline in the number of original publications during the last fifteen years of Luther's life was very gradual with no sharp discontinuity in, say, 1537, that might point to the effects of renal failure or the onset of acute senility or manic-depressive psychosis. From 1531 to 1535 some 74 original works appeared, from 1536 to 1540 the figure dropped to 61, and in the last five years, 1541 to early 1546, there appeared 49 original works (see Figure 7).

It seems likely that aging and ill health played some role in the gradual decline during the last fifteen years of Luther's life. The

*Figure 7.* First editions by five-year intervals: Literary type (In parentheses: *rounded-off* percentage of total for each period)

| Period: | 1516–1520 | 1521–1525 | 1526–1530 | 1531–1535 | 1536–1540 | 1541–1546 |
|---|---|---|---|---|---|---|
| Treatise | 29 | 45 | 25 | 7 | 11 | 13 |
| | (40%) | (23%) | (26%) | (10%) | (18%) | (27%) |
| Sermon(s) | 23 | 84 | 25 | 25 | 12 | 9 |
| | (36%) | (44%) | (26%) | (34%) | (20%) | (18%) |
| Foreword | 3 | 14 | 22 | 24 | 17 | 13 |
| | ( 4%) | ( 7%) | (23%) | (32%) | (28%) | (27%) |
| Lectures | 2 | 0 | 1 | 3 | 6 | 1 |
| | ( 3%) | ( 0%) | ( 1%) | ( 4%) | (10%) | ( 2%) |
| Published letter | 5 | 33 | 13 | 5 | 3 | 5 |
| | ( 7%) | (17%) | (14%) | ( 7%) | ( 5%) | (10%) |
| Biblical exposition | 5 | 7 | 7 | 6 | 1 | 2 |
| | ( 7%) | ( 4%) | ( 7%) | ( 8%) | ( 2%) | ( 6%) |
| Disputation or theses | 5 | 2 | 0 | 3 | 8 | 4 |
| | ( 7%) | ( 1%) | ( 0%) | ( 4%) | (13%) | ( 8%) |
| Woodcuts | 0 | 1 | 0 | 0 | 0 | 1 |
| | ( 0%) | ( 1%) | ( 0%) | ( 0%) | ( 0%) | ( 2%) |
| Glosses, etc. | 1 | 6 | 2 | 1 | 3 | 0 |
| | ( 1%) | ( 3%) | ( 2%) | ( 1%) | ( 5%) | ( 0%) |
| Totals | 73 | 192 | 95 | 74 | 61 | 49 |

quantitative evidence does not allow us go beyond this bland conclusion. The evidence does not support any hypothesis positing a sharp discontinuity in the late 1530s indicating the onset of senility or mental illness.

## Luther's Mental Health

Luther's psychological health during the later years is even harder to diagnose than his physical health, although some investigators have confidently concluded that Luther suffered from a manic-depressive psychosis.[16] Among the symptoms of this illness in his later years they list his frequent bouts of depression and spiritual temptation, his death-wish, his vulgar and scatological language, his outbursts of rage and vilification, and his visions of and contests with the devil. These behaviors—or symptoms, perhaps—can all be easily verified by anyone willing to take the time to page through the collections of table talk or through the volumes of Luther's correspondence for these later years. There is frequent occasion in later chapters to become acquainted with all these behaviors or symptoms. But the question that must be posed here is whether they point to mental illness, or manic-depressive psychosis, or the onset of senility.

Luther was often melancholy during his later years. His melancholy took the form of spiritual temptations and doubt, desire for death, and contempt for the world. Generally, ill health and apocalyptic fears played a large role in his bouts of melancholy. For example, most of Luther's prayers for death occurred, understandably enough, during periods of acute illness.[17] But illness was not the only occasion. At times when he prayed for the Lord to take him, his concern was less for his own physical weakness or incapacity to read or preach, and more for the wicked condition of the world.[18] "I wish that I and all my children were dead!" he exclaimed quite publicly in the winter of 1542-1543. His daughter Magdalene had died just a few months earlier and plague was active in Wittenberg, but his upset and anger were directed more at the ingratitude with which Germany had received the restored Gospel. Luther was convinced that he was living on the threshold of the End Time. "For marvelous things are yet to happen in the world," he continued.

> Those who live shall see that things will get worse. For this reason our Lord God now removes his own and proves what John says: "He has his winnowing shovel in his hand." Now he collects his grain in his shovel, into his granary, but he will deal

marvelously with the chaff: "He will burn it with an inextinguishable fire," says the text. This is also what he did with Rome . . . And so he will also do with Germany. He will take up the pious and then make an end to Germany, for it well deserves the punishment, and still there is no end to [its wickedness].[19]

As is seen in later chapters, apocalyptic views and his vision of his own role in the final drama of the world play a highly significant role in his polemics. At this point there is need only to consider whether these views might in themselves be regarded as symptoms of psychological imbalance: an odd mixture of paranoia and delusions of grandeur.

The older Luther did firmly believe that he was living on the eve of the Last Judgment. Once the papacy had been exposed by the Reformation as the antichrist seated within the church, the final battle had been joined. Satan had unleashed all his minions in a last, desperate attempt to defeat the servants of Christ. Luther's polemics were part of this final struggle.

His apocalyptic convictions were integrated into a larger Augustinian view of the dynamics of history. Early in his career as a reformer his reading of the Bible had convinced him that practically from the beginning of the world there had been a perpetual, unchanging struggle between the true and false church.[20] He saw this struggle as involving a recurrent contest between true and false prophets and apostles. Believing that mankind did not change and that the devil never slept, he could trace this struggle from the biblical histories into his own time. What happened to the prophets and apostles in their day could and would happen to the church of his day. Their experiences established a paradigm of the dynamics of all sacred history.

Within this paradigm the papacy was the antichrist described in Scripture, the Turks were Gog and the little horn in the Book of Daniel, contemporary Jewry was the remnant of a rejected people suffering under God's wrath, and his Protestant opponents were contemporary false prophets and apostles, like those who had plagued the true prophets and apostles. They were all members of the false church. He understood his disagreements with them in the context of this struggle between God and Satan. And behind them all loomed the figure of the devil, the father of lies. Furthermore, since Luther was always drawing comparisons and parallels between these opponents and the opponents of the prophets and apostles, it was only natural that he would see the true prophets and apostles as having provided a precedent for the way in which one should deal with such opponents. As a result he could explain and justify his polemics and his stubbornness on points of doctrine by pointing to the example set by these men of God.

Personal disappointment and fears strengthened his conviction that he was living on the eve of the Last Judgment. Although he had never entertained much hope for the mass of sinful humanity, events from the mid-1520s onward still shocked and disappointed him. He was made particularly indignant by what he saw as widespread indifference and ingratitude toward the renewed Gospel. The "ingratitude of the Germans" is a complaint heard with increasing frequency as he moves through the last decade or so of his life. This ingratitude, conjoined often with what seemed to him to be open blasphemy, was interpreted as further signs of the imminentness of the Last Judgment.

Luther's apocalyptic mood may also have been reinforced by his fears for the fate of the Reformation movement after his own death. These fears were shared by others. Elector Johann Friedrich commissioned the "Schmalkaldic Articles" partly to serve as Luther's "last testament" both against Catholics and against deviants within the Protestant ranks.[21] Luther himself viewed as his last testament against these different opponents his anti-Jewish treatises of 1543, his *Short Confession on the Supper* of 1544, and his 1545 *Against the Papacy at Rome, Founded by the Devil* along with the associated cartoons.[22] For example, he often directed his attacks not at his human opponents but at the devil who he saw as their master. Even some of his language may be attributed to this biblically based view of the strug- and its kingdom. For this reason he had published these pictures, each of which said a whole book's worth. They were his testament.[23]

As we shall see in later chapters, this Augustinian and apocalyptic view of the world and his own role helps to explain much of the mood and some of the elements in the polemics of the older Luther. For example, he often directs his attacks not at his human opponents but at the devil who he sees as their master. Even some of his language may be attributed to this biblically-based view of the struggle. When he rebuked his age for its failings, it was a prophet like Jeremiah from whom he borrowed his style, his tone, often the language itself. When he blasted the papacy as a wanton whore, he was borrowing language from Hosea and Ezekiel.[24]

But are these views symptoms of mental imbalance? If someone in the twentieth century espoused these views with the vehemence and conviction that Luther did in the sixteenth century, one might justifiably doubt the individual's touch with reality. By contemporary standards, such a view of the world would be highly aberrant. By sixteenth-century standards, however, such views are in no way unusual. On the contrary, such a biblically-based view of the world, conjoined with apocalyptic hopes and fears, was common among both Catholics and Protestants. And Luther's view of his own special role within the struggle between the true and false church was shared by many other Protestants.[25]

As for Luther's report of nighttime bouts with the devil, they may simply refer to the anguish caused by Meniere's syndrome (assuming this was the illness responsible for his dizziness and ringing in the ears). Or, alternatively, it may refer to doubts and anxieties that frequently plagued Luther and often took the form of such questions as "Are you alone wise?" Anxiety, doubt, and temptation were, Luther believed, requisite for a proper understanding of the Scripture and had afflicted many men of God before himself, including St. Paul. Is such a belief a rationalization and projection of neurotic symptoms or an acute theological insight? Or could it be both? In any case, historians of Luther's theology have long recognized that temptation or *Anfechtung* plays a significant role in Luther's theology.[26]

It is, of course, quite possible that Luther was referring to what he believed were actual physical encounters with the devil. He was quite credulous in some matters, accepting as a matter of fact the existence of witches, the reality of demonic possession, the disturbances of poltergeists. He was convinced that he had encountered a few poltergeists himself, and had on one occasion seen a black sow and on another a black dog, both of which were actually the devil.[27] But are such examples of superstitious credulity symptoms of mental illness? Since most of his contemporaries shared these beliefs, one should be careful about concluding that these experiences of the "demonic" testify to psychotic hallucinations or delusions.

Even the old Luther was never consistently violent or vulgar in his polemics. Throughout his last years he produced both violent and temperate polemics. Consider his attacks on Duke Heinrich of Braunschweig-Wolfenbüttel. In 1541 he produced *Against Hanswurst,* a politically inspired treatise and one of the coarsest Luther ever wrote. Four years later he wrote the moderate *To the Elector of Saxony and the Landgrave of Hesse Concerning the Captured Heinrich of Braunschweig* (1545).[28] The differences between these two treatises can best be explained not by changes in Luther's physical or mental health but by changes in external circumstances. The abuse and coarseness found in the earlier treatise was a deliberate polemical tactic, and perfectly in keeping with the general low tenor of the larger dispute. In the later treatise Luther sought to dissuade the landgrave from releasing Duke Heinrich, who had recently been taken prisoner. This called for a calm, reasoned argument, which Luther produced. Furthermore, every polemic Luther wrote during these later years contained sections devoted to clear and persuasive exposition of doctrine and exegesis of Scripture. Once again, his *Against Hanswurst* (1541) is illustrative. Fully two-thirds of the treatise is given over to violent, uninhibited (and often unedifying) attacks on Duke Heinrich and his Catholic allies. Yet, sandwiched between the invective and abuse is a lucid discussion of the characteristics of the true and false church and a briefer comment on the distinction between person and office. The independent worth of this section on the true and false church was attested to by its later publication in combination with the "Schmalkaldic Articles."

It would appear, therefore, that the vulgarity and violence was by choice. Luther could turn it on and off as it suited his purposes. His illnesses may have made him more irritable and less inhibited, but he had not lost complete control.

When all is said and done, the common description, and explanation, for the polemics of the older Luther—that they are the product of an ill and aged man—is not particularly illuminating historically. This explanation fails particularly to explain the wide range among the polemics of the older Luther and, more importantly, the function the polemics performed within the larger Reformation movement. In subsequent chapters we must turn to a consideration of political context and apocalyptic conviction to achieve a more satisfying historical understanding.

CHAPTER TWO

# The Question of Resistance

After 1530 Luther's correspondence and his published polemics reflected a shift in the character of the Reformation itself. A much larger percentage of his total correspondence was directed to secular authorities.[1] A similar change occurred with his polemics; the previous decade or so included a significant number of treatises that were directed towards the unconverted, at open-minded Catholics, and were dedicated to the exposition of Protestant faith. In contrast, the polemics of these later years were largely works of exhortation, aimed at the converted, at convinced Protestants, and were most often politically inspired and politically significant.

This shift in the character of his polemics and their intended audience was manifested also in the locations where the works were printed and reprinted.[2] In an age well before copyright and with shipping over land expensive and printing relatively cheap, a work generally spread through reprinting. If, for example, there was interest in southern Germany for a work first published in Wittenberg, it was more common for a printer in, say, Augsburg to reprint the work than it was for the printer in Wittenberg to ship a large number of copies to southern Germany. Since, as a general rule, printers printed works with the expectation of sale, the printing or reprinting of a particular work in a particular place suggests at the very least that the printer believed that there would be a demand for that work in his area. If the work is reprinted more than once in a particular area, it seems doubly reasonable to assume that an actual demand existed for the work. Based on these assumptions, an examination of Luther's publication statistics is striking.

In contrast to the earlier years where a number of printing centers throughout Germany accounted for a substantial percentage of works

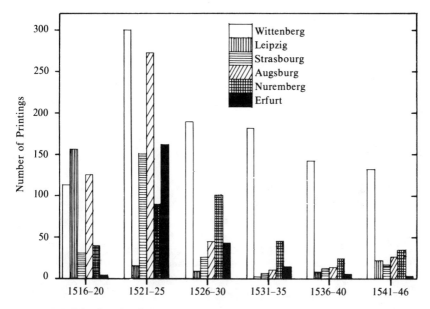

*Figure 8.* Publications by city

by Luther, the later years saw most of the printings and reprintings coming from Wittenberg, supplemented by the production of a few staunchly Lutheran cities, mostly in central and northern Germany. The bar graph of publications by city (Figure 8) and the individual graphs for the cities of Wittenberg, Nuremberg, Augsburg, and Strasbourg illustrate this trend (Figures 9 through 12). In the period 1516 to 1530, Wittenberg accounted for only 25 percent of the printings and reprintings of Luther's works, followed by Augsburg (18 percent), Nuremberg (9 percent), Strasbourg (8 percent), and Erfurt (8 percent). In contrast, in the period 1531 to 1546, Wittenberg accounted for fully 55 percent of the printings and reprintings, followed by Nuremberg (12 percent), Augsburg (6 percent), Magdeburg (6 percent), and Strasbourg (4 percent). If one examines only the last six years of Luther's life, 1541 to 1546, this change is even more apparent: Wittenberg (43 percent), Nuremberg (11 percent), Frankfurt a.M. (9 percent), Augsburg (9 percent), Leipzig (7 percent), Strasbourg (5 percent), and Magdeburg (5 percent)—to list the top seven centers for the printing and reprinting of Luther's works. Luther, these statistics suggest, had gradually become the publicist for an established, territorially defined party.

# Publication in Four Separate Cities

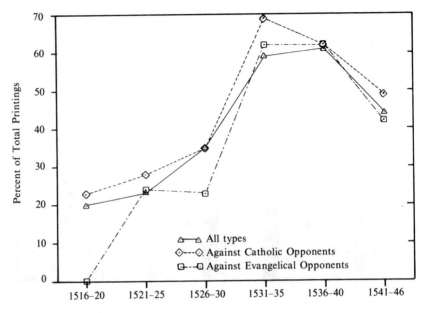

*Figure 9.* Wittenberg

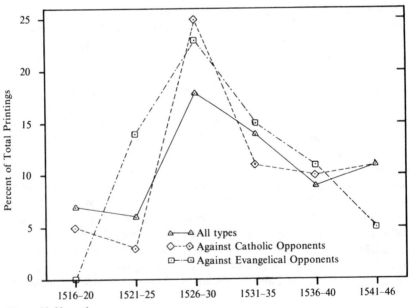

*Figure 10.* Nuremberg

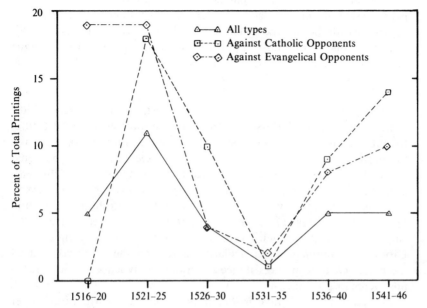

*Figure 11.* Augsburg

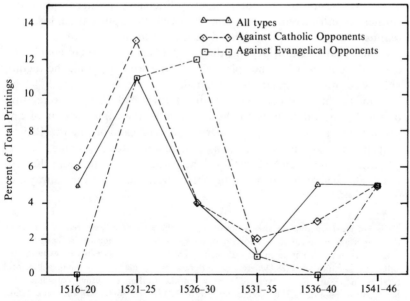

*Figure 12.* Strasbourg

Of course the greatly heightened role of politics, and the accompanying shift in the character and audience of Luther's polemics, came a good decade before the 1540s. Of the many events involved in this transition, one of the most important was the formation of the League of Schmalkalden in 1531, which was preceded by Luther's public volte-face on the issue of resistance to the emperor in defense of religion.

Among the leaders of the Protestant estates in the late 1520s, Landgrave Philipp of Hesse was the one who most encouraged Luther to publish on issues of interest to the estates. Philipp was also the foremost advocate of a Protestant League, seemingly little bothered about the licitness of armed resistance to the Emperor. He fully realized that Luther was an obstacle to his plans, that the Saxon Reformer harbored severe reservations about a Protestant League and opposed on theological and practical grounds armed resistance to the emperor, especially in defense of their faith.* At the same time it was Landgrave Philipp who particularly insisted on the propriety, indeed the necessity, of armed resistance to an imperially led attempt to reimpose Roman Catholicism.

For years the landgrave made strenuous efforts to win Luther over to this position. Finally in October 1530 in a meeting at Torgau, Luther and Melanchthon were prevailed upon by Hessian and Electoral advisors and politicians to leave the question of the propriety of armed resistance to the jurists and politicians.[3] To accomplish this Luther in effect redrew the line between the spiritual and secular realms. He described the right of resistance to the emperor as a political and legal question beyond the competence of the theologians. To avoid the confusion of the spiritual with the secular realm, the theologians were not to regulate the secular law.

Prior to this October 1530 meeting Luther had viewed the relation of the Protestant princes to the emperor as the same as that of any subordinate authority to its superior: he had categorized the Protestant princes as "private persons" in relation to the emperor. As "private persons" and Christians, then, the princes had the duty to obey all secular commands of their ordained superior, always of

---

*It is not clear whether he also realized that he, the landgrave, was seen by Luther as one important practical reason for opposing a Protestant League or, at least, for opposing Saxon participation in such a league. Thanks to Luther's experiences in the so-called Pack Affair of 1528, where the landgrave nearly managed to involve Electoral Saxony in a surprise "preventive" attack on the Catholics, Luther considered the landgrave to be a dangerous young hothead (e.g., WABr 5:76-77. On the Pack Affair, see Kurt Dülfer, *Die Packschen Händel* [Marburg, 1958]).

course with the stipulation that such obedience must not violate their higher duty of obedience to God, as set down in Acts 5:29. When these two duties conflicted, the princes should refuse obedience to the lesser authority and passively suffer the consequences. They had no more right to resist the emperor actively than the mayor of Wittenberg had the right to resist actively the elector of Saxony.

At the October 1530 meeting Luther first recognized the princes as "political individuals" who were obliged to obey positive law, even if that obedience lead to active resistance to the emperor. Ample evidence shows that Luther was initially uncomfortable with this change, however consistent it may be with his theology of the two kingdoms.[4] At Torgau Luther's uncoerced opinion was apparently not sought, rather he was expected to provide Scriptural sanction for a policy that had already been determined. The politicians would not accept theological objections to resistance. Some of them were willing to carry on without the theologians' approval, and some even stated in the theologians' presence that they considered this matter to be beyond the theologians' competence.[5] Under these circumstances, Luther saw no need to provide a written opinion, and finally did so only without grace and with much resistance.[6] In subsequent letters Luther insisted that he had not changed his position,[7] and he refused as a theologian and preacher to judge the validity of the positive law argument or to advocate the formation of a League.[8]

Landgrave Philipp was certainly aware of Luther's feelings. Nevertheless within weeks of the October 30 meeting he was urging Luther to publish a public treatise on the matter.[9] Obviously he expected that whatever reservations it might contain such a treatise would be of service to his and the Protestant estates' cause. As it turned out, Luther was intent on publishing such a treatise in any case, but the landgrave's entreaties probably strengthened his resolve.

The treatise, *Warning to His Dear German People,* was everything the landgrave could have hoped for under the circumstances.[10] In it Luther once again voiced some of his reservations in respect to resistance to the emperor and placed responsibility for determining the licitness of resistance squarely on the shoulders of the Protestant rulers and their jurists. At the same time, the wording of the treatise and many of its arguments could be, and, indeed, were used in two ways: first, to strengthen the Protestant resolve to resist, and, second, to quiet the consciences of any who might worry whether resistance to the emperor in defense of religion would be a violation of God's ordinance.

Scholars disagree about the theological convictions that underlie Luther's argument in his *Warning.* Most agree, however, that there are tensions in his argument. Some of the treatise was based on what for Luther was a "counter-factual" assumption—"as if there were not God and as if idly imagining in a dream, that their [the Catholics'] plans and undertakings will begin and continue by force."[11] His discussion concerning rebellion, then, if limited by this assumption may have been valid for him only in terms of "worldly wisdom," that is, in juridical rather than in theological terms. In places Luther seems to argue that the whole question, at least in these "worldly" terms, was not within his competence. Twice he referred his readers to the jurists or to the law. He wrote, "I will not have rebuked as rebellious those who offer armed resistance to the murderous and bloodthirsty papists, but rather I will let it go [uncensored] and allow them to call it self-defense, and will thereby direct them to the law and to the jurists," and one senses a concession in the statement that he would "allow" them to call it self-defense.[12] He said further, drily and perhaps a little sarcastically, "It should have another name [than rebellion], which the law will surely find."[13] And at one point he seems to contrast his advice as a theologian with that a jurist might give.

> Not that I hereby wish to incite or provoke anyone to such resistance or to justify it, for that is not my office, much less even mine to pass sentence or to judge —a Christian knows well what he should do, that he give God what is God's and the emperor, too, what is the emperor's, but certainly not the bloodhounds what is not theirs—rather that I am offering a distinction between rebellion and other actions and do not wish to allow the bloodhounds the pretense of boasting that they were waging war against rebellious people and were justified by secular and divine law as they would gladly maintain.[14]

What was the advice he gave, then, in his office of theologian? "A Christian knows well what he should do," he wrote, "that he give God what is God's and the emperor, too, what is the emperor's, but certainly not the bloodhounds what is not theirs." Although defiant in its language, this counsel strikes a note different from that struck by the analysis surrounding it. And when he insisted that one should not accept as rebellious everything that the "bloodhounds" rebuked as rebellious, he explained that not all transgressions of the law were rebellion. He was suggesting perhaps that even if the "self-defense" were not rebellion, it might still be a transgression of the law.[15]

What is significant here is how contemporaries may have understood this treatise. It seems safe to assume that Luther's theological subtleties, qualifications, and reservations were not what first struck the sixteenth-century readers, whether friends or foes. Rather what seems most likely to have struck them, and it has relatively little to do with theology, was Luther's righteous anger, coloring the whole treatise, and his almost joyful conviction that the papists would be resisted, whether or not such resistance was proper.

With respect to the first point, Luther's righteous anger, the treatise fairly bristled with abusive and disparaging characterizations of the Catholics and their cause. At the outset Luther announced that God had apparently given the papists over to their sins, since they had dissolved the Imperial Diet at Augsburg without a peaceful resolution and even with increased discord and defiant threats. Therefore Luther and his adherents now had to withdraw their prayers for the impenitent papists as God commanded (1 John 5:15). Because of their bad conscience and wrongful cause, the papists themselves did not and could not pray to God. Needing no God they proceeded with haughty defiance against flesh and blood. "We, however, are completely certain," Luther wrote, "that their rabid undertaking is not within their power but in God's hand, and they will not so quickly attain what they wish."[16] Their conscience was too burdened not only with lies, blasphemy, blood, murder, and all abominations but also beyond that with hardened, impenitent hearts and sins against the Holy Spirit. They would, Luther claimed, have as much success against the Lutherans as the Germans had had against "Saint John Hus" and the Bohemians. "Nor will I along with my [adherents] take a rest from praying and imploring God that He give them a despondent, timid, cowardly heart when they are on the [battle] field, [and] that here one and there another be touched and stung by his conscience."[17]

No language uttered against the papists was harsh enough, and Luther had no apology for his words. "Such scolding is nothing," he wrote, "in comparison to the unspeakable wickedness [of the papists], for what sort of scolding is it when I scold the devil as a murderer, rogue, traitor, blasphemer, and liar? It is just as if a breeze blew on him. What are the papal asses but pure and simple living devils who are impenitent and have nothing but obstinate hearts and [who] knowingly defend such obvious blasphemy and seek protection for it from the emperor and from you."[18]

Luther also appears to take grim satisfaction in his prediction that the papists would meet with resistance whether licit or not. Were the papists to attempt to carry out their designs by force, Luther announced early in the treatise, there would be a war or a rebellion or both. "For it is indeed likely (we are speaking now in the dream where there is no God)," Luther wrote, emphasizing the "counterfactual" nature of the discussion, that if the papists started a war, both they and the Protestants would be likely to perish in mob uprisings. "For in such a case they [the papists] may not rely on our teaching as if they were now assured that no one would oppose them because we have strenuously written and taught against rebellion, also [that] one should suffer the crimes of tyrants and not defend oneself." Such were his teachings, he said, but given how few people followed his other teachings, he could not guarantee the papists that he would be followed in this.[19]

Were he to die in such a war or rebellion, Luther would, he assured his readers, take a multitude of bishops, priests, and monks with him. For it was to be expected that rebels who killed him would not spare many priests. "And so in the end [we] shall make a little pilgrimage together—they, the papists, into the abyss of hell to their god of lies and murder, whom they have served with lies and murder; I to my Lord Jesus Christ, whom I have served in truth and peace." The papists "have blundered badly, for my life shall be their hangman, my death shall be their devil!"[20]

A bit further on Luther announced defiantly that, although it was not proper for him as a preacher to wage or counsel or incite war, he intended, since his enemies desired war rather than peace, to remain silent in the event of war and not to intervene as he had done in the Peasants' War. "Instead I will let occur what occurs," he warned,

> even though no bishop or priest or monk should remain, and I myself should also perish. Furthermore should it come to war—which God forbid—I will not have rebuked as rebellious those who offer armed resistance to the murderous and bloodthirsty papists, but rather I will let it go [uncensured] and allow them to call it self-defense, and will thereby direct them to the law and to the jurists. For in such a case, when the murderers and bloodhounds wish to wage war and to murder, it is also in truth no rebellion to oppose them and to defend oneself. Not that I hereby wish to incite or provoke anyone to such resistance or to justify it, for that is not my office, much less even mine to pass sentence or to judge—a Christian knows well what he should do, that he give God what is God's and the emperor, too, what is the emperor's, but certainly not the bloodhounds what is not theirs—rather that I am offering a distinction between rebellion and other actions and do not wish to allow the bloodhounds the pretense of boasting that they were waging war against rebellious people and were justified by secular and divine law as they would gladly maintain. Likewise, I do not wish to allow the conscience of the people to be burdened with the peril and concern that their resistance may be rebellious. For such a name is too evil and too harsh in such a case. It should have another name, which the law will surely find. One must not accept as rebellious

everything that the bloodhounds rebuke as rebellious, for they thereby wish to bind the mouth and fist of all the world so that no one should censure them in sermons or defend himself with the fist, [while] they maintain an open mouth and free hand. They wish in this manner to frighten and ensnare all the world with the name of rebellion but to comfort and make themselves secure. No, dear fellow, one must submit to you another definition and interpretation. It is not rebellion when one breaks the law, otherwise all transgressions of the law would have to be called rebellion. Rather he is called a rebel who does not wish to tolerate authority and law but rather attacks them and battles against them and wishes to suppress them and to become lord himself and establish law, as Müntzer did. A usurper is one thing, a transgressor another. That's how one properly defines a rebel, so that resistance against the bloodhounds cannot accordingly be rebellious. For the papists begin and wish to wage war and not maintain peace or to let be the others who would gladly have peace, so that the papists are much closer to the name and virtue called rebellion.[21]

How are readers likely to have reacted to this language, these predictions, and this fascinating examination of rebellion? Prediction, of course, is not incitement. But when coupled with such language and arguments was it likely to have left the reader unmoved? Might it not be assumed that the violent verbal attack on the papists, the lurid description of their misdeeds and intentions, easily canceled out any reservations that Luther expressed about the legitimacy of armed resistance. Readers who accepted Luther's characterization of the papists should have had little trouble overcoming any scruples they might have had about defending themselves against such wicked people engaged in so evil a cause.

It is here that the distinction between what Luther actually said and how he went about saying it becomes crucial. The intricacies of his argument may suggest to the twentieth-century scholar and perhaps even to some careful readers in the sixteenth century that Luther still harbored doubts about the propriety of Christians offering armed resistance to persecution by the emperor, and that he still had an unwillingness, first announced in Torgau, to urge Christians to offer such resistance.[22] But the polemical force of this treatise, which found expression in Luther's characterization of his opponents and in the arguments he employed, including the "dream" in which there was no God, favored resistance. In fact, it was an incitement to resistance. This was realized by Catholic opponents, who made some telling points about the provocative effects of Luther's violent and abusive language. Consider, for example, what the staunchly Catholic Duke

Georg concluded in his anonymously published *Against Luther's Warning to the Germans That They Should Not Be Obedient To the Emperor, Another Warning That They Should Not Allow Themselves To Be Misled By It Nor To Be Moved To Disobedience, ₁Written₁ by an Obedient Nonpartisan* of April 1531. The Gospel was to be maintained not by the sword but by the power of God, "as Luther himself . . . had often indicated."

> But now one sees well that he does not trust the power of God but rather thinks to protect himself with the sword and in that fashion to confirm his undertaking in the empire so that one would have to look upon him as a prophet and holy man. How holy he is and what spirit resides in him, if one otherwise does not sense [it], he could nevertheless guess from his treatises in which one finds not much sign of love, peaceableness, gentleness, [and] patience, which the spirit of God usually gives, but rather nothing but cursing, scolding, abuse, slander, shameless tales and lewd sayings, not to mention the insidious tricks and presumptuous lies by which he gladly wishes to make subordinates disobedient to their authorities and to bring [them] together at one place to the devil's advantage so that the pious with the evil would be exterminated through murder and bloodshed.

The harshness of Luther's treatise and its language betrayed Luther's true intention. In another treatise, the Catholic publicist Johann Cochlaeus argued that Luther sought to incite the population to rebellion by slandering Duke Georg, calling him the enemy of the gospel, a devil's apostle, a murderer, and a liar. Who could be well disposed toward a robber or murderer, or toward an enemy of the gospel and the devil's apostle? he asked. Luther's language disclosed his true intentions.[23] Even more to the point, perhaps, the rhetorical effect of the treatise was recognized by the League's leaders, who saw to it that the publication was reprinted numerous times both in 1531 and in 1546, when war actually broke out.[24]

In his later pronouncements on resistance, Luther became more comfortable with the positive law argument but never fully satisfied. In 1536 and again in 1538 he added his signature to joint opinions of the Wittenberg theological faculty,* probably written by Melanchthon,

---

*In signing the 1536 opinion along with the other theologians, Luther added a belligerent postscript: "I, Martin Luther, will also assist with prayer, [and] also (if it should be [necessary]) with my fist." This unequivocal subscription is all the more interesting since the opinion relies heavily on natural law arguments not normally used by Luther (who to this point had allowed only a positive law justification) and, in advocating not only the *right* of resistance by the Protestant princes but the *responsibility* of resistance

that advocated resistance partly on the basis of natural law.[25] But as a theologian, Luther seems to have wished to develop a *theological* justification for his position. At the same time, he wished as much as possible to remain true to his earlier convictions. He found his solution in his understanding of the apocalyptic situation in which he lived.

The decade or so before the outbreak of the Schmalkaldic War in 1546 saw considerable religious and political maneuvering. The threat of religious civil war loomed large in the late 1530s and tensions were only partially eased by the Frankfurt Standstill signed on 19 April 1539. In these troubled years the threat of Catholic attack was always present, and Luther and the other Protestant theologians were often asked for advice at times of particular danger. On 8 February 1539 Luther sent Johann Ludicke, pastor of Kottbus in the Electorate of Brandenburg, suggestions how he might publicly or privately advise Elector Joachim II[26] concerning resistance to the emperor in the event that the emperor proceeded against the Protestant princes "forcibly and tyrannically." In a revealing way he did not fully embrace these suggestions as his own. "I, to be sure, have previously written my opinion on this matter while Duke Johann was living," he began, referring most likely to his opinions of 1529 and 1530. "Now it is too late to inquire into this matter since it has already been decided among them [the Protestant princes] that they wish and are able by law to resist and defend themselves, and nothing would come of my saying anything new [*et ad meum denuo dicere nihil sequetur*]. Why should I then vex you and me in vain?" For himself he hoped that Christ would see to it that this advice was not necessary and would not permit the emperor to wage "such a furious war." He was, he admitted, comforted by this thought.

> And nonetheless I have the most weighty reasons not to oppose the inclination and determination [*voluntatem et consilium*] of our [princes], one of which being that the emperor may not nor can [he] be the person which brings about or is able to bring about this war but rather [it must be] the pope and bishops who wish to use the emperor as a soldier in order to defend their horrible tyrannies and diabolic abuses in opposition to the acknowledged truth. For the emperor as emperor has no reason [to proceed] against the [Protestant] princes, but the pope wishes to have a reason when

---

in defense of religion, advances a position much less qualified than Luther's usual stance (Wolgast suggests that Luther's belligerent postscript refers not to the whole opinion but only to the concluding remarks about a possible prohibition by the council of priestly marriage [Wolgast, *The Wittenberger Theologie,* p. 228]. This suggestion makes considerable sense.). For more on these opinions, see note 25.

*31*

there is none [*sed papa vult habere non causas pro causis*] and thus involve the emperor in this dangerous war. If, therefore, it is permitted to wage war or defend oneself against the Turks, [it is] even more so against the pope, who is worse. . . . Therefore our [princes] have decided [that] the emperor in this case is not the emperor but a soldier and mercenary [*latronem*] of the pope.

He had previously given advice concerning the emperor, Luther said, not concerning a soldier of the pope. He had also been moved by the example both of the pope and of Cardinal Albrecht of Mainz, who, under Christ's name, blasphemously took pleasure in persecuting Christians. Were the pope, cardinals, bishops, emperor, and so on, to renounce the name of Christ and to admit that they were what purchased slaves of the devil, then Luther would recommend, as he had done before, that the Protestants submit to them as to pagan tyrants. But if they continued to persecute Christians under Christ's name, they should expect to receive the punishment appropriate for blasphemy. With this assertion, Luther was returning, with a significant qualification, to his earlier opinion that it was the Christian responsibility of subordinates, including the princes in relation to the emperor, to submit even to tyrannical authority. What was new in this argument was Luther's insistence that the papacy and its soldier, the emperor, by persecuting Christians *under the name of Christ,* committed blasphemy and thereby forfeited claims to obedience on the part of their Christian subjects.

Luther also told Ludicke that although this was not the only thing that moved him, he did not wish to put everything down in writing lest it reach "those most wicked servants of Satan for whom it was fitting to be punished with the punishment of Cain, namely, fear and trembling." It was also not necessary for Ludicke to know everything in this matter as long as he did not fortify the "hands of the godless" against the Protestant princes, but rather gave room to God's wrath and judgment. After citing examples from the Old Testament that should terrify their opponents, Luther insisted that the German princes, as those who by common counsel governed the empire with the emperor, had more right to oppose the emperor than the populace had to oppose Saul [1 Sam. 14:44-45] or Ahikam to oppose Jehoiakim [Jer. 26:16, 24]. The emperor was not a monarch, Luther contended, nor was he able to change the form of the empire by removing the electors—nor would it be tolerated if he tried. This was enough on the matter, Luther concluded. The rest should be left to God and they should teach to give unto Caesar what was Caesar's—for the rest, "*Secretum meum mihi.*"[27]

This letter gives the impression once more that Luther had said his piece a decade earlier. The princes had decided, however, despite his reservations, that they had the legal right to offer armed resistance to the emperor. There were weighty reasons, he had told Ludicke, not to oppose the princes on this. First, the emperor would not be acting in his office as emperor if he attacked the Protestants. Second, by persecuting Christians under the name of Christ, the emperor, as the pope's servant, would be committing blasphemy and thereby earning the punishment appropriate for this sin. Luther had then declined to give his other reasons, explaining that he did not wish to give comfort to his opponents. Probably, one of the unstated reasons for not opposing the inclination of the princes was his earlier stated conviction that it was better for the Protestant princes to fight a war with a good conscience than without. It appears that Luther still had his doubts about the cogency of some of the arguments advocating resistance to the emperor. He was willing, however, to keep silent because he would accomplish nothing if he were to insist on his reservations but strengthen the papists and trouble the consciences of the Protestant princes without dissuading them from their resolve. In the meanwhile he was comforted by the hope that God would prevent a war from occurring and thus make this advice unnecessary.[28]

Luther's last major pronouncement on the question of resistance came in the spring of 1539 while the Protestants were negotiating with imperial representatives in Frankfurt and there was widespread fear that religious war was imminent. Luther was not present at these negotiations but he received regular, and fairly gloomy, reports from Melanchthon, Myconius, and Bucer.[29] Hence it was in an atmosphere of tension and anticipation of religious war that Luther composed his *Seventy Propositions for Debate, Concerning the Three Hierarchies, Church, State ₍Politica₎, Household ₍Oeconomica₎, and that the Pope Belongs to None of Them But is the Public Enemy of Them All.* Intended for the quarterly disputation at the University, which was Luther's responsibility that April, these theses laid out once again Luther's position on the right of armed resistance.[30] In theses 51 to 70 he claimed that the papacy did not belong to the divinely ordained orders.

> It is evident [that] the pope is not an authority [*magistratum* or *Oberkeit*], either of the church or of the state or of the household. For God ordained three hierarchies [*hierarchias/ Regiment*] against the devil, namely the household, the state, and the church. That he [the pope] condemns and tramples upon the Gospel with his blasphemies in the canon law proves that [the pope] is not of the church. That he wishes to subject the civil law

> to himself just as [he does] the Gospel proves that [he] is not of
> the state. That he prohibits weddings and marriage as he pleases,
> [and] not only of priests, proves that [he] is not of the household.
> Rather he is that monster of which Daniel speaks, which opposes
> all that is of God and the God of gods [Dan. 11:36].[31]

The papacy was no true authority at all but rather the antichrist.
Hence normal considerations concerning resistance to superior authority did not apply to him. In fact, the papacy was a beast which all
should resist as they would a possessed beast. "Thus," Luther concluded in thesis 66, "if the pope stirs up a war, he ought to be resisted
just like a furious and possessed monster or a true werewolf." One
should not be concerned if the pope has as his soldiers princes, kings,
or even emperors themselves, enchanted by the name of the church.
"For he who soldiers under a highwayman (whoever he may be) must
expect the risk of his military service along with eternal damnation,"
Luther contended. "Nor does it save kings, princes, or even emperors
that they boast [that they are] defenders of the church, since they are
obliged to know what the church is."[32] With this argument,[33] Luther
had provided a *theological* justification for resisting the emperor *but
only if he were acting in this apocalyptic context as a servant of the
papal antichrist.** For obvious reasons, the theses as a whole and the
most relevant subsets were reprinted in both Latin and German in
1546 during the Schmalkaldic War.

In the question of resistance Luther's convictions came in conflict
with circumstances. He believed that it was contrary to God's law to
resist duly constituted superior authority. Injustice was to be suffered
in patience by true Christians. God could be trusted ultimately to save
them. He continued to believe this to his death. By 1529, however, the
issue was no longer whether true Christians, such as Luther himself,
should suffer martyrdom patiently,** but whether Christian city-states

---

*The original series of theses ended with this attack on secular rulers, including the em-
peror, who undertook to fight for the papacy. But in late April or early May Luther
added an additional twenty theses attacking the papacy. This addition was probably occasioned by news of the Frankfurt Standstill, which was agreed to on 19 April. According to this agreement, the emperor granted to all adherents of the Augsburg Confession
a Standstill or truce for fifteen months beginning on 1 May. With this agreement the
threat of religious war receded greatly for the moment. The need for Luther's advice on
resistance to a Catholic attack was thus less urgent. By adding twenty articles in which
he attacked the papacy's right to establish laws that were binding on the church or individual consciences and by arguing again that the papacy did not belong to any of the
three divinely ordained "governments," Luther shifted the focus of the treatise from
those who supported the papacy to the papacy itself (WA 39/2:35-38).

**Some of Luther's earliest pronouncements dealt exclusively with this more limited
question, whether the elector should resist an imperial attempt to capture Luther or

and territories, political entities, could be reasonably expected to adopt this same ethic.[34] Luther believed that they, too, should trust in God and not resist. But the rulers and their advisors most strongly disagreed.

Luther then had a painful choice. Either he accommodated himself to this stubborn fact or he stood by his principles. There were high costs whatever he did. Failure to make compromises and accommodations meant surrendering influence over the movement that bore his name. Too great a readiness to make concessions, to modify his teachings, or to reach accommodation would have opened him to the charge of hypocrisy and insincerity, accusations that would also cost him influence and would damage the reputation of the movement itself.

Luther was very hard pressed to adjust to these painful circumstances. Almost everything he did was on the basis of principle, on the basis of his understanding of the Bible. Moreover, it was not in his character to compromise or make concessions on matters of theology. Yet the times required concession and accommodation. Somehow Luther had to adjust while remaining as true as possible to himself and his beliefs.

At the level of theology he adjusted to political realities, first, by "allowing" a positive law justification for such resistance, and, then, by arguing that if the emperor attacked the Protestants on account of their faith, he would not be acting in his capacity as a superior secular authority but rather as a servant of the papal antichrist. Neither position entailed the abandonment of Luther's fundamental convictions concerning resistance or his doctrine of the two realms. But both rested on some convoluted arguments and some strained rationalizations. Luther, of course, was a master of plausible theological rationalization, but he was not always comfortable with his efforts. The

---

other individual Protestants. This had first become an issue in 1522, when Luther had returned to Wittenberg after hiding some ten months on the Wartburg. Although he had left the final decision up to Luther, Elector Friedrich had strongly recommended against Luther's return and had outlined the possible legal and political consequences for himself and for Electoral Saxony should the emperor demand that he turn Luther over to imperial authorities (WABr 2:449-53). In his famous letter to the elector justifying his return, Luther had rejected the elector's protection arguing that such a spiritual matter could not be decided by the sword but only by God. He had admonished the elector to be obedient to the emperor, his sovereign, and not to offer any resistance should the emperor capture Luther or put him to death. No one should resist authority except Him who established it, otherwise it was rebellion and an offense to God. At the same time, the elector should not actively assist the imperial authorities to capture or punish Luther; it was enough if the elector did not interfere if the imperial authorities came to seize him. See note 34 for other early pronouncements.

accommodations gave rise to considerable internal tensions, to internal dissonance, which in turn spilled over into the polemics themselves, increasing their passion, their vehemence, their shrillness.

Significantly, Luther's talents as a polemicist, as a shaper of passions and emotions through words, were put to use for ends different from those his theological beliefs, even the more convoluted among them, would lead one to expect. For as a practical matter, all of his polemics on the issue of resistance *encouraged* Protestants to resist a Catholic attack, even if led by the emperor.

Moreover, with their impassioned language, abusive characterizations of opponents, and almost summary discussions of the theological issues involved, they were obviously intended to be treatises of exhortation rather than explanation. They may have deepened convictions already held, but they were unlikely to have converted anyone from outside the Protestant ranks. In short, their intended audience was Protestants, not Catholics or any third party. And their intended purpose was to rally Protestants to the defense of their faith, not to convince them to resist passively an unjust attack by the Catholic emperor. They were political polemics. They were written at the request of Landgrave Philipp or Luther's elector. They served the interests of these Protestant leaders of the League of Schmalkalden and were reprinted whenever there was a threat of Catholic attack. Publication statistics for the older Luther's works suggest that his audience had become more narrowly Lutheran, territorially defined. The polemics on resistance fit this pattern.

Of course there is nothing surprising about polemics of this sort, more exhortation than explanation, aimed at the converted rather than the unconverted, written in response to political circumstances. They are just what one would expect in the consolidation phase of an ideological movement.

What is surprising, perhaps, is that they were written by Martin Luther. While it is almost a cliche in Luther studies to point to Luther's delight in paradox and his ability to hold in creative tension seemingly conflicting ideas, what we find in the question of resistance is a paradox, a tension of another sort. Here we see his ability to *really* say one thing but to say it in a manner that conveyed a different message. I do not think we should label this hypocrisy, as many of his Catholic opponents did. Yet it requires some explanation.

Luther hated the pope as antichrist and Catholics as the agents of Satan. On the level of conscious theological reflection, he believed it wrong to resist duly constituted superior secular authority, even if it was Catholic and unjust. But on the visceral level he may have felt differently. The language of his polemics, and his search for a theological rationalization of the right of resistance, certainly suggest this. As we shall see in the next chapter, Luther tended to become furious with those who misunderstood what he claimed to have said. Perhaps some of this fury was born of an almost unconscious awareness that his message lent itself to misunderstanding or, even worse, that his message, at least on one level, was just what his opponents said it was.

## CHAPTER THREE

# Princes and Polemics: Luther, Duke Georg, and Elector Johann Friedrich

Duke Georg of Saxony, assisted by several of his churchmen and scholars, including the learned Johann Cochlaeus, led the Catholic counterattack to Luther's *Warning*.[1] The controversies between Luther on one side and Duke Georg and his supporters on the other, which is examined in this chapter, illustrate some of the dynamics typical of the polemics of the older Luther.

By the 1530s the differences between Catholics and Protestants were irreconcilable. Each side claimed to be of the true church. Each believed that its opponent was in league with the devil. Each felt that justice was on its side. Each had a long list of grievances against the other. Such convictions left little to be discussed.

At issue in the disputes between Luther and Duke Georg was the obedience due to secular authority. On the basis of his doctrine of the two kingdoms Luther distinguished between secular and spiritual affairs and counseled disobedience to coercion exercised by Catholic secular authorities in spiritual matters. His Catholic opponents either missed this distinction or thought it hypocritical. The practical effect, they claimed, of Luther's advice, and the violent language in which the advice was couched, was to promote rebellion. Luther was enraged by such a claim, and saw the apparent unwillingness or inability of the Catholics to recognize and honor this distinction between the two kingdoms as a sure sign of Catholic allegiance to the devil. Each side, then, viewed the other as the true rebel. Each side charged the other with a desire to foment disorder, sedition, and war.

Given such opposed convictions, it is not surprising that the language and form of argumentation employed by the publicists— Luther, Duke Georg, Cochlaeus—suggest that each was speaking more to his own party than to one another. Expressions of righteous indignation, liberal use of insult and name-calling, lengthy recitals of old grievances, rehashing of past disputes, repetition of familar arguments—such material may appeal to the converted and may reinforce convictions already held. But it is unlikely to move the unconverted. And it will only enrage the opponent.

## Duke Georg and the Reformation

Duke Georg and Elector Johann were cousins. Albrecht, the father of Georg, and Ernst, the father of Johann, were brothers, who, for a time, had ruled all of Saxony together. In 1485, however, they had divided the territory between themselves with Ernst receiving the electoral title along with his share. The territorial division itself was extremely complex, leaving Ernestine and Albertine Saxony intermingled, as one scholar aptly put it, like Siamese twins. Very roughly speaking, Ernestine or Electoral Saxony resembled a bone grasped in the jaws of Albertine or Ducal Saxony, with the lower "jaw" being much larger than the upper. To travel, then, from Dresden, the ducal seat, in the lower jaw to Leipzig in the upper, the traveler had to cross through Electoral Saxony. To complicate this simile but also to bring it closer to reality, various blemishes, large and small, must be imagined in bone and jaws. Some of these represent territories that were independent of both Saxonies, others that were under partial jurisdiction of one Saxony or the other, and still others that were under the common lordship of the two Saxonies.

Duke Georg was one of Luther's very earliest opponents, and he remained until his death in 1539 a constant and often penetrating critic of all Luther did. His character and conviction were strongly influenced by his parents and by a religious education unusual for a firstborn son of a major German prince. His father, Duke Albrecht, had been a close friend and supporter of Maximilian of Habsburg, emperor from 1493 to 1519, and Duke Georg throughout his reign continued the family tradition of unswerving loyalty to the emperor. As a result, he was never able to forgive Luther's disobedience of the emperor.[2]

The duke's mother, Sidonie, certainly contributed to his considerable personal piety, and may also have been responsible for his intense aversion to anything smacking even faintly of heresy. She was the daughter of the excommunicated Hussite Utraquist King Georg Podiebrad of Bohemia and evidenced throughout her life great concern for the ultimate fate of her father's soul.[3] If he had not already done so, Luther lost Duke Georg's good will during the Leipzig debate when he asserted that among the articles of John Hus he had found many that were plainly Christian and evangelical and could not be condemned by the universal church. "That's the plague," the duke reportedly exclaimed. And he wrote to Elector Friedrich on 22 December 1519 that Luther's teaching was quite "Praguish."[4]

Despite being the firstborn son, Duke Georg had spent much of his early life preparing for an ecclesiastical career. As a result he remained throughout his life a competent lay theologian.[5] His knowledge of Latin was good—he was able to follow the debate at Leipzig easily—and he later took offense when Luther implicitly questioned his knowledge of the language. He was also a lifelong supporter of humanism, both at the University of Leipzig and at his own court.[6] He corresponded with Erasmus, the "Prince of the Humanists," repeatedly urging him to attack Luther in print and criticizing him for his reluctance to do so. When Erasmus finally attacked Luther on the question of the freedom of the will, the duke was pleased, and even more pleased by Erasmus' 1526 *Hyperaspistae Diatribe Against M. Luther's Bondage of the Will.* This was the first part of a long and cranky reply to Luther's *On the Bondage of the Will.* It earned Erasmus the duke's congratulations and a drinking cup as a gift.

Duke Georg's involvement in secular and ecclesiastical affairs within his own territory showed both traditional and humanistic elements. He was a very talented, very honest secular ruler, which even Luther acknowledged.[7] His internal politics aimed at maintaining traditional law and political order. This policy greatly endeared him to his estates, who rewarded him with considerable loyalty even in religious matters. In the ecclesiastical sphere he sought to improve the moral standards of the clergy and was something of a "specialist" in cloister reform.[8] In common with the older humanists such as Erasmus, he vigorously sought a reformation of the church but shied away from a reformation of the faith. At the Diet of Worms in 1521 he had introduced twelve *gravamina.* These were so critical of the practices of the Roman church that the papal legate, Aleander, had complained that the duke had given a bad example to others.[9] In the subsequent years he continued to criticize what he saw as failings in the church and in the papacy, to support reforms and even lay-directed visitations in his own territory, and to add his voice to the call for a general council of the church. In his many disputes with Luther he was always scrupulously concerned about documenting his charges, and he never resorted to extralegal means to combat Luther. As he himself once pointed out, had he wished to execute the Edict of Worms and have Luther captured or killed, he could easily have done so—Luther was literally his next-door neighbor. He was unwilling, however, even in such a "good cause" to compromise his standards and conscience.

In the years preceding 1531 Luther and Duke Georg had had several conflicts. As early as 1519 the duke had complained to Elector Friedrich about Luther's *A Sermon on the Highly Revered Sacrament of the Holy True Body of Christ*,[10] and in 1522, though with notable lack of success, he had ordered the confiscation in his territory of Luther's German translation of the New Testament. Luther's March 1522 (published) letter of consolation to Harmuth von Cronberg[11] had also aroused Duke Georg's ire. This is hardly surprising since in one of the editions, published outside of Wittenberg, the duke was characterized by name as a "water bubble" and a "straw and paper tyrant" who wished to gobble up Christ as a wolf did a gnat. The duke and Luther exchanged most ungracious letters on the matter, and the duke lodged one more complaint with the elector, the latter giving rise to a lengthy and ultimately inconclusive correspondence between the two princes. The duke had also complained to the Imperial Governing Council [*Reichsregiment*] that Luther's 1523 *On Secular Authority: To What Extent It Should Be Obeyed* had slandered the princes in general as "rogues," but his complaint had had little effect. There were occasional lulls in this running feud. At one point, in 1525, Luther had even been induced by friends to send the duke a relatively polite letter. He had done this, however, in the mistaken belief that the duke was becoming more receptive to the Protestant position. The duke's uncompromising rejection of his advances had quickly disabused Luther of his false hopes for the duke.[12] Of all these earlier incidents, however, the two that most rankled both men and had the greatest influence on subsequent debate were Duke Georg's 1527 foreword to Emser's Catholic version of Luther's translation of the New Testament into German and the so-called "Pack Affair" of 1528-1529.

In his foreword to Emser's version of Luther's translation, Duke Georg had sought to justify his prohibition and confiscation of Luther's New Testament translation within Ducal Saxony, for which Luther and his adherents had labeled him a "tyrant, persecutor, and enemy of the Holy Gospel and word of God."[13] The duke charged in the foreword that Luther's translation perverted and added and subtracted from the text approved by the holy Christian church, contained poisonous and heretical glosses, rejected entire books, and reviled and found fault with the canonical writings of the holy apostles, calling them "straw epistles which contain no apostolic office or character."[14] He contended furthermore that this perverted translation had been especially successful in misleading both common people and potentates. The duke expressed the hope that people would recognize that it was only the false teaching of Luther and his adherents that he sought to suppress in his lands. He gladly supported and encouraged the gospel and word of God approved by the Christian church.[15] Emser's translation was now being published, Duke Georg explained, so that none of the duke's subjects could complain in the future that the gospel or word of God was being kept from them and so that they could easily recognize the perverted translations, glosses, and interpretation of Luther and the other heretics.[16]

Luther had been greatly incensed by this foreword and by Emser's plagiarism of his own German translation. He had contemplated a response,[17] but had finally decided to let the matter rest. All of his dislike of the duke and his resentments, and the reasons therefor, were, however, thoroughly aired in the Pack Affair of 1528-1529.

In March 1528 Otto von Pack, vice-chancellor to Duke Georg, had presented Landgrave Philipp of Hesse (the duke's son-in-law) and Elector Johann of Electoral Saxony with evidence that the Catholics, including Archduke Ferdinand of Austria, Cardinal Albrecht of Mainz, and Duke Georg of Saxony, had formed a secret alliance. The reputed purpose of the alliance was to restore Catholicism within Electoral Saxony and the Landgravate of Hesse and to force the elector to hand over to them "the archheretic Martin Luther along with all the heretical preachers, priests, apostate monks [and] nuns, and other clergy who had changed their habit, religion, and spiritual character."[18]

Having learned of this alleged alliance, the two Protestant princes had decided to anticipate the Catholic attack with one of their own. In their planning, however, they had not reckoned with Melanchthon and Luther. When apprised of the princes' plans, these two Wittenbergers had argued that such a preventative attack would be unchristian. They had advised the elector and landgrave to wait for the Catholic princes to make the first attack, and they had threatened to quit Electoral Saxony if the elector persisted in these agressive plans.[19] There had followed a flurry of opinions and meetings. Finally, on 17 May 1528, Philipp had confronted his father-in-law, Duke Georg, with his evidence for the secret alliance.[20] The duke, however, had denied that there was any such alliance, and had branded the document supplied by Pack as a forgery. He had then published the correspondence between himself and Philipp to reveal "with what deceitful falsehood the children of this malicious world endeavored to awaken unrest between kings, prelates, and spiritual and secular princes to the ruin of poor people in the empire."[21]

If, through this public apology, Duke Georg was able to convince Landgrave Philipp and others of his innocence in the matter of the alleged Catholic alliance, he had failed to convince Luther.[22] In a letter to Wenzeslaus Link in Nuremburg Luther had written that he interpreted the duke's "most frigid apology" as a confession.

> But let them deny, excuse, fabricate, I have certain knowledge that that alliance is not a mere nothing or chimera, although the monstrosity is sufficiently monstrous. Then the world knows that they have so far attempted and done such things publicly by mind, deed, edict, and most pertinacious zeal, and still do. For they wish the gospel extinguished, which no one can deny. But what is this to you who are without doubt certain about all these things? You should only know that neither do we believe those impious [princes], although we offer, desire, and grant peace. God will confound that most foolish fool [*Moron Morotaton—* Duke Georg], who like Moab dares more than he is able, and boasts not according to his powers, as he has always done. We shall pray against those murderers, and so far allowance had been made for them. If they undertake anything anew, we shall pray to God, then we shall warn them that they may be destroyed without mercy since the insatiable bloodsuckers do not wish to cease until they see Germany soaked in blood.[23]

Link had circulated this letter among friends in Nuremberg, and somehow a copy reached Duke Georg.[24] Feeling himself slandered, the duke had then exchanged terse, hostile letters with Luther and had initiated a lengthy correspondence with the elector on the matter.[25] He had finally published in his defense a placard entitled somewhat awkwardly *What Character ₍gestalt₎ In Regards the Fictitious Alliance We, Georg, by God's Grace Duke of Saxony, Landgrave of Thuringia, and Margrave of Meissen, Were Groundlessly Alleged ₍To Have₎ In Writings by Martin Luther, And Our Answer Thereto.*[26] Luther had responded with his treatise *On Private and Stolen Letters,* a furious piece of polemic in which, among other things, he accused the duke of having stolen and improperly published Luther's private letter.[27]

Luther's attack set off another round of correspondence between the two Saxonies, and Duke Georg published a reply to Luther's treatise.[28] The elector had finally felt constrained to write Luther about his "rather sharp" attack on the duke. He had requested that in the future Luther not publish anything concerning Duke Georg or other princes and persons without having first sent it to the elector and received permission for publication. As for treatises dealing with Christian doctrine, they would continue to be censored by a panel composed of the rector and other University members, a practice that had been established under Elector Friedrich the Wise.[29]

Following this exchange there was a lull in the public hostilities between Luther and the duke which lasted for a couple of years. With the appearance of the *Warning,* and with Luther's *Glosses on the Alleged Imperial Edict* (also 1531), which was a thorough refutation of the Recess of the Augsburg Diet, however, the feud was resumed with, if anything, greater passion and acrimony than before.

## Against Luther's Warning to the Germans

On 8 April 1531 Duke Georg wrote Elector Johann about two profane letters written to the abbess of the Riesa cloister and signed "M.L." The duke doubted that the letters were in fact Luther's. He requested the elector to make inquiries, however, since the letters were addressed from Wittenberg and "it often happens that in such matters the perpetrator betrays himself."[30] Five days later he forwarded another complaint, this time concerning Luther's *Warning to His Dear Germans* and his *Glosses on the Alleged Imperial Edict.* Luther's two treatises were, in Duke Georg's view, "truly not a little conducive to rebellion." In addition, they contained "so much abuse against both higher and lower estates" that the duke had not seen their equal. To avoid imperial displeasure, the elector should indicate his own displeasure to Luther, the printer, and the sellers of the books.[31]

The elector sent the two complaints to Chancellor Brück, who happened at the time to be in Wittenberg. He requested the chancellor to discuss the matter with Luther and to forbid him from issuing such sharp and hot-tempered treatises in the future. On 16 April Brück conferred with Luther as ordered, and on 18 April Brück sent the elector Luther's written reply, a report of his meeting with Luther, and a draft of a possible reply to Duke Georg. In his report Brück observed that although Luther was "somewhat sharp," the elector knew how loyally and well he meant it. For that reason Brück asked the elector not to be displeased with Luther since he was a "dear man" [*teurer man*].[32] Curbing Luther was a difficult if not impossible task, one for which Brück apparently had little heart.

Luther's reply to the elector on this occasion reveals much of his thinking on the matter of polemics and on the polemical contest in general. Luther denied that he had dealt with anything rebellious in the two treatises, and he pointed out that he had greatly praised the emperor in the two treatises and had only attempted "to give Christian instruction to consciences and to disclose the evil machinations of those who misused the imperial name so that pious hearts might remain unalarmed and unseduced."[33]

Luther reminded the elector how badly the elector and his allies had been treated in the "threatening, cruel, bloodthirsty, [and] false edict" of the Diet of Augsburg. They had remained silent in the face of all this for longer than half a year and had displayed "all too much dangerous and hazardous patience." Although the elector and his allies might wish to bear with this forever, it was not given to Luther to do so. "For if I were forever to remain silent to such a public condemnation of my teaching," Luther said, "it would be equivalent to my forsaking and denying it. Before I am willing to do and endure that, I would prefer to burden myself with the anger of all the devils, of all the world, not to mention of the imperial rabble [councils? *keiserisschen rotte*]."[34]

Luther agreed with those who considered his two treatises as "sharp and precipitous [*scharf vnd geschwinde*]." "I did not write them with the intention that they be dull and mild and I am only sorry that they are not sharper and more hot-tempered, for whoever looks closely at the sharpness and precipitousness [*Geschwindigkeit*] of the dealings on the other side will not consider my treatises to be particularly sharp or precipitous, unless it is considered mild and gentle dealings to have published against Your Electoral Grace and your allies such a cruel edict and condemnation without a hearing or an opportunity to reply and thereby to draw the sword and fury of the whole empire against Your Electoral Grace's life and limb and to undertake to make Germany full of innocent blood, widows, [and] orphans and to destroy and devastate the whole empire."[35] When would the Catholics judge their own treatises as sharp? This led to a series of interesting rhetorical questions:

> When has the emperor censured or forbidden the treatises that are continually being published in the whole empire and in the emperor's hereditary lands and in Italy and which attack us most sharply and abusively? When has His Royal Majesty of Bohemia deemed too sharp the mendacious, slanderous, asinine treatises of Dr. Faber and the like? When have the dukes of Bavaria restrained or censured the treatises of Dr. Eck and others, which are full of lies and the most bitter slander? When does Margrave Joachim censure his Wimpina and Mensingen, the poisonous adders and liars? When had Duke Georg ever been annoyed with what Emser, Dr. Cochlaeus, and many others in his lands have written so sharply, bitterly and abusively against us, in which also the honor of the sensitive, pious prince, Duke Friedrich of blessed memory, was not a little injured, not to mention how

*45*

Your Electoral Grace was lashed and cuffed thereby? Even Duke
Georg himself has now often written against me in such a fashion
that even a good-for-nothing [*loser*] Emser or "Snot-spoon"
[*Rotzleffel*=Cochlaeus] ought to be ashamed to write, but he too
is still not to be given [any rebuke].

From this Your Electoral Grace sees well that the opinion
of such people is [that] if on their side a hundred thousand
authors, yes, when every leaf and blade of grass wrote and cried
out against us in the most venomous, bitter, abusive, [and] mendacious fashion and we remained silent and assented to it, that
would be right and fine. But when I, poor man, alone against so
many enormous monsters and abominations, cry out even once,
then no one has written sharply except Luther alone.[36]

Luther went on to point out that the Catholics were not stupid and
would like to have such a one-sided arrangement.[37] About the two
letters to the abbess or about the abbess herself, Luther professed to
know nothing.

In this reply is clearly seen Luther's sense of responsibility to speak
out whenever he thought the gospel message was threatened, even if to
do so were to displease his prince. One also glimpses the apocalyptic
dimensions of the contest, as Luther viewed it. The evil on the other
side called for the sharpest possible attack. Rather than being too
harsh, the treatises were, in Luther's opinion, not harsh enough by
half. Finally, one finds an expression of Luther's strong conviction
that Catholic complaints, even if understood solely in human terms,
revealed a double standard. They wished to hold Luther to standards
that they themselves were unwilling to observe.

The elector's brief, and somewhat vague, reply to Duke Georg's two
complaints left the duke unsatisfied.[38] He finally decided, it would
appear,[39] to issue an anonymous treatise attacking Luther's two
treatises. In late April 1531, there was published his *Against Luther's
Warning to the Germans That They Should Not Be Obedient To the
Emperor, Another Warning That They Should Not Allow Themselves
To Be Misled By It Nor To Be Moved To Disobedience, [Written] by
an Obedient Nonpartisan*. The pastor at Cölln, Francis Arnoldi, provided a short afterword in the second edition of the treatise. This edition happened into Luther's hands in time for him to prepare a
response that could appear at the Leipzig Book Fair along with Duke
Georg's attack.[40]

In the very first paragraph of his anonymous treatise, Duke Georg
summarized his argument:

Luther has now recently published a treatise once again which he called "A Warning To His Dear Germans," but which with more justice might be called an enticement and guide to disobedience and rebellion. For in it he basically seeks nothing else but to make us Germans disloyal to the emperor and insubordinate to all authority. Now with what insidious perfidy, lies, screams, and bawling he does this and how often he used the devil's name besides, I shall let others, who are always saying that he is a holy man and possesses the Holy Spirit, offer some explanation.[41]

It was the Lutherans, the duke maintained, not the Catholics, who were arming, rising in rebellion, and depriving people of their possessions.[42] If the emperor were to take up arms, it would be to punish this rebellion and theft, and not, as Luther claimed, to persecute the gospel,[43] or to defend the "knavery of the papists"[44] or to extinguish the good among the Lutherans.[45] There were good and bad people among both Catholics and Lutherans. For each side to attack the other on account of the ill will or misdeeds of some among them would lead to mutual destruction. "For this reason, I wish here neither to defend the vices and misdeeds of the papists nor to inveigh against the good teaching of the Lutherans, if there is some, but only to say that even if the papists were such people as Luther describes, it still should not induce any Christian to refuse due obedience to the emperor."[46] Luther was doing the emperor a gross injustice by giving the people the impression that the emperor wished to protect the knavery of the papists and to exterminate the good teaching of the Lutherans (if, the duke added, any could be found among them). Luther did the emperor and the papists an even greater injustice when he accused them of being unable to tolerate the article "that faith that works through love alone makes [a person] righteous and free from sin."[47] "For indeed they not only can tolerate it," the duke protested, "but they teach and preach it themselves, but in fact with a greater improvement of the people than Luther accomplishes, who so over-stresses it at the expense of love. Such faith [as Luther's] St. Paul and also [St.] John considered a dead faith." Since Luther left out love, the duke almost had to conclude that Luther wished to extinguish and exterminate true faith, which did not exist without works of love, as he falsely accused the emperor and papists of wanting to do.[48] 
It was the emperor who desired peace, the duke claimed. It was the Lutherans who armed for war and thought to maintain their gospel against the emperor with the sword. The gospel was not, however, to be maintained by the sword but by the power of God, "as Luther himself . . . had often indicated."

47

But now one sees well that he does not trust the power of God but rather thinks to protect himself with the sword and in that fashion to confirm his undertaking in the empire so that one would have to look upon him as a prophet and holy man. How holy he is and what spirit resides in him, if one otherwise does not sense [it], he could nevertheless guess from his treatises in which one finds not much sign of love, peaceableness, gentleness, [and] patience, which the spirit of God usually gives, but rather nothing but cursing, scolding, abuse, slander, shameless tales and lewd sayings, not to mention the insidious tricks and presumptuous lies by which he gladly wishes to make subordinates disobedient to their authorities and to bring [them] together at one place to the devil's advantage so that the pious with the evil would be exterminated through murder and bloodshed. If he might accomplish this, dear God, how he would afterwards shout for joy and exult, how he would be pleased that he had so well accomplished the work of his lord, the devil![49]

The harshness of Luther's treatise and its language betrayed Luther's true intention.*

Duke Georg requested all good Christians to maintain the peace and obey their authorities. He also asked them not to adhere to either the so-called papists or to the Lutherans, but to take what was good and Christian from each and let the rest go. In a sentence: "Because you are not forced to believe in your heart other than what God has commanded you [to believe], may you indeed always stick to those things that serve obedience and peace, so long as God gives the grace to separate the evil from the good; and the matter will go forward everywhere in a good and Christian fashion."[50]

---

*At another point Duke Georg restated this criticism: "For who does not realize that all his abuse, slander, cursing, scolding, and incitement to disobedience, which he has in [his writings], is done with the sole intention that, if the pious princes and lords, which he had attracted to himself, did not wish themselves to instigate war or rebellion, he should nevertheless cause the emperor and other lords [to do so], so that in any case the plans of his lord, the devil, would be successful? Were he, however, that which he claims to be, namely, a true preacher of the gospel, he would undoubtedly do nothing of the sort. Instead he would chastise the shortcomings and misdeeds of his adversaries with complete patience and gentleness. He would seek their improvement not destruction. But since he on the contrary does nothing but scold, curse, rave, and rage, it is to be feared that he will lead to eternal and irreparable destruction not only his adversaries but also his closest adherents. For if they otherwise bore no guilt in the matter, still one does not see it as in accordance with their responsibilities that they tolerate, protect, and use in their lands such a one, who most harshly scolds, abuses, and slanders the emperor, kings, princes, and all other authority, not to mention how some incite him to this" (WA 30/3:421).

In sum, there was little love or peaceableness among the Lutherans; rather there was nothing but an insubordinate will and an inclination to rebellion. This was proved by Luther's treatise "in which he to be sure appears to warn the common man that if the emperor summons him against the Lutherans, he should not obey him. But in truth he basically seeks nothing else than that the common man not await the coming war with the emperor, which he himself has fabricated and imagined, but instigate it himself and exterminate all higher and lower authority. [This he wishes] so that a new government [will be] formed according to his pleasure and he, Luther, will be considered an over-lord of it and a new Turkdom will finally be established in Christendom."[51]

Clearly this was not the work of a nonpartisan, whatever the claims of its title. On the other hand, it was also not a totally partisan work lacking in all balance or objectivity. The duke was a Catholic moderate. He disapproved of the excesses of both parties, Catholics and Protestants. And he was genuinely conservative in political matters. The subversive aspects of Luther's treatises did not escape his notice. As we have seen, Luther's *Warning* was in fact an inflammatory and provocative piece of writing. While the duke was not at all right about Luther's motives in writing the *Warning,* he was not all wrong about the effects of the *Warning.* The extreme vehemence with which Luther responded to the duke's attack was due at least in part, I believe, to his awareness that the duke had made not such a bad case for himself.


## Against the [Character] Assassin at Dresden

As mentioned earlier, a copy of this treatise fell into Luther's hands early enough for him to prepare a rebuttal that appeared simultaneously with the publication of the anonymous treatise in late April or very early May. In the rebuttal Luther professed not to know the identity of his attacker and simply entitled his treatise *Against the [Character] Assassin at Dresden* since Dresden was the place of publication of the duke's original attack. Luther most likely knew that Duke Georg was the author.[52] It served his purpose, however, and allowed him more latitude in his attack, to pretend ignorance. Luther's treatise was published and causing a stir in Dresden before Elector Johann even knew of its existence.[53]

The treatise was a point-by-point refutation, framed in vehement, abusive language. Its thesis was that it was the papists, not the Lutherans or Luther himself, who were disobedient and arming to attack the Protestants. When they claimed otherwise, they were lying and slandering the Lutherans. "Practically the whole world knows," Luther asserted, "that no one has written so grandly about the emperor and obedience than I have. And what the papal asses knows about this, they have learned from me. Earlier, they had known nothing about it."[54] He had taught that only in the special case where the emperor or other secular authority sought to wage war against God and justice, should one refuse to obey.[55] Whether the Protestants were arming or not, Luther wished the papists to suffer the fear and anxiety that they were. Such was the fear that had plagued Cain, Annas, and Caiaphas. "So, too, our murderers, who have shed so much innocent blood and gladly wish to shed more, should be plagued by the anxiety and fear that there will be a rebellion. And even if the Lutherans were not to arm themselves, they [the Catholics] should still be fearful that Germany was full of armed Lutherans."[56] On the other hand, that the Catholics sought the armed destruction of the Protestants could not be denied. To support this claim Luther listed some twelve pieces of evidence, including the "Catholic Alliance" disclosed by Pack and the recent edict of the Augsburg Diet.[57]

To this historical evidence Luther added that Holy Scripture testified that the world was either Cain or Abel, either of the children of the devil or of the children of God. There had to be a murderer and bloodhound lurking within that which was Cain and of the devil; there had to be a pious, peaceable heart within that which was Abel. By their fruits one could determine which was Cain or Abel. The papists had not wished peace but had concluded the Imperial Diet with threats. The "assassin" himself could not deny this. The Lutherans, on the other hand, unceasingly begged for peace and furthermore they tolerated all sorts of abuse. The papists' attempts to present themselves as friendly or peaceful must be considered pure treachery or the product of the fear that they could not accomplish what they desired to do. "I know that I do not lie," Luther insisted, "unless the Scripture be false."[58]

He had written this treatise, Luther explained again, to defend his earlier treatises against the character assassin. He announced his intention soon to issue another attack on the book "in which there are still many good papistic virtues."[59] And he closed with a response to Duke Georg's charge that his treatises contained nothing but evil words and references to the devil. His reply is worth quoting at some length:

> It should be my fame and honor, [and] so I also wish to have it, that one should say of me from now on how full I am of evil

words, abuse, and cursing for the papists. For more than ten years I have often humbled myself and have used the very fairest words with the result that the longer [I have done so] the worse I have made them. . . . Now, however, since they are impenitent [and] have decided to do simply no good but rather nothing but evil so that there is no hope [for them], I also wish from now on to occupy myself with cursing and rebuking those rogues to my grave [*wil jch auch hin furt mich mit den bösewichten zu fluchen und zu schelten bis jnn meine gruben*], and no good word more should be heard from me. I wish to ring them into the grave with my thunder and lightning.

For I cannot pray without thereby having to curse. If I say: "Holy be Thy name," I must in addition say: "Cursed, damned, and disgraced must be the papists' name and all who slander Thy name." If I say: "Thy kingdom come," then I have to add: "Cursed, damned, destroyed must be the papacy with all kingdoms on earth that are opposed to Thy kingdom." If I say: "Thy will be done," then I must add: "Cursed, damned, disgraced, and to nothing must be all thoughts and plots of the papists and all who strive against Thy will and advice." In truth, I pray thusly daily without fail [both] orally and in my heart, and with me [pray in the same manner] all who believe on Christ, and I also feel indeed that it will be heard. . . . Still I hold a good, friendly, peaceful, and Christian heart towards everyone. Even my greatest enemies know that.[60]

To a casual reader, however, this passionate treatise might well seem to belie this last claim.

## *Vindication Against Duke Georg's [Charge of] Rebellion*

In 1532 Johann Friedrich succeeded his father, Johann, as Elector of Saxony. His relationship to Luther was different from that of his uncle, Friedrich the Wise, and that of his father. For one thing, he was much younger, only twenty-nine when he began his reign.[61] He regarded Luther, who was twenty years his senior, as his "spiritual father."[62] He had grown up with the Reformation movement and had been one of its staunchest advocates from the very beginning. Moreover, he was more aggressive than were his uncle or father in voicing his support for the Reformation. He was willing to go on the offensive. He was willing to encourage Luther to attack the Reformation's opponents. He was willing aggressively to defend Luther from his Catholic and Protestant detractors. He was directly responsible for many of the polemics of the older Luther. He commissioned them, he circulated them, he defended them. This new phase in the history of Luther's polemical writings began in 1533 with another dispute between Luther and Duke Georg, this time over the issue of rebellion.

On 23 March 1533, Duke Georg directed the Leipzig Council to have clergy note during the upcoming Easter period those who confessed and communed in one kind, receiving the bread alone.[63] Those who refused to adhere to the Catholic faith were to sell their goods and possessions and be banished from Ducal Saxony.[64] Underlying this order was Duke Georg's conviction that all members of his principality should at least outwardly conform to the uses of the one church accepted by the government, in this case the Roman Catholic church. Protestant princes in dealing with Anabaptists and Catholics, it should be noted, expected no less.

Luther learned of this new measure on 3 April through a letter from Peter Gengenbach, one of the leaders of the Protestants in Leipzig.[65] Several days later he received a request forwarded by the Wittenberg goldsmith Christian Düring for his opinion on whether the Leipzig Protestants could in good conscience commune in one kind "under the appearance of having received both kinds"[66] in order to satisfy their authorities. Luther's reply is worth quoting at length since it sparked another exchange between himself and Duke Georg, this time on the question of rebellion.

> Because I do not know any of you and do not know how it stands with your heart and conscience, my best advice is [that] he who has been informed and believes in his conscience as God's word and institution that both kinds is proper should indeed by body and soul not go against his conscience, that is, act against God Himself. Now since Duke Georg also dares to investigate the secrecy of the conscience, he would well deserve that one tricked him as the devil's apostle, as one could always still do. For he has no right at all for such a demand and sins [thereby] against God and the Holy Spirit. But since we are not to think of what other evil people do, be they murderers or robbers, but of what it is appropriate for us to endure and to do, it would thus be best in this case that one defiantly say to the face of the murderer and robber: "That I will not do. If you on that account take my body or goods, then you have taken from another than me, whom you must dearly repay. As Peter says, 'Jesus Christ has been ordained [*paratus est*] to judge the living and the dead.' Therefore go ahead, dear robber, what you want, I do not want; but what I want, God, too, will one day want—you should be informed of that." For one must make the sign of the cross in the devil's face [literally: one must strike the devil in the face with the cross], and not hoot [*pfeifen*] or flatter much, so that he knows

with whom he is dealing. May Christ our Lord strengthen you and be with you, Amen.[67]

On 26 April the Leipzig Council sent Duke Georg a copy of this letter together with a report of their own efforts to determine who had solicited the letter, to whom it had been written, and who had it now.[68] Upon receipt of the copy and report, Duke Georg sent a complaint to Elector Johann Friedrich on 30 April. He reminded the elector of the agreement reached in 1527 between himself and the elector's father, Johann, that stipulated that the elector request Luther and his supporters to refrain from writing treatises that were abusive or conducive to rebellion. They were also to have no dealings with Duke Georg's subjects.[69] He also pointed to the 1531 Grimma agreement that ended the controversy between Luther and Duke Georg of that year.[70] Describing Luther's letter as "unchristian and rebellious," the duke requested that the elector, in accordance with the cited agreements, indicate to Luther his displeasure in regard to "such a malicious, uncalled-for, and disobedient undertaking, in which in addition to greatly slandering and abusing us, he dared to make our subjects antagonistic toward us."[71]

The elector forwarded the letter together with a draft reply to Chancellor Brück and requested Brück to show them to Luther, Jonas, Bugenhagen, and Melanchthon and solicit their opinion on what the elector should do when Duke Georg made his predictable response. In his letter to Duke Georg, which had been corrected by Brück, perhaps in consultation with the Wittenberg theologians, the elector stated that the 1527 agreement between his father, Elector Johann, and Duke Georg did not apply to this case. Elector Johann would not have forbidden Luther or anyone else to advise and comfort suffering and persecuted Christians. He further reminded the duke of the slanderous books [*Schmähbücher*] published in Dresden and elsewhere, especially by Francis Arnoldi. Finally, he expressed pity for the duke that in his old age when he was near death and should be seeking reconciliation with God, he should escalate his attacks and dare to persecute and outlaw his subjects for adhering to the clear gospel truth and institution of Christ concerning the holy Sacrament of His body and blood. The elector would assiduously pray to God to grant the duke understanding of His divine word and to make a Paul out of a Saul.[72] In content and even tone, this letter could practically have been written by Luther himself; certainly he would have disagreed with little in it.

In the meanwhile Luther had exchanged letters with Wolf Wiedemann, the mayor of Leipzig. Wiedemann had written on 25

April to confirm that Luther's 11 April letter to the Leipzig Protestants was in fact his.[73] Luther had responded two days later, asking at whose command Wiedemann was making inquiry, at command "of the pastor at Cölln [Francis Arnoldi] or of the assassin at Dresden or of your Junker Duke Georg?"[74] This exchange prompted another complaint from Duke Georg, written on 2 May, and a reply from the elector four days later. The elector simply acknowledged receipt of the duke's complaint and referred him to his letter of 3 May. To Duke Georg's comment, however, that although Wiedemann had no command from him to send the letter to Luther, he had not done anything improper or inappropriate to his office, Elector Johann Friedrich replied that if the mayor wished to investigate and inform on injured Christians, as his letters indicated, then he should do so in some place other than Wittenberg and the lands of Electoral Saxony.[75]

In his reply of 8 May to this and to the elector's letter of 4 May Duke Georg gave as good as he had received. He would have to allow Luther, he wrote, to comfort those whom he brought into his sect, as best as Luther was able, so long as it caused no rebellion or other injury to Duke Georg or his subjects and he was not abused or libeled and his subjects were not aroused against him and the elector did not encourage Luther in these endeavors. As for the elector's expression of pity for him, he replied that as many of the young died as of the old. No one knew who would go first. So it was fitting for him to pity the elector that he had allowed an apostate, forsworn monk to seduce him away from the obedience and order of the Christian church. He would pray to God daily that God grant the elector grace to return to the unity and obedience of the Christian church and to obedience to the imperial majesty as the divinely established authority.

> Martin Luther has called us an enemy of the gospel and the devil's apostle and compared us with murderers and robbers. But you compared us to Saul, a persecutor of the Christian church, as he himself confessed. But we have never, may God be praised, persecuted members of the true Christian congregation.

In closing Duke Georg observed that it seemed closer to Saul's persecution of Christians that one allowed "churches, cloisters, and the persons and goods belonging to them to be demolished, persecuted, banished, and turned to worldly splendor."[76]

Elector Johann Friedrich replied on 11 May, professing disingenuously some surprise at the duke's unfriendly comments. Since the duke continued to insist that Luther's letter of consolation was seditious, the elector felt constrained to elaborate on his previous replies. In no way could he see that Luther had given cause for the interpretation the duke was placing on the letter. On the contrary, no one could rebuke as rebellious the advice that the duke's subjects should rather leave house and land, wife and child than deny the holy gospel and the institution of Christ in the holy Sacrament.

> In order that you should recognize that we, too, do not wish to tolerate rebellion in our electoral principality, we are intending to send your letter to Dr. Martin and require his answer to it. . . . If it turns out, as we expect, that injustice was being done him, then you will know to spare us further on the matter and will have excused the good man. If it turns out, however, that he does desire to incite rebellion, we will know how to proceed against him, too, in an irreproachable fashion.

He closed again with his warning that the duke should consider his age and the approach of death and stop plaguing and burdening his subjects concerning the clear gospel truth.[77]

As he had indicated was his intention to Duke Georg, the elector sent Luther a copy of the duke's letter of 8 May and a copy of his reply. In his accompanying letter, he gave Luther clear instructions:

> Now if you should be of the mind through your writings to incite to some rebellion the populace of our relative or of others, we could in no way tolerate that from you, and it could very conceivably happen that we would not neglect to impose the appropriate penalty on you on that account. We would expect, however, that that is not your intention. Therefore, you will, as required [*Euer Notdurft nach*], know how indeed through your writings to justify and give answer for yourself to our relative and to each and everyone else concerning these charges and attributions so that your innocence is apparent, for we would have to consider you guilty in the matter if such an apology of yours were not to appear.[78]

Luther promptly accepted the elector's charge, and by 14 July his *Vindication Against Duke Georg's ₁Charge of₁ Rebellion, Including a Letter of Consolation to the Innocent Christians Driven by Him from Leipzig* had left the press.[79]

This treatise was brief, but no less aggressive or pugnacious for this fact. As was the case with his letter to Wenceslaus Link in 1528, Luther no longer had the original, nor had he kept a copy. He accordingly warned the reader that Duke Georg's copy was not a certain foundation on which to build since it had passed through so many hands.

Luther next replied to each of Duke Georg's complaints. A child of seven knew, Luther claimed, that his advice that for the sake of God's word people should suffer and risk life and goods and not oppose their authorities and tyrants was a proper Christian teaching. He denied that he had infringed on the duke's honor: "We indeed grant Duke Georg that in the presence of the world he sits in princely honor and is a laudable, honorable prince of the empire; but in the presence of God and in spiritual matters we grant him no honor unless it be the honor of Pilate, Herod, Judas, and similar people who condemned and put to death Christ and his apostles on account of God's word."[80] He had not said that one should hit Duke Georg in the face but rather the devil; Duke Georg could not apply this to himself unless he wished to call himself a devil, which Luther's letter did not do. And he charged that Duke Georg had imposed an oath on his subjects at Leipzig and forced them to swear that they would help condemn and persecute the Lutheran teaching.[81]

While he himself bore no grudge towards anyone, he wrote, he had to innocently bear the title of rebel, a title that Christ himself had had to bear. "For he himself was also crucified as a rebel and hanged between two murderers, and his rebellious title was: 'King of the Jews,' that is, that he wished to oppose the emperor, his authority, to make his subjects disobedient and disloyal, and to make himself king, etc."[82] In fact, since the time of the apostles no one had more magnificiently upheld secular authority than had he.[83] The real rebels were the Catholics who condemned the lay estate and tried to turn rulers into monks.[84]

In the second half of the treatise Luther consoled those who had been unjustly exiled from Leipzig and were suffering for Christ's sake.[85] As Luther saw it, the papacy had not done anything since its founding over six hundred years ago but shed blood, and not only the blood of heretics. Even Duke Georg, as Luther claimed he had discovered at Worms and subsequently at Augsburg, would have gladly caused calamity and bloodshed in the German lands. "Thereafter Duke Georg would have shed tears," Luther commented sarcastically, "and lamented the blood of the disobedient and perhaps would have sent, say, a thousand gulden to Meissen to buy requiem masses for the slain Lutheran heretics, as though it were so sorrowful to him, [and] afterwards God would be placated, and he [Duke Georg] would have attained the reputation for unheard-of mercy. Who believes, however, that God would allow Himself to be so easily played the fool and deceived?" Only the emperor had forestalled this.[86] Luther urged his readers to wait and see what God would bring about.[87] If the Last Judgment itself did not intervene, Luther expected that the same thing would happen to the papists as had happened to the Jews at Jerusalem, who also were unable to cease from murder and bloodshed until they had put Christ himself and his apostles to death. Then the Romans had come along and given them sufficient death and bloodshed.

## Duke Georg's Honorable and Thorough Apology

Duke Georg read Luther's *Vindication* shortly after it was published, and immediately began investigating Luther's charge concerning an oath imposed on the Leipzig Protestants.[88] When both the Leipzig Council and the bishop of Merseburg, who had headed the examining commission that had on 30 May negotiated with the Leipzig Protestants, denied knowledge of any oath, the duke sent a formal delegation to the elector to demand that he proceed against Luther as a "mendacious, forsworn, and apostate monk" who had circulated "an obvious, unfounded [*unerfindlichen*] lie about the concocted oath." The next day, 10 August, the elector replied through Chancellor Brück:

> That the elector of Saxony wished to let be Doctor Martin Luther's writing in [the matter of] his *Vindication;* but as for Doctor Martin Luther himself, His Electoral Grace knew of no way to regard him other than as one who had never done anything but preach, teach, and write against rebellion, as his writings also testify. And the elector of Saxony intended to remain all the way to his grave in the belief that Luther is he, whom God has selected as a special man to preach his holy word clearly, purely, and faithfully.[89]

After such a declaration of unqualified support for Luther by the elector, Duke Georg had no recourse except to bring his case before the court of public opinion. He accordingly roused his stable of writers against Luther and even drafted a reply himself under the name of Francis Arnoldi of Cölln, although this reply was never published. Amnicola and Cochlaeus, however, did enter the public lists for their Duke.

Cochlaeus's first treatise, completed on 6 September 1533, bore Duke Georg's coat of arms and the title *Duke Georg of Saxony's Honorable and Thorough Apology Against Martin Luther's Seditious and Mendacious Letter and Vindication.* Given this title it is hardly surprising that Luther mistook the treatise, at least initially, to be by Duke Georg himself, although on the top of the first page after the

*57*

*Protestatio Autoris* Cochlaeus's name is prominently displayed. As the title itself indicated, the treatise was a thorough reply to Luther's letter and *Vindication,* running some one hundred pages in length. Although Luther later characterized Cochlaeus's writings as "pure twaddle, lies, or abuse" and claimed not to have read the treatise but only to have paged through it, this treatise was in fact a serious, well-argued, and occasionally telling attack on Luther. It also displayed an impressive knowledge of Luther's own writings, of the Bible, of church history and law. In this treatise Cochlaeus explains in detail why Catholics held Luther responsible for much of the contemporary unrest in Germany.[90]

Here are some of the major points in this vituperative and long-winded treatise. It was evident, Cochlaeus claimed, that in his letter Luther had slandered the duke and attempted to incite the population to rebellion by calling the duke the enemy of the gospel and a devil's apostle, a murder, and a robber. Who could be well disposed toward a robber or murderer, or toward an enemy of the gospel and the devil's apostle? he asked. Such evil words spoiled the whole letter.[91]

Turning to Luther's *Vindication,* he scored Luther for refusing either to acknowledge or deny that the letter was his, and compared this with contradictory statements that could be found in Luther's earlier and later writings.[92] Quoting Luther's *Confession Concerning the Lord's Supper,* Cochlaeus observed that Luther himself had condemned such contradictory writing in the Sacramentarians' publications with the argument that the devil was the father of disunity and the contradictions in the writings of the Sacramentarians allowed one to detect this spirit of disunity among them.[93] Luther was, in fact, a faithless man, forsworn in his oaths to God, pope, cloister, and university.[94]

It was a good Lutheran trick, he charged, for Luther to distinguish between Duke Georg and the devil who allegedly possessed him. In this way he could hypocritically argue that when he taught that one should not obey Duke Georg's mandate, he did not mean Duke Georg as a secular authority but rather the devil who used Duke Georg as a mask. It was a similar case when he taught that one should strike the devil in the face with the cross and then claimed that he was not referring to Duke Georg. If such an excuse were valid, however, then any prince or gentleman could be slandered and reviled in the worst possible fashion without danger of punishment for the slander, and all rebellion and vice could be introduced among the populace under such a specious distinction [*zwyfachen hüttlein*].[95] The oath Luther alleged to have been imposed on the Leipzigers was a Lutheran fabrication, intended to incite his allies against Duke Georg and to make the duke's subjects rise in rebellion.[96]

At great length Cochlaeus disputed Luther's claim to have "magnificently" upheld secular authority, citing past controversies and reproducing numerous excerpts from Luther's works in an attempt to prove the contrary.[97] These quotes indicate that it is Luther's often pungent comments about the limits of secular authority in the spiritual sphere that Cochlaeus found most objectionable. And in the selective citation of quotes, often drastically severed from their original context, Cochlaeus allowed little of Luther's distinction between the kingdoms to come through.

These are but a few of the arguments that fill this treatise. Cochlaeus's language is rich with insult, a clear attempt to repay Luther in his own coin. Two examples suffice. To Luther's assertion that he was certain that Duke Georg was damned, Cochlaeus, likening Luther to the great heretics of the past, argued on the contrary that it was Luther who was certainly damned unless he reunited with the church. By supporting the Bohemian schism, Luther condemned himself. But Luther did not recognize, Cochlaeus asserted,

> that he more closely resembled Judas than did Duke Georg, not only in [his] many traitorous actions, in which he has done much, from [the time of the Diet of] Worms to this very hour, but also in "hanging," for as Judas hanged himself after he had betrayed Christ and burst right in two [*vnd barste mitten entzwey*], in the same manner Luther hanged himself right after he had betrayed the poor peasants. Where [did he hang himself]? On a runaway nun, Katherina von Bora, on whom he still hangs until he one day bursts on her, the unchaste rooster [*an ein ausgeloffene Nonn/ Kethen von Bore/ doran er noch hangt/ biss er der tag eins auff yr zerbyrstet/ der vnkeusch Göker*][98]

And when Cochlaeus dealt with Luther's assertion that he had no bitter or evil inclination of his heart against Duke Georg or anyone else on earth, Cochlaeus observed:

> That may be believed of him by his adherents, to whom he has pandered with fleshly freedom [and] allowed all [sorts of] church robbery, and he justifies in advance everything done even publicly in violation of both laws, spiritual and secular, divine and human, if it involves attacking priests and monks. But if one asks the pope in the bulls, the emperor in the edict, the princes and estates in their recesses, the king of England in his little book and

his epistle, and many other honest people of higher and lower standing [and] of diverse nations who have written against him and have given public testimony before many concerning what a good and sweet heart Luther has; yes, if one asks his reverend archdeacon Doctor Karlstadt, as his initially closest advisor; and his tender little sons, his little brothers, his golden little friends (as he calls them) Oecolampadius, Zwingli, Bucer, Balthasar Hubmeier, etc.; also, his disciples the rebellious peasants; and, which is much more certain, if one asks his own books and letters, the fruits of his heart, then one truly discovers most clearly that in fifteen hundred years there has been, next to the bitter heart of the betrayer Judas Iscariot, no more bitter, harsh, base, venomous, bloodthirsty, restless, seditious heart on earth than Luther's heart. For although we do not see the heart within, nevertheless we recognize it as [we do] a tree by its fruit.[99]

The treatise abounds with such language.

Since Cochlaeus chose to respond to Luther's *Vindication* point-by-point, his treatise was quite long and does not read well. Still, it deserved more than the contemptuous dismissal that Luther was to give it. True, Cochlaeus gives no indication that he understood the crucial difference between the two kingdoms in Luther's thought. As a result many of his criticisms miss the mark. On the other hand, he is able to point to contradictions between the older and the younger Luther and then use with embarrassing effect Luther's own argument against his Protestant opponents that such or similar contradictions proved that their spirit was the spirit of the devil. Although his remarks about Luther's claim to harbor no bitterness towards any man are laden with partisan venom, Cochlaeus still has a point. Luther might claim that he was not ill-inclined towards anyone, but his polemical treatises, filled with such incredible passion and *ad hominem* abuse, seem to belie his claim. As Cochlaeus himself remarked, we cannot know Luther's heart. But the fruits of his heart, which include his polemics, point to passions and hatreds that are as much a part of Luther's personality as the compassion and love shown friends and supporters.

### Brief Reply to Duke Georg's Next Book

Cochlaeus himself sent a copy of his *Apology* to Elector Johann Friedrich in order, as he had announced in the treatise itself,[100] to initiate the legal proceedings concerning Luther's writings to which Luther himself had offered to submit. The elector received the treatise on 16 September. Luther, too, laid hands on a copy of the treatise, or at least parts of it, about the same time, and prepared a reply that was to appear at the Leipzig Fair at the same time as Cochlaeus's treatise. It seems likely from his *Brief Reply,* as this treatise was titled, and also from his own admission,[101] that Luther neither read Cochlaeus' *Apology* carefully nor examined the separate attack by Cochlaeus on Luther's letter to the Leipzig Protestants with its discussion of both kinds.

> My ungracious lord, Duke Georg, has now published his reply to my letter of consolation to those banished at Leipzig, and he marked this reply on the outside with his name and coat of arms, and nevertheless the master of this book styles himself Dr. Cochlaeus, whom I am accustomed to call Doctor Snotspoon [*Rotzleffel*] or Dr. Clown [*Gauch*], which is his proper name by which one may best know him; and Duke Georg is so entirely enraged that he is not satisfied publicly to accuse me and orally to condemn me before my gracious lord, Duke Johann Friedrich, Elector of Saxony, etc., and the whole court through his envoy to Aldenburg [on 9 August] but also lets me be taken to task in writing or print [*buchstablich*] before all the world by his little clown and fool. If I were not by now accustomed to the anger of the devil and the world, I would indeed learn something from such great seriousness.

So Luther began his *Brief Reply to Duke Georg's Next Book.*[102]

He first enumerated some of the charges lodged against him: he was mendacious, forsworn, and an apostate monk who was not to be trusted. As Luther saw it, the one new charge was that he himself had fabricated and mendaciously attributed to Duke Georg the oath that supposedly was imposed on those who were banished at Leipzig. Leaving aside the question whether the oath was a forgery or had simply not been carried out, Luther asked (aware, perhaps, that his charge had been mistaken) whether he should on its account be rebuked as and considered to be false and mendacious in all matters? Neither Duke Georg nor any other lord could be so pious and holy, Luther observed, that he would be willing to tolerate such a harsh law.[103]

He next turned to the charge that he was forsworn since he had not kept his monastic vow. He was honored, he replied, to be so accused.

> For I would prefer that the hangman thrust me onto the rack or burned me to powder than that Duke Georg should praise me as a pious, faithful monk. 'Tis true [that] I was [once] a pious monk, and I kept so strictly to [the rules of] my Order that I

> may state [that] if ever a monk got into heaven through monk-
> ery, i, too, would have gotten in. All my colleagues in the cloister
> who knew me will bear me out on this. For I would have
> martyred myself to death with vigils, prayers, reading, and other
> work, etc., if I had kept on longer.[104]

After a few remarks about the duke's double standard in the matter of
polemics, Luther launched into a lengthy and elaborate criticism of
monasticism and monastic vows. At best, this was a reply to a section
in Cochlaeus' treatise defending monasticism. At worst, this section
had nothing to do with Cochlaeus' treatise at all. The criticism itself
was essentially a restatement of his earlier attacks on monasticism.
Monks considered their (uncertain) good works to be equal, if not
superior, to Christ's sacrifice and hence they were the truly forsworn,
apostate, and runaway Christians. Luther's view was that a monk
denied Christ, was an apostate from Christian faith, and thus an ally
of the devil. Monks compared their monastic vow with Christ's baptism, yet the vow conveyed no security.* He concluded his attack on
monasticism with a diatribe against the distinction between commandments and counsels, the former allegedly applicable to all, the latter
only to monks.[105] And in the final pages of the treatise Luther also
defended Elector Johann from charges that had arisen from the 1528
Pack Affair.[106]

Although this treatise is one of the less edifying pieces to flow from
Luther's pen, it is still has value. Luther's discussion of monasticism
and the monk's lack of certainty of salvation, although not new, is
well-put and informative reading. The same cannot be said for his
attacks on Cochlaeus and Duke Georg. If he had taken the trouble

---

*Luther here referred to his own experience: "And I, too, was therefore wished luck,
after I had made my profession, by the prior, assembly, and confessor, [to the effect]
that I now was like an innocent child that just came pure from baptism. And in truth I
would have been greatly pleased about the magnificent deed, [namely], that I was such
an excellent man who had himself through his own work without Christ's blood made
himself so splendid and holy so easily and so quickly. But although I gladly heard such
sweet praise and magnificent words about my own works and allowed myself to be regarded as a miracle worker who could so easily make himself holy and gobble up death
along with the devil, etc., yet I could not hold firm. For when only a tiny temptation
[*anfechtung*] came along concerning death or sin, I fell apart and found neither baptism
nor monkery that could help me. Thus I had long ago also lost Christ and his baptism.
There I was, the most wretched man on earth. Day and night there was nothing but
moaning and despair so that no one could prop me up. Thus I was bathed and baptized in my monkery and had the true sweating sickness. My God be praised that I did
not sweat myself to death, otherwise I would long ago have been in the abyss of hell
with my monk's baptism. For I knew Christ only as a strict judge from whom I wished
to flee and yet could not escape" (WA 38:147-48).

actually to reply to the points made by Cochlaeus the treatise would have been much more informative for us, although perhaps less effective as a polemical work. In its organization, the treatise shows signs of hasty composition, a characteristic common to much of the polemics of the older Luther. This hastiness may reflect the need to prepare the work in time for the Leipzig fair.

Duke Georg, of course, did not find this to be a mild treatise, whatever Luther's claims for it. Given the elector's unswerving support for Luther, however, there was little the duke could do about it. Cochlaeus replied to Luther, but Luther chose to ignore him.

## Luther and His Prince

Between the polemical battle in 1531 over Luther's *Warning* and *Glosses* and the clash in 1533 over Luther's letter to the Leipzig Protestants there occurred a change in Luther's rulers. In 1531 he had to answer for his polemics to Elector Johann. In 1533 it was Johann's son, Johann Friedrich. This change is significant for the history of the polemics of the older Luther.

Consider the controversy of 1531. As mentioned earlier, Luther had acknowledged on 16 April 1531 Elector Johann's command forbidding him to publish "hot-tempered [*heftig*], sharp treatises" like his *Warning* and *Glosses*.[107] Then, however, a printed copy of Duke Georg's anonymous attack on the treatises came into his hands. This was probably sometime after 16 April since there was no mention of it or of Luther's counterattack in Luther's letter to the elector or in Brück's report of their conference. At this point Luther disregarded the electoral command and swiftly composed and published his *Against the ₍Character₎ Assassin at Dresden*. A letter written by Luther to Chancellor Brück on 8 May began with an apology for the treatise having reached Dresden before it reached Torgau. From this it appears that the electoral court at Torgau first learned of the treatise from the ducal court at Dresden.[108] Luther hoped that the apology was not necessary, for Brück had been away too long, he wrote, and he had expected his absence to continue.[109] "I also think," Luther continued, "that if my little books had to come to the court first, they would find so many masters [critics] that nothing more would come of them and [they] would make innumerable other people suspicious of me, their author.[110] Now if they appear to be exclusively Lutheran [in origin], however, everyone can offer the excuse that he had nothing to do with them."[111]

With this reply Luther appears to be completely ignoring, even defying, Elector Johann's order prohibiting the publication of such treatises without prior electoral censorship. Certainly, he apologizes (and then half-heartedly) only for the fact that the treatise reached Dresden before reaching Torgau and not for his violation of the electoral prohibition. He may have felt that he had sufficiently justified his actions in his 16 April letter to the elector and that the electoral prohibition was no longer in force. Or, Luther may have believed that the treatise did not violate the command because it was not explicitly directed against the duke (although Duke Georg was attacked by name several times in the treatise). It seems most plausible, however, that Luther had simply and knowingly disobeyed the elector. As he had said to the elector on 16 April, he felt that if he were to remain silent in the face of a public attack on his teaching that would be equivalent to denying and forsaking it. This he was unwilling to do. Therefore, since Duke Georg had branded him and his last two treatises as rebellious, Luther may have felt constrained to reply despite the electoral command. This would also explain how he could have the temerity to ask Brück to supply him with assistance for his promised sequel to *Against the Assassin*. Specifically, he asked Brück for information concerning Duke Georg's charge that the Lutherans intended to reestablish Duke Ulrich in Württemberg. "Theologically I can handle it well," Luther wrote, "but to deal with it historically [your assistance] would be very useful to me." [112]

Luther, then, had no intention on 8 May to refrain from "hot-tempered, sharp" polemics against the "assassin" at Dresden, whatever the instructions from Brück. He did agree, however, to spare Cardinal Albrecht of Mainz, but perhaps only because he was too preoccupied with other writings. [113]

The case for a belief that Luther's violation of the electoral prohibition was deliberate is strengthened by a 29 July letter from Luther to the elector. From 2 to 17 July representatives of Electoral and Ducal Saxony had met in Grimma and had reached an agreement on most points in dispute between them. As a consequence of this agreement Luther was instructed through Chancellor Brück to refrain in the future from "sharp writings" and especially those that might concern Duke Georg but only, as Luther put it, "to the extent that it possible in respects to my conscience and the [Lutheran] teachings." Luther agreed with the following, revealing qualifications:

> Now it is indeed true that Duke Georg has much to settle for with me. But in order that they see that I, too, desire peace and am not in the habit of writing my 'evil books' out of meddle-

someness [*Furwitz*], I am willing to let all that go and be for-
given so long as Duke Georg also leaves me in peace from now
on and causes no new unpleasantness, also with the proviso that
if other papists do not wish to keep peace with me, I am free to
deal with them. For in so doing I do not wish it to be taken as
an attack on Duke Georg; and he should not interpret it as
such.[114]

Clearly Luther intended to respond to Catholic attacks in the future,
whatever the elector's commands, and he reserved the right to reply
even to Duke Georg if his conscience or teachings demanded it.* With
all his professed respect for the commands of secular authority, the
commands of the gospel and of conscience came first. Elector Johann
seems to have acquiesced in this position.

As late as summer 1531, then, Elector Johann had requested Luther
to refrain from "sharp writings" against Duke Georg. When Luther
had not complied, Johann accepted Luther's position with seeming
good grace, but he did nothing to encourage Luther in this course. In
contrast, his son, Johann Friedrich, who had succeeded him to the
rule of Electoral Saxony in 1532, had instructed Luther in 1533 to
respond publicly to Duke Georg's charges that he was promoting
rebellion. Cochlaeus recognized that this was a new policy. In the epi-
logue to his *Duke Georg's Honorable and Thorough Apology* he cas-
tigated Luther for publicly attacking the duke while the duke was
attempting to resolve the matter privately. Cochlaeus also criticized
the elector for his handling of the affair and especially for ordering
Luther to respond publicly to the duke's charges.[115] In the negotiations between Albertine and Ernestine Saxony surrounding this affair,
Elector Johann Friedrich gave his full approval and support to everything that Luther did. For the last fourteen years of his life Luther's
polemics were to enjoy Johann Friedrich's unswerving support. For
his part, Johann Friedrich was to call upon Luther repeatedly to issue
public statements on issues in dispute between Catholics and Protestants. He was also more prone than his predecessors to solicit
Luther's written opinion to provide sanction and support for policies
that had been arrived at without consulting Luther or the other theo-

---

*In a coda to this dispute, Luther was approached by Alexius Chrosner, a preacher at
Altenburg, for assistance in publishing an attack on Francis Arnoldi, who had written
against Luther's *Against the Assassin* and had dropped a couple of slurs against Chrosner in the process. Due to the agreement at Grimma, Luther felt he could not assist in
the publication of Chrosner's treatise in Wittenberg and wanted nothing directly to do
with Chrosner's treatise. He was willing, however, to write to Amsdorf in Magdeburg
to see if the treatise might be printed there (WABr 6:158f.). Melanchthon was opposed
to its publication.

logians. "Time and again," Eike Wolgast concludes in his fine monograph *Die Wittenberg Theologie und die Politik der evangelischen Stände,* "there is an obvious effort to commit the theologians to decisions already made, to win their approval for them, and to use them to accomplish the elector's ends among the other Protestant estates. The original function of the Wittenberg opinion, to advise conscience, was increasingly transformed by Johann Friedrich into the function of relieving consciences, as a religious sanction and reassurance for otherwise autonomous and often previously made decisions of the politicians."[116] In a way markedly different from the preceding decade and a half, Luther was to spend the last years of his life as a counselor to princes and a publicist in service to a religious movement that had become inextricably entangled in political interests.

## The Dynamics of the Disputes

These exchanges over Luther's *Warning* and *Glosses* and over his letter to the Leipzig Protestants illustrate two characteristics of all Luther's exchanges on the issue of obedience to secular authority. First, Luther, on the basis of his theology of the two kingdoms, could with complete consistency argue that no one had advocated obedience to secular authority more forcefully than had he. Yet, at the same time, he could violently attack individuals in authority and advise that Christians disobey such "robbers and murderers" when they attempted to coerce consciences in spiritual matters. He wished from now on, he announced defiantly, to occupy himself for the rest of his life with cursing and rebuking such impenitent men. Second, Catholics, whether maliciously or not, failed to recognize this consistency. For them, Luther's distinctions were hypocritical. The practical effects of his treatises, whatever his theological arguments, was to promote resistance and rebellion toward duly constituted authorities. With a certain plausibility they argued that attacks on secular authorities in the religious sphere necessarily carried over to secular affairs. Who, Cochlaeus asked, would obey a robber and murderer? Duke Georg and Cochlaeus pointed particularly to Luther's harsh language, which, they insisted repeatedly, betrayed Luther's true rebellious spirit. While missing the whole force of Luther's theological argument, they nonetheless raised a practical issue that Luther never addresses. Luther insists that his polemics be judged on the basis of what he said—not an unreasonable request in most cases. But what of how his treatises might be understood by the general populace? By attacking

Catholic authorities in such forceful terms, he was running the risk that his readers would be so carried away by his attack that they failed to realize the boundaries Luther set. Catholic fears were not totally inspired by partisan considerations. As the Peasants' War demonstrated, especially in the Twelve Articles,[117] there could be serious discrepancies between what Luther intended with his publications and how they were understood by others.

Luther's arguments had force—for other Protestants. Duke Georg's and Cochlaeus's arguments had force—for other Catholics. They were responding to, but no longer communicating with, each other. The lines had been long drawn. The goal now was not to encourage defections across the line but to exhort the troops on one's own side of the line. The content and style of the treatises themselves suggested their purpose and intended audience. They are replete with the epithets and name-calling that delights the ears of the partisan and closes those of the opponent. With righteous indignation the dominant tone, old grievances and past disputes are exhumed and paraded before the partisan reader to remind him of the long history of injustice and wickedness practiced by their opponents, of which the current dispute is but the latest example. Old and familiar arguments, both theological and political, are rehearsed once again. Where there are attempts at education, they are to deepen and add sophistication to beliefs already held. Whatever the author's conscious intention, such treatises are not designed to reach the unconverted.

## CHAPTER FOUR

# A Matter of Substance:
# The Convening of a Council

From the first years of the Reformation movement, the appeal by Protestants to a future general council of the church both served the nascent movement and threatened it. It served the movement by reinforcing the widespread impression that the issues in dispute would remain undecided until a council met and pronounced on them, an impression hotly contested by advocates of the doctrine of papal supremacy and infallibility. It served the movement by gaining support from reform-minded Catholics and conciliarist circles within Germany. These groups believed, along with many members of the new movement, that a general council of the church offered the only possibility for the reestablishment of ecclesiastical unity and for the realization of needed ecclesiastical reforms. As a result, they were willing to join with the Protestants in calling for a general council and to oppose attempts to settle the dispute by force. Finally, it served the movement by securing time for it to spread and take root and by providing legal justification for armed resistance if there were an attempt to reimpose Catholicism by force while the appeal to the council was still pending.

The threat posed by the Protestant appeal to a future general council was, of course, that it would be answered, not with a "free Christian council" as the Protestants understood it, but with a council on the model of the Council of Constance that would treat the Protestants as the Council of Constance had treated Hus and the Hussites.

In the 1530s Luther and his fellow Protestants were forced to come to terms with this threat. The convening of a general council of the church was no longer such an unlikely possibility as it had once been. The papacy seemed to be moving, however reluctantly, to answer the chorus of voices clamoring for a council. Now the Protestant estates and the Protestant theologians were confronted with the delicate problem of remaining faithful to their repeated calls for a "true Christian council" while discrediting the council called by the pope, and justifying their refusal to participate in it.

The rulers and theologians were of different minds on how best to deal with this problem. The rulers, such as Luther's own prince, Elector Johann Friedrich, tended to view the problem in political and legal terms. For the elector the papal invitation to a council and the papal council itself was a legal snare, set to capture the Protestants. He feared that a meeting with the papal legate who bore the invitation or an acceptance of the invitation would be a tacit acknowledgment of the papal claim to be head of council and church. The invitation itself he viewed as a devious attempt to divide the Protestant princes and estates from their preachers and scholars. Once the Protestants had agreed to participate they would have to support the citation and condemnation of the Protestant preachers, as had been attempted at the Diet of Augsburg and as had actually occurred with the Hussites in Constance. The elector further expected that a Catholic majority would dominate the council, even if the laity were allowed to vote, and would force its will on the Protestant minority. And by their attendance the Protestants would have lost their right to appeal to yet another council. He also feared that once the council convened the Protestants would lose the protection of the Nuremberg Standstill, which would no longer be in force. For these and other weighty political and legal reasons, the elector and his fellow Protestant rulers thought it best to protest the papal council and to refuse participation.[1]

The elector's theologians, including Luther, disagreed. They expected nothing good from a papal council, but they nonetheless urged their prince not to refuse the invitation. For them it was a question of faith and appearances. It would simply look bad to refuse a council after having called for one for so many years. It would also suggest a lack of faith and trust in God's ability to protect them or an unwillingness to risk martyrdom for their belief.[2] Not surprisingly they lost the argument with their prince. And they acquired the task of justifying this decision and discrediting the papal council.[3] Luther's attacks on the papal council, although heavily theological in their argumentation, were meant to serve this political decision.

Luther employed a variety of literary forms to meet this challenge: the preface, marginalia and glosses, theses for disputation, the parody, the treatise. The works Luther produced against a papal council were more overtly theological than most of the polemical works in his later years; this is not surprising given that the issue in dispute was the nature of a general council, its authority, who would convene it, and who might participate. Luther was in his element, and it shows. These writings lack the forced and tense quality of his writings on resistance and rebellion.

There is also novelty in these writings. Luther has developed into a powerful polemical weapon a form of argumentation that he had employed but little in his earlier polemics: the "historical argument." Of course he had discovered the liberating power and polemical utility of historical knowledge as early as the 1519 Leipzig debate.[4] But it was only years later that he found the opportunity to study church history in detail. To his professed satisfaction, historical sources appeared to support the theological convictions that he had developed directly out of his reading of Scripture. In his writings on the council Luther eagerly shares these *a posteriori* confirmations of his *a priori* convictions. Moreover, in a striking number of these writings Luther's argument develops in the analysis of historical documents, from both the recent and remote past. Historical documents, faithfully reproduced, are used both as evidence to buttress other arguments and as polemical pieces in their own right, conveying directly to the reader Luther's message about the papal council and the papal church. The argument from Scripture and from reason is accordingly being augmented by the argument from history and from documental evidence.

## Luther's First Appeal to a Council

Martin Luther first appealed on 28 November 1518 from a "misinformed" Pope Leo X to a future council to be held "at a safe place." This appeal followed his interview in Augsburg with Cardinal Cajetan when it became apparent that the pope and his representatives intended to allow Luther only the option of recanting or of being arrested and sent to Rome.[5] In his appeal Luther asserted that the "sacrosanct council legitimately assembled in the Holy Spirit [and] representing the holy catholic church is superior to the pope in matters concerning faith" and he denied that the pope had the authority to forbid appeals from his decrees to a council. Luther had the appeal printed for use only in case he was actually excommunicated, but the printer sold a number of advance copies, thus making the appeal public.[6]

Two years later Luther received the bull *Exsurge, Domine* which gave him sixty days to recant and which, incidentally, rejected his earlier appeal to a council on the basis of Pope Pius II's and Pope Julius II's prohibitions of such appeals. On 17 November 1520, Luther renewed his appeal to a "Christian council."[7] He asserted that "the power of the pope is not superior or contrary to, but rather for the sake of and subordinate to Scripture and divine truth."

In the interval between these two appeals Luther had publicly asserted, first in the Leipzig debate[8] and then in published treatises,[9] that councils had erred in the past and could err in the future. As a result, he was accused in the bull *Exsurge, Domine* of having appealed to a council after publicly confessing that he did not grant credence to councils.[10] At issue here were conflicting conceptions of a general council and, underlying them, conflicting conceptions of the church.[11]

Very briefly, for sixteenth-century Catholics the universal church was the visible community of the baptized, recognizable by its celebration of the sacraments. The council when properly convened was the visible representative of the universal church and as such was assured by God's promise to possess the Holy Spirit and could accordingly pronounce on matters of faith. For conciliarists, the council was superior to the pope and was to be proclaimed and assembled by the universal church. For advocates of papal supremacy, the pope was superior to the council and it was his responsibility to convene and lead the council and to promulgate those of its decrees he agreed with. Once the council was properly convened and its decrees properly promulgated, however, its decisions were, both conciliarists and advocates of papal supremacy agreed, binding on all Christians.

For Luther, too, the church was the community of the baptized. But among the baptized Luther distinguished a subgroup, the community of the faithful, those who had been won by the word to true faith in Christ. This subgroup he variously called the "assembly of the righteous," the "people of faith," the "body of Christ," and the "spiritual church." Strictly speaking, the spiritual church was, for Luther, the only true church. The assembly of the baptized, which included both the righteous and the unrighteous, made up the visible church, the "universal church." The spiritual church was an invisible, hidden subgroup of the universal church and could not be separated from the universal church, nor could it be discerned by human reason but only discerned by faith.

For Luther as for Catholics, the council was the visible representative of the universal church. The spiritual church, however, remained hidden and was not represented by any council. But since the spiritual church was a subgroup of the universal church, it was possible for a council, in which members of the spiritual church, enlightened by the Holy Spirit, played the determining role, truly to "represent" the community of the faithful. Since, however, the spiritual church was invisible, the one valid test for its presence and influence in a council was the conformity of the council's decrees with Scripture. Only a council that reached its decisions on the basis of Scripture was, in Luther's view, a council "legitimately assembled in the Holy Spirit." Given this criterion it followed that every member of the spiritual church had the right and the responsibility to test the decisions of a council for their conformity to Scripture. That a council was a true Christian council, then, was not determined by its form and procedures, as Catholics believed, but by the content of its decrees. It was to such a free council whose decisions were based on Scripture that Luther appealed. It was to such a council that he was willing to grant full credence.

In August 1520, a few months before he renewed his appeal to a general council, Luther had published his highly influential *To the Christian Nobility of the German Nation Concerning the Improvement of the Christian Estate.*[12] In this treatise he characterized as the "third wall of the Romanists," by which they attempted to protect themselves from reform, their argument that no one but the pope could convene a council.[13] They had, Luther asserted, no basis in Scripture for this claim. When necessity demanded it and when the actions of the pope were an offense to Christendom, the first person who had the opportunity should do what he could "as a faithful member of the whole body" to see that there would be "a proper free council." Secular authorities, he argued, were in the best position to do this "especially because they, too, are fellow Christians, fellow priests, fellow members of the spiritual estate, fellow potentates [*mit-mechtig*] in all things."[14] And he also provided a lengthy list and discussion of those reforms that should be undertaken by a council.[15] This treatise was nicely calculated to appeal to sentiments for reform that were widespread within Germany as well as to the sharply anticlerical and anti-Roman sentiments that also existed there.

## The Imperial Diets and the Council

At the Diet of Worms in 1521 in which Luther made his famous appearance, the question of a council was widely discussed.[16] "The whole world shouts 'Council, Council,'" the papal legate worriedly reported. Many of those present at the diet were convinced that the whole Luther affair could only be resolved with a council. A significant group of reform-minded Catholic princes, bishops, and cities, including in their number Duke Georg of Saxony, attempted in vain to induce Luther simply to accept the authority of a council. He was only willing, however, to accept a council that would judge his teachings on the basis of Scripture, a clear indication of the divergent conceptions of a council held by the Catholics and by Luther and his fellow Protestants. Several lists of complaints and grievances concerning the church and suggestions for reform were drawn up by the diet, but the papal legate managed to forestall a joint demand by the secular and clerical estates for the convening of a general council. Even so, the sentiment both for ecclesiastical reform and for resolving the Luther affair by means of a general council remained widespread among all the German estates and was there to be tapped by the growing Reformation movement.

With the end of the diet, Emperor Charles V left Germany not to return for nearly a decade. In his absence the German estates, both Catholic and Protestant, called repeatedly for a general council to settle the religious disputes and to reform the church. On 5 February 1523 the German estates assembled at the Diet of Nuremberg and demanded for the first time that the pope, with the consent of the emperor, should convoke within a year if possible "a free Christian council in a city on the German border, such as Strasbourg, Mainz, Cologne or Metz."[17] The diet also drew up a list of grievances to be submitted to the pope. Both the call for a council and the list of grievances were antipapal and anticlerical in spirit.[18]

The estates renewed their request for a "free general council" the next year at another Imperial Diet at Nuremberg, and added a demand for a "national council" to consider the issues until the general council could meet. Despite the strenuous objections of the papal legate, the diet even proclaimed an "assembly of the German Nation"—a euphemism for a national council—to be convened at Speyer on 11 November 1524. It was only the emperor's blunt prohibition that headed off this plan for a national council.[19]

At the Diet of Speyer in 1526 the estates once again demanded the convocation of a general or national council within a year and a half. In the meanwhile, each of the estates was to act in relation to the Edict of Worms in such fashion as it could give answer for "before God and before the imperial majesty." The effect of this ambiguous formula was to leave reforms up to the discretion of each city and prince, and the Protestants gained the legal justification, as they saw it, to introduce reforms within their lands.[20]

The second Imperial Diet of Speyer in 1529 annulled the recess of the first Diet of Speyer that had so favored the Protestants, and thus prompted the Protestant estates—Electoral Saxony, Hesse, Brandenburg-Ansbach, Lüneburg, Anhalt-Köthen, and fourteen cities—to lodge a protest. Despite this show of hostility, the Catholic majority was still unwilling to proceed with force and once again requested that the emperor urge the pope to proclaim within one year a "free general council in the German Nation" which would be convened within two years. They also proposed the convening of a national assembly in the event that no general council were held.

It is clear by the 1526 and 1529 Diets of Speyer, if not before, that the demand for a "free general council" meant one thing to the Protestants and another to the Catholics. For the Protestants including Luther, it meant a council free of papal control in which the laity might participate and vote and the clergy were freed of their oaths of obedience to the pope and, most important of all, in which all decisions were made on the basis of Scripture. For the Catholics, on the other hand, it meant a council that followed the traditional procedures and in which the authority of the pope was not challenged and only the clergy had votes. For Protestants a "true council" would reform the abuses of the papacy and sustain the Protestant teachings; for Catholics a "true council" would reform the abuses of the church and, once and for all, pass judgment on the Protestant heresy.

With the return of the emperor to Germany and the convening of the Imperial Diet of Augsburg in the summer of 1530, the question of a general council had to be tackled once again. In the preface to the *Augsburg Confession* submitted to the emperor on 25 June 1530, the emperor was reminded both of the requests made by the estates at past diets that the emperor promote and bring about a "general, free, and Christian council." He was reminded also of the commitments made by his representatives that he would do what the estates had requested. The signators to the Confession offered to participate obediently in such a council.[21] In the subsequent negotiations the emperor and the Catholics held out the promise of a council on the condition that the Protestants in the interim return to the practices of the old faith. This the Protestants refused, and they repeated their appeal to a council. When all attempts at compromise failed, the emperor considered resolving the dispute with force, but neither the Catholic estates nor the pope were willing to give him meaningful assistance in such an enterprise. He was forced to turn once again to the convening of a general council as "the only remedy" for the schism.

In the recess of the 1530 Diet of Augsburg Emperor Charles V committed himself to urging Pope Clement VII that "for the purpose of Christian reformation [he] announce within six months a general Christian council at a suitable location, which was to be held as soon as possible and at the latest within one year after such an announcement."[22] Although the emperor attempted on repeated occasions to fulfill this promise, dilatory and obstructionist tactics by Pope Clement VII and by Francis I of France, both of whom had strong political and personal reasons for fearing the likely effects of a council, brought his efforts to nought. When the Imperial Diet at Regensburg opened on 17 April 1532, the emperor was no closer to fulfilling his promise than when it was made. The Protestant estates were in the process of negotiating the Nuremberg Standstill with the emperor and remained away from the diet. But the Catholic estates present at the diet forced Charles to renew his promise and even suggested that if the pope failed to convene a council, then the emperor should do so, or, if he felt unable or unwilling to, then he should convene a national council. In the Nuremberg Standstill with the members of the League of Schmalkalden the emperor also committed himself to working for the convocation of a "free Christian council." Both Catholic and Protestant princes had once more placed the responsibility for seeing that a council was convened squarely on Charles's shoulders.

## *The Publications of 1532-1536*

From 13 December 1532 to 28 February 1533 Emperor Charles and Pope Clement negotiated with each other in Bologna over the convocation of a council. The most the emperor was able to get from the pope was an agreement to sound out the various Christian princes about their willingness to attend a council. Count Ugo Rangoni, Bishop of Reggio-Emilia, was chosen for this purpose as the nuncio to Germany. On 3 June in Weimar Rangoni submitted to Elector Johann Friedrich orally and in writing eight articles from the pope setting forth the conditions under which he would convene a council.[23] Luther's advice on these articles was solicited by the elector, but only partly followed. Drawing on the example of recent councils including the Fifth Lateran and the councils of Constance, Basel, and Ferrara-Florence, Luther drew a bleak picture of what to expect from a papally convened council, but urged nonetheless that the papal proposal not be rejected out of hand.[24] He and his Wittenberg colleagues wished the Protestants to take no steps that could be interpreted as attempts to impede the convening of a council and could thereby be used by the the papacy to discredit them.[25] But they were overruled. While not completely ruling out their own participation in a papal council, the League of Schmalkalden on 30 June roundly attacked the papal proposal and renewed their request for a "free and Christian council."[26]

The League also decided to have published in Latin and German an account of the negotiations between Elector Johann Friedrich and the envoys as well as the eight papal articles and the formal reply of the League. This pamphlet was to be sent to all the Protestant estates and to a number of foreign potentates.[27] Melanchthon provided the foreword to the Latin edition[28] and Luther the foreword to the German.[29] In his foreword, which was anonymous and clearly aimed at a broad readership, Luther pointed out that there was a long-standing wish among pious Christians for a "general Christian Council." Some people were of the opinion, he continued, that the pope and his allies had impeded such a council up to now because they feared the example of the Council of Constance. In that instance, he pointed out, a council had been placed over the pope and had dealt very harshly with him as its subordinate. Another general council, the papists feared, might behave in a similar manner. However, Luther continued, the emperor had pursued the matter of a council "with true Christian seriousness and courage" until he had induced Pope Clement VII to agree to holding a council although under unacceptable conditions. All Christians should support the emperor and his efforts with their prayers, and they should also pray and work against "the enemy of truth, who would not willingly allow the chief issues of faith and the abuses opposed to them to be dealt with."[30]

More significant than Luther's foreword and the accompanying documents for its impact on the public's view of the papal council and the Protestant's rejection of it was a meeting between Pope Clement VII and King Francis I of France. They met in Marseilles from 11 October to 12 November 1533, and while no record was kept of the conversation between them, it is clear that the question of a council was discussed.[31] The pope later reported that Francis had rejected a council, arguing that it could not serve any useful purpose while tensions remained between him and the emperor. With this convenient excuse, the pope postponed the council indefinitely. His decision gave rise to great disappointment and bitterness even among the most committed Catholics in Germany. Duke Georg is reported to have commented on 14 June 1534, "While a hundred thousand souls perish, the appointed shepherd of souls makes common cause with our avowed enemy!"[32] For the rest of Clement's lifetime—he died unexpectedly on 25 September 1534 at the age of fifty-six—the prospects of a council were dead.

With the election, 13 October 1534, of Cardinal Alessandro Farnese as Pope Paul III, however, the prospects of a council took on new life.[33] In the spring of 1535 the pope sent the papal nuncio, Pietro

Paolo Vergerio, to Germany to secure approval from the major German princes for a council to be held in Mantua. His tour through Germany even included a stop in Wittenberg in October and a meeting with Luther himself.[34] In the sometimes amusing and sometimes heated exchange between Vergerio and Luther, the nuncio managed to provoke a promise from Luther that he would attend the council wherever it might be convened.[35] But once again the League of Schmalkalden overruled its most prominent theologian and offered to participate in a "free Christian council in German lands" but attacked and rejected the papal proposal.

The year 1535 also saw the first of a growing number of published attacks by Luther on past councils, especially the Council of Constance, and on the Catholic conception of a council in general. In midyear, Luther published in both Latin and German a series of disputation theses against the Council of Constance's decree on communion in both kinds.[36] Luther viewed this decree as historical evidence for his harshest judgments about the hypocrisy and faithlessness of recent Catholic councils, of Catholic beliefs, and of his contemporary Catholic opponents.

Accordingly, in the foreword to the theses Luther "rebaptized" the *Constantiense Concilium* [Council of Constance] as the *Obstantiense Concilium* [the "Withstanding" or "Resisting" Council], playing on the phrase *tamen hoc non obstante* [nonetheless this not withstanding]. The decree first admitted that Christ may have instituted the Sacrament after supper and his disciples may have administered it to the laity under both kinds, but it then asserted that, *tamen hoc non obstante,* the church had by long custom ordained that this should no longer be the case. *Obstantia*, Luther said, meant "resistance" [*widderstand*], and in its decree the Council had not only resisted Christ and his church in deed but had boasted of the fact. It had confirmed that Christ might well establish what he wished but the "lords of the *Obstantiense* Council" would oppose it and would pay no regard to Christ or to his church.

The other major charge Luther lodged against the Council of Constance was spelled out in the first few theses:

> At this time one may no longer ask whether it is proper or improper to maintain or to permit the command of Christ concerning both kinds. Rather whether it is Christian or unchristian forcibly to drive people away from Christ's command. And whether Christ's command [is] heresy, and Christ himself along with all those who follow his command were and should justly be called heretics.[37]

The true church, Luther contended, did not force people from God's command, and it was the church of the antichrist, "Satan's school," the "devil's furious whore," that labeled as heretics all who followed Christ's command. In the theses themselves Luther passionately and sarcastically attacked Catholic practices and motives. A righteous anger runs through all the theses as can be felt, for example, in the concluding ones. "And if someone thinks that the papists should not be called antichrists for condemning one article, since they believe many others, that helps nothing. For he who knowingly denies or condemns Christ in one issue has denied and condemned all of Christianity and believes no other article rightly. . . . In any case they have not only taught against this article [on both kinds] but have suppressed practically all the others. . . . There is no ship that sails the sea large enough to be able to carry even the chief books used to rule the papal church. Yet one would not find in all of them even two correct lines about Christ and faith, the rest is all against Christ. . . . And their own decretals teach how Christ did not say, 'I am the custom' but rather 'I am the truth.' They also state that custom should yield to the truth, as all reason must also acknowledge. But in the 'Resisting' Council the truth had to yield to custom. And custom there became articles of faith and truth became heresy. Custom must help to save those who obey and follow it. Truth must lead here to death and there to hell all who believe and follow it."[38]

Probably in late 1535 Luther penned a foreword to Robert Barnes's *Lives of the Roman Pontiffs,* a patchwork of earlier sources organized around the thesis that the popes were the personification of the antichrist.[39] Barnes was at this time, in his third stay in Wittenberg (September 1535 through early April 1536), chaplain to King Henry VIII, and was one of his king's representatives to the League of Schmalkalden. It was his task to induce the League members to refuse participation in a papal council.[40] Barnes's compilation greatly pleased Luther, since the history Barnes laid out confirmed Luther's view of the papacy.

> To be sure, in the beginning I attacked the papacy *a priori* (as they say), that is, on the basis of Holy Scripture [since I was] not really knowledgeable [*gnarus*] or trained in histories. Now I am extraordinarily pleased that others have done this *a posteriori,* that is, on the basis of histories. And it seems to me [that I] clearly triumph when I recognize by the evident light that the histories agree with Scriptures. For that which I, with St. Paul and Daniel [as] teachers, have disseminated and taught, [namely that] the pope is that adversary of God and all things, the histories,

proclaiming by the deeds themselves, point just like a finger and exhibit not the genus or the species but the individual himself, not an uncertain thing (as they say).[41]

Gradually, Luther was building up a full historical and theological picture of the papacy and the papal councils.

In 1536, probably early in the year,[42] Luther held another disputation on the question of a council, this one on the "power" of a council or, as it was expressed in the German translation of the theses, on the "power and authority of a general council." These theses provide an excellent summary of Luther's view of a council and anticipate many of the arguments Luther advanced in his 1539 masterwork, *On the Councils and the Church*. The theses were published immediately in both Latin and German. Cochlaeus republished the German theses in 1537 along with his refutation,[43] and Georg Spalatin published his own German translation in 1538. The issue was of obvious contemporary importance.[44]

In the second half of 1536, after the 2 June proclamation by Pope Paul III of a council to be convened in Mantua in 1537, Luther published in Latin another historically based polemic, a group of letters written by John Hus while imprisoned in Constance.[45] Early in Luther's career as a reformer he had accepted and championed the Bohemian Hus as a good Christian and as a forerunner to himself. It is hardly surprising, therefore, that he came to believe that the Council of Constance and its treatment of Hus and the Hussites had set the pattern likely to be followed by a papal council in its treatment of himself and his fellow Protestants. In Luther's preface he explained to the reader that he was publishing these letters so that kings, princes, and bishops would be on their guard lest similar or worse abominations came out of the recently proclaimed council at Mantua than had come out of the Council of Constance. Following Luther's preface were four letters by Hus urging his readers not to be dismayed by the burning of his books and not to surrender them, describing the disorder and injustice and hypocrisy of the council's proceedings, admonishing them to lead a good Christian life, and sharing with them his thoughts and mood as he awaited death. There was also a copy of a letter written to the council by a group of Bohemian nobility. The nobles declared their support for the recently executed Hus and for his teachings, protested the Council's treatment of Jerome of Prague, denied the existence of heresy in their lands, and announced that they would defend their preachers not only with their goods but also with their lives. Luther had probably included this letter by the Bohemian nobles to encourage the German nobility to do the same.

For this treatise fully to have its desired effect, it had to be translated into German. On 29 November 1536 an anonymous German translation was published in Nuremberg.[46] But the Wittenbergers were not taking any chances in their efforts to influence as wide a public as possible. Luther's friend Johann Agricola also translated the collection into German and in late 1536 or early 1537 Luther provided a German postscript for this edition. Hus had done nothing worse, Luther claimed, than to teach that if the pope were not pious, then he was not the head of the *holy* church although he remained head of the church, just as a wicked pastor remained a pastor although not a member of the true saints within his parish. For this, Luther charged, the Council of Constance had burned Hus.

Luther next recounted how Hus had come to this fate, stressing, as he saw it, the injustice and hypocrisy of the whole proceedings.* Hus had been more learned, he claimed, than all the doctors in the council. This was proved by his book on the church and by his sermons.[47] Drawing on the account in the recently republished *Acts of the Councils* by Ulrich von Richenthal, he then described Hus's execution as the death of a martyr and saint.

All this, Luther stated in his final paragraph, he wished to say as a warning to "our spiritless lords who perhaps will be in the council."

> For if they perpetrate another Council of Constance, it will also happen to them that afterwards people will speak of what they have done and of what they have forbidden others to say. For those at Constance were also certain that no one would ever be allowed to write or speak against them much less sanctify and praise John Hus or condemn them. . . . But John Hus had prophesied otherwise, as has come to pass through many others and also partly through me.

This translation by Agricola, an effective piece in the Protestant attempt to discredit the papal council before it even convened, was first published in Wittenberg in early 1537 and reprinted the same year in

---

*Luther also recounted an anecdote about his own past. "Once as a young theologian in the cloister at Erfurt he had come across a book of Hus's sermons in the library and had wished, out of curiosity, to see what the 'archheretic' had taught. There, in truth, I found so much that I was shocked that such a man was burned who could adduce Scripture in such a powerful and Christian fashion. But because his name had been so horribly condemned that at that time I also thought that the solstice would be black and the sun would lose its shine if one spoke well of Hus's name, I shut the book and left with a wounded heart, but I comforted myself with such thoughts: Perhaps he had written such things before he became a heretic. For I did not yet know the history of the Council of Constance" (WA 50:37f.).

southern Germany. Cochlaeus, disturbed by the potential influence of this and other recent publications on Hus and the council of Constance, published his own *True History of Master John Hus* (1537), in which, among other things, he accused Luther of having forged Hus's letters.[48]

## The Publications of 1537

Soon after his return from the February, 1537, League meetings in Schmalkalden, probably in April but certainly no later than early May, Luther published *The Lie-gends of St. John Chrysostom, To the Holy Fathers in the Putative Council in Mantua.*[49] In his sarcastic foreword dedicating the treatise to Pope Paul and the cardinals, archbishops, and other prelates who would supposedly be assembling in the Council at Mantua, Luther explained that it had been his original intention personally to attend the council, as he had promised the nuncio Pietro Paulo Vergerio. But his great weakness and lack of sufficient resources prevented his physical presence. Still, he had to come as best he could, if not by foot or horse or wagon then by paper and ink. So he was sending "this John Chrysostom" to the council as a "harbinger and foretaste" of what he intended to deal with in the council.

> For such gross, undoubted lies and idolatry you have not only taught but have also confirmed with pardons and indulgences and filled the whole world with it. But now, thank God, the whole world comprehends and you yourselves also know and understand well that such are true lie-gends, stinking, devilish lies and pure seductive idolatry.

He then reproduced the legend of St. Chrysostom with occasional sarcastic marginalia.

The legend, as Luther reported it, was indeed spectacular. Before Chrysostom's birth, a soul suffering the agonies of purgatory informs the pope that he will be released only when Chrysostom has sung sixteen masses. Once Chrysostom is born, he is raised by the pope. Originally a very inept student, he acquires not only marvelous learning by kissing the lips of a portrait of the Virgin but also a gold ring about his lips—hence his name Chrysostom, "golden mouth." After celebrating his first mass at age sixteen, he flees into the wilds where he lives as a hermit. The emperor's daughter is then conveyed to his hermitage by a great wind. After a period of chaste cohabitation, the couple, prompted by the devil, make love. Both are stricken with guilt, and Chrysostom, to remove temptation from his sight, pushes the princess off a cliff. In penance for this heinous sin, he begins to go on all fours and turns into a hideous animal. After many years the emperor has another child. But the baby refuses to be baptized by the pope, insisting that Chrysostom should perform the rite. Meanwhile, a hunter has captured Chrysostom and, thinking he has captured some rare beast, has brought him to the emperor. When the "beast" is presented to the court, the baby recognizes him to be Chrysostom and announces that the saint has done sufficient penance. Chrysostom regains the form of a young man, the princess is found to have miraculously survived her fall and to have been preserved by God through all the intervening years, and Chrysostom finally performs fifteen more masses and releases the soul from purgatory.[50]

In his postscript Luther distinguished between "human lies" that did bodily and material injury and "devilish lies" that did spiritual injury. The papal church was full of "human lies," he charged, but the real damage came from "devilish lies" on which the papal church and the papacy were founded and based. People did not recognize these lies until it was too late and they were brought to the eternal flames of hell. The legend of St. Chrysostom was such a lie, fabricated to flatter the pope and strengthen the devil's church with its masses and purgatory. And even though they themselves recognized such legends to be shameless lies, Luther charged, the papists were not only unwilling to improve anything, they also knowingly defended recognized lies and forced people to believe and to worship such apparent lies. On their account, they killed, exiled, and burned people.* Luther drew a pointed conclusion for his readers. They should understand without any doubts that if there were a council, then nothing would occur in it other than the confirmation of such lies to the very letter and the condemnation to death and hell of all those who would not believe such things.

The sensationalism of this little tract proved popular, and reprints were quickly issued in Strasbourg and Augsburg.[51] The central thesis of the tract—that such legends were articles of faith within the papal church, to be believed on pain of burning—was of course untrue, as

---

*"Now to be sure, one laughs at such lies and no one will believe them, but especially you, dear young people, who now have the light and have not been under the lying kingdom of the pope as I and others like me have been. If even twenty years ago one had believed of this legend of Chrysostom that a single little piece were fabricated, he would have had to have been burned to ashes without any mercy. Then neither Emperor, king, prince, doctor, etc., cunning nor force would have helped, so strictly did the 'tonsurelings,' preacher monks [Dominicans], inquisitors of heretical depravity deal with the matter, so earnestly had we to believe the lies and fear and worship their father, the devil, and, in addition, praise his 'tonsurelings' and 'baldies'" (WA 50:63).

the indefatigable Johann Cochlaeus took pains to point out in two treatises of his own.[52] The Catholic understanding of the mass and of purgatory that underlay the legend, however, could not be so easily denied. To fit his attack on the mass and purgatory, and on the proposed papal council, to such an outrageous legend was a shrewd piece of propaganda by Luther. His exaggerated charges contained enough fundamental truth to do serious injury to the Catholic cause.

In May or June 1537 Luther also did a German translation from Gratian's *Decretum* of excerpts from the so-called "Donation of Constantine" and published this translation with an extended, historically based attack on the papacy. The Donation—in fact a late eighth- or early ninth-century forgery—purports to be an edict of the emperor Constantine conferring on Pope Sylvester and his successors, as the vicars of St. Peter, primacy over all the Christian churches including the four principal sees of Antioch, Alexandria, Constantinople, and Jerusalem, and temporal lordship, with all its perquisites and trappings, over the western half of the empire. It had been branded the forgery it was on various occasions through the middle ages, and in the mid-fifteenth century the great Italian humanist Lorenzo Valla had attacked it on the grounds, among others, that it used Latin terminology that was unknown in Constantine's lifetime. This *Declamation* by Valla had been republished by Ulrich Hutten in 1518 as part of the humanist-knight's paper war against the Italian papacy. On 24 February 1520 Luther had written Spalatin about this edition of the *Declamation,* expressing his astonishment that "such an impure, such a crass, such an impudent lie" could have prevailed for such a long time, supplanting true articles of faith. He felt constrained, he had announced to Spalatin, to conclude, almost without a doubt, that the pope was the true antichrist.[53]

Seventeen years later, Luther of course harbored not the slightest doubt that the pope was the antichrist and that the Donation of Constantine, along with a wealth of other historical evidence, all supported this conclusion. As in other instances, Luther took less exception to the forgery itself than to the "fact" that the papacy had forced people to accept the Donation as an article of faith. Those who had not wished to believe "such a shameless, devilish lie and blasphemy of God" were stigmatized as the worst heretics, he charged, and those people still living under the power of the pope had to "worship such obvious devils" or be burned to ashes, or at least they had to keep silent and not contradict them.[54] Once again Luther was using hyperbole to good polemical effect. Although Cochlaeus rightly pointed out in his published rejoinder that the Donation had never been made an article of faith, his denial could scarcely affect the unfavorable impression made on many nationalistically-minded Germans by papal claims to spiritual and temporal authority—the authority of the "two swords"—whatever the justification. Additionally, Cochlaeus' argument, although basically correct, could easily be called into question by the embarrassing fact that the Donation was included in the canon law.[55]

The significance of this treatise lies largely in Luther's effective use of history to undermine papal claims and to portray the papacy as the kingdom of the antichrist. Although he occasionally has his facts wrong and he consistently places the least favorable construction on events as far as the papacy is concerned, Luther does demonstrate a broad knowledge of papal history, especially of its less admirable moments. For instance, he dwelled at length on the excesses of Pope Boniface VIII, a fairly easy pope to fault. He also discussed the various papal claims to temporal lordship and recounted incidents of papal interference in secular rule. Ruling groups in Germany, who had submitted lists of complaints about the Roman Catholic church at diet after diet, were unlikely to read this section without being put off by the events recounted. As Luther himself put it, he had written this section so that his readers saw how the papacy was founded on lies and idolatry and had grown into a true kingdom of the devil which aimed not only at the ruination of the Christian church but also of the secular realm.

To bring this point closer to home, Luther also enumerated examples of papal misconduct within recent years. He passed on rumors about Pope Clement VII's alleged incestuous birth and lack of baptism, and branded as fraud all the papal taxes allegedly collected to support war against the Turks. He interpreted all the papal claims of authority as a sign that they were living in the last days, and he announced his intention at sometime to do a treatise on the pope as the antichrist.*

Luther also cited evidence from early church history to prove that at that time the pope was no more than one bishop among many, all equal in authority to each other. In this connection he cited St.

---

*"The pope had to be emperor and through his god, the devil, had to bring into play this fraudulent Donation of Constantine, for he is certainly the highest authority over emperor and kings and all worldly lordship (I do not speak now about how he has become the antichrist in the church. Soon I will write about that, God willing), and also has greater goods than all the emperors, greater honor, greater power, and everything that is high in the world. He is closest to a god pure and simply, as they also flatter him that he is king of all kings, lord of all lords, and an earthly god and more of the horrible names that were painted on the forehead of the red, shameless whore in Revelation, chapter 17" (WA 50:83).

Jerome's letter to Evagrius in which Jerome denied that the bishop of Rome held more authority than any other city bishop. In fact, he felt that this letter was such a telling piece of evidence against papal pretensions that, in 1538, he published it as a separate treatise.[56] Since the time of Jerome and Irenaeus, who had rebuked Bishop Victor of Rome for excommunicating the Greeks for holding Easter on a date different from that celebrated by the West, the devil had, Luther charged, elevated the pope over the councils, the church, and the Scriptures. For Luther it was always this last point—that the pope claimed not to receive his authority from Scripture but, on the contrary, that Scripture received its authority from the pope—that conclusively identified the papacy as the antichrist. This was the *a priori* grounds for his rejection of the papacy as the antichrist; historical examples provided the *a posteriori* confirmation.

On 27 April 1537 Spalatin wrote the elector that Luther was at work on a treatise "on the three symbols and faith of the apostles, of the council at Nicaea, and of St. Athanasius."[57] Although not actually published until early 1538 due to problems at the printers, the treatise *The Three Symbols or Confessions of the Christian's Faith* also belongs to the hectic period immediately following the meetings in Schmalkalden. He was publishing this treatise, Luther explained, "so that I may once again bear witness that I am in agreement with the true Christian church that has kept such symbols or confessions until now and not with the false, arrogant church (that is, indeed, the true church's worst enemy), which has introduced much idolatry along side such beautiful confessions." The confessions he published, and to which he declared his unswerving allegiance, were the Apostles' Creed, the Athanasian Creed, and the *Te Deum Laudamus,* known also as the hymn of St. Ambrose and St. Augustine since, according to legend, the two saints had sung this hymn at St. Augustine's baptism. Following the creeds themselves he appended a relatively lengthy discussion which ended with the Nicene Creed. Clearly, Luther was attempting to fend off the Roman Catholic charge that the Protestants were breaking with the church that Christians had confessed for centuries. Luther and his fellow Protestants were turning this charge on its head and arguing that it was the Catholics who had broken with the church of the ancient creeds.

While Luther was busy penning these various attacks on a papal council, the immediate reason for this flurry of activity, the proposed Council at Mantua, ran into serious obstacles from another quarter. Once again it was the French, not the Protestants, who were responsible for scuttling the council. Although Francis I had at one point given his qualified assent to the proposal of a council in Mantua, once the legates arrived in France to deliver the bull of convocation, Francis returned to his standard position that neither he nor his bishops could attend a council while war with the emperor continued. He also rejected Mantua as the council's site. Although his objection was sufficient to doom the council, it was the duke of Mantua who was ultimately assigned the blame. In the middle of February 1537, when detailed preparations were first being made for the council's opening, the Duke let it be known that a very large guard would be necessary to maintain adequate security. A guard as large as he proposed, however, would call into serious question the freedom of the council. So on 20 April the pope postponed the council until 1 November 1537, explaining that an "armed council" was unacceptable. On this occasion it appears that the pope was truly not at fault. But, as Aleander expressed it, "however loudly we may blame the Duke of Mantua for the postponement, in the opinion of the world the real culprit is the pope."[58]

Aleander was right. Around midyear Luther anonymously published a copy of Pope Paul's bull proroguing the council. It is clear from the preface and sarcastic marginalia that this prorogation had confirmed Luther's judgment that the pope was not serious in desiring a council. On the contrary, he asserted, the pope had no intention of holding a council since he feared that a council would treat him as the Council of Constance had treated the three contending popes during the Great Schism. Luther simply branded the whole story about how the Duke of Mantua had forced the postponement as a contrived fraud. This little Latin pamphlet was first published in Wittenberg and then immediately reprinted in Nuremberg.[59]

While Luther was busy in the summer of 1537 ridiculing and attacking the papal council, the pope was trying to put together an acceptable set of conditions for the council. He now suggested as possible sites a city in the Venetian or papal territories. Francis I, however, rejected any Italian site and suggested instead cities in either Germany or France, locations unacceptable either to the pope or to the emperor. On 29 August the pope requested the Venetians to allow the council to meet in one of their mainland cities, and on 29 September he was offered Vicenza. Since it was now too late to inform participants of the new site in time for the scheduled 1 November convocation, the pope postponed the council once more, this time until 1 May 1538.

The effects of this further postponement on both German Catholics and Protestants were predictable. Good Catholics like Johann Eck were greatly depressed by the news. "Many people are scandalized," he wrote Aleander, "when they see the council gone with the wind."[60]

The Protestants, on the other hand, interpreted this postponement as just one further proof of the pope's aversion to holding any council.

The year 1537 also saw a few lesser salvoes by Luther in his war with the papacy and its council. Soon after his return from Schmalkalden he may have anonymously composed a brief satire purporting to be a letter from "Beelzebub, prince of all devils," to "his faithful subjects," the pope, cardinals, bishops, and other members of the papal church; the authorship is not certain, however.[61] In this "letter," Beelzebub, who is in the field with his army warring against "the new Galileans, called the Lutheran heretics," writes to the pope about reports that the pope intends to reform the papal curia. Such action, Beelzebub informs the pope, would be treachery. To his relief, his legate Belial had reported that the pope was not serious about this Reformation but only intended to pull the wool over the eyes of the world and its kings and to dupe the German fools into eating horse manure instead of figs. Beelzebub gave his approbation and promised to attend the Council at Mantua to provide the pope with assistance, for he had reliable report that the Holy Spirit would not be attending.

In 1537 Luther did published with his postscript an excerpt from the late fifteenth century treatise by the Italian Dominican John Nanni of Viterbo that prophesied (incorrectly as it turned out) a great Christian victory over the Turks.[62] In the excerpt published, Nanni attempted to demonstrate on the basis of logic and Scripture that the pope as Christ's vicar on earth possessed temporal power by divine right. He also argued that with his future kingdom in mind Christ had, with his resurrection, relaxed the prohibition against the use of money and the sword by the church. In his postscript to this excerpt Luther attacked what he viewed as the popes' centuries-long fleecing of the Christian sheep, labeled as "shit, dung, and crap" the papal decretals that asserted the primacy and authority of the pope, and identified the papacy as the great whore of the Book of Revelation. He insisted that Charlemagne had owed nothing to the papacy; on the contrary, the papacy had been completely dependent on Charlemagne. In this regard he took to task the claim advanced by Aeneas Silvius Piccolomini, later Pope Pius II, that the Germans should be grateful to the papacy for transfering to them the Roman Empire. In its polemical tone and in some of its arguments, this little postscript anticipates Luther's 1545 *Against the Papacy at Rome, Founded by the Devil.*

Finally, in 1537 Luther provided a brief foreword to the Hessian pastor Johann Kymaeus's treatise *An Ancient Christian Council Held Twelve Hundred Years Ago at Gangra in Paphlogonia Against the Highly Regarded Holiness of the Monks and Anabaptists.*[63] This local council held in Paphlogonia around 345 had passed canons condemning the extreme asceticism advocated by Eustathius, bishop of Sebaste. Kymaeus had used the council's decrees as a springboard from which to attack the Anabaptists. But Luther devoted his foreword to (occasionally coarse) attacks on papal councils and on papal claims of authority over councils and Scripture. His strategy seems fairly clear. In addition to attacking recent councils such as the Council of Constance, it was useful also to point to ancient, nonpapal councils which gave witness to how he thought true councils and true fathers of the church behaved. He was to elaborate greatly on this approach in his *On the Councils and the Church.*

## The Publications of 1538

Shortly after issuing the 2 June 1536 bull proclaiming the council at Mantua for May of the next year, Pope Paul had summoned a group of reform-minded clerics to Rome to form a committee to draw up, in advance of the council, recommendations for the reform of the church.*

On 9 March the product of the committee's deliberations was presented to the pope. It dealt exclusively with administrative reforms and especially with the reform of abuses in the use of papal dispensations, particularly for money, that led to improper ordinations, improper bestowal of benefices, nonresidence, pluralism, and the like. Unchastity in the cloisters, the teaching of "godless matters" by teachers and philosophers (especially in Italy and France), the lack of proper censorship of books, and dispensations for monks who committed apostasy, for consecrated people who wished to marry, and for marriage within the prohibited degrees were also faulted. The report set a bold agenda for reform.

The pope had ordered that all the cardinals be given a copy of the report with the request that they prepare individual opinions on the matter. Until all opinions were collected and a definitive text of the

---

*Headed by Cardinal Caspar Contarini, the committee included John Carafa, James Sadoleto, and the Englishman Reginald Pole—all three raised to the cardinalate in December 1536—and, to bring expertise to the committee on concerns in Germany, Jerome Aleander, Archbishop of Brindisi and occasional legate to Germany. The reforming bishop of Verona, John Giberti, was also a member as were Frederick Fregoso, Archbishop of Salerno, Gregory Cortese, abbot of St. George in Venice, and the Dominican Thomas Badia, Master of the Sacred Palace.

report were prepared, the report was to be kept secret. In the process of discussion and consultation, however, a copy leaked out and was published in Milan in early 1538 and soon after in Rome. Luther received a copy almost immediately, and on 23 February he had announced to Nicholas Hausmann his intention to publish the report. By 27 March a German translation with his preface and sarcastic marginalia was off the press.[64]

Luther's preface began not with the report itself but with the papal council and its repeated postponement. He likened the pope to the legendary Markolf, who, granted one wish before his execution, requested the opportunity to choose the tree on which he would be hanged. Markolf could never find a tree that suited him; so, too, Luther charged, the pope would never find a council's site that suited him. At issue, he contended, was the question of papal infallibility. If at a council the pope should be found in error in even the least significant issue, then the whole papacy would collapse. So either the papacy had to avoid holding a council in which the question of papal infallibility might be discussed or had to hold a council, like the Fifth Lateran, in which nothing contrary to its wishes would occur. For Luther it was the desire of the pope to be above all law, subject only to his own will, and lord over Scripture that revealed him to be the antichrist. The report of the committee was the latest subterfuge which deceitfully advocated the reform of the whole church so that, if people believed "such lies," it would no longer be necessary to hold a council. If, nevertheless, a council were to be held, there would be nothing for it to do for the reform of the church since the pope had already begun such reforms. In fact, Luther concluded, the whole report was so much hypocrisy. In his marginalia to the report, he contemptuously mocked all the suggestions for reform.

Of course Luther was not being fair to claim that all the proposals for reform were hypocritical, even though the failure of past proposals justified considerable scepticism about the likelihood of the actual implementation of the proposed reforms.[65] On a more profound level, however, the proposals, even if sincerely made and actually implemented, would make no significant difference in Luther's evaluation of the papacy. The root error of the papacy, as Luther saw it, was not administrative but theological. It was not simply that the papacy needed to reform its process of ordination, assignment of benefices, residence, and the like. Rather the papacy had to accept a different, for Luther the only correct, understanding of Christian faith.[66] The committee had neither dealt with this question nor was it ever supposed to.

In its negotiations with Imperial Vice-chancellor Held at its February 1537 meetings in Schmalkalden, the League of Schmalkalden had drawn attention to Pope Adrian's admission, made by his legate at the 1522-1523 Diet of Nuremberg, that the sins of the priests and the prelates were especially responsible for the current state of the church and that the sins of the head had infected the members.[67] This admission had been embodied in Pope Adrian's Instruction to his legate Francis Chieregati. This Instruction along with an apostolic brief dated 25 November 1522 from Adrian to the diet, the estates' first reply of 5 February 1523, the legate's rejoinder and the estates' second reply, the estates' lengthy list of gravamina about the state of the church, and, finally, a list of annates was published in Nuremberg in 1523.[68] Since this treatise combined, first, the pope's admission of sin among the Roman Catholic church's higher clergy, second, the estates' detailed grievances against the Roman Catholic church, and, third, their calculations of the massive amount of money that flowed from Germany to Rome in payment of annates (234,518 gulden is the calculated sum!), it could easily serve as a devastating indictment of the papacy. It was with this purpose in mind that, in mid-1538, Luther republished this treatise in both a Latin and a German edition and supplied angry forewords to both.[69] These were historical documents, published for posterity, to make sure that future Germans would never forget from what horrible tyrany God had freed them.* The papists tried to cover their sins but documents such as these exposed their ignominy. Combining imagery from the prophets of the Old Testament and from Revelation of the New with some of his own coarseness, Luther wrote:

---

*For example, just as Moses had admonished his people never to forget their distress in Egypt from which God had freed them, Luther said in his German foreword, "So, too, must we now act with the papacy and always remember in what a horrible tyranny we were under him, and never again forget from what misery and distress of our consciences the Lord once again freed us through his holy word. Therefore we should zealously keep and preserve this and similar booklets so that our descendents also see what type of roguery and tyranny the pope has produced and practiced, and to help us praise and glorify God [and] also to learn to be on guard in the future against the papacy and other errors. For the papists are now starting to spruce themselves up. . . . In addition [they] are stealing from our books [things] that they never knew or taught before, as if they could thereby cover their previous infamy and deceive the people with promises as though they had never troubled any waters. But it will and shall not help. There are too many books and other tokens extant, also their own decretals and bulls that cannot be spruced up or covered over. Thus even now they do not cease their impudent stinking lies, feigning to reform the Roman curia and the whole church, also to hold a council, thus pursuing their mockery and derision of all Christendom as if they [members of Christendom] were mere toy jugglers and dolls who simply could not perceive what false roguery they [the papists] were practicing" (WA 50:361).

The leather has become too short for them so that one sees the Roman whore exposed both front and back. If they wish to spruce themselves in front, they uncover themselves in back. If they wish to cover the rear, they stand naked in front. They hire lots of scribblers and want very much to produce something stinking, but they just don't have anything in their belly. Their hour has come, as is stated in Revelation.[70]

Also in 1538 Luther published a series of articles, which, as the title of the publication indicated, "were to have been presented by our party at the Council of Mantua or wherever it was." These articles had been written at the request of Elector Johann Friedrich, who sought a definitive statement of Luther's beliefs to be used, if necessary, at a future council and after Luther's death.[71] After Luther's death, they received the title "Schmalkaldic Articles," and gained the status of an official confession of faith during the second half of the sixteenth century and were finally incorporated into the 1580 *Book of Concord,* which became the standard of faith for most Lutheran churches thereafter.

In the first section Luther dealt with the "high articles of the divine majesty" set forth in the Apostles' Creed, the Athanasian Creed, and the Catechism concerning which, he claimed, there was "no quarrel or dispute since we both confess them."[72]

In the second section he presented articles dealing with the "office and work of Jesus Christ" or with "our redemption." In the first and "chief" article in this section, Luther laid out the doctrine of justification by faith alone. "One cannot yield or give way on anything of this article," he stated, "even though heaven and earth should fall and all temporal things should be destroyed." On this article rested everything that they taught and practiced against the pope, the devil, and the world.[73]

In the next article he characterized the mass as the "greatest and most horrible abomination" in the papacy since it conflicted with the "chief" article concerning justification by faith alone. "There is to be no yielding or giving way on this article either," he wrote, "for the first article does not permit it."[74] In the third article he called for the restoration of foundations and cloisters to their original purpose: the rearing of learned men and chaste women. Otherwise, he concluded, they should be abandoned or destroyed.[75]

Turning in the fourth article to the papacy—which the elector had explicitly asked him to discuss—Luther asserted that "the pope is not the head of all Christendom by divine right or according to God's word (for that belongs to one only, who is called Jesus Christ)." The pope was solely the bishop or pastor of the churches of Rome and of those churches that had "joined with him voluntarily or through a human institution (that is, secular authority)." With this comment, Luther was probably referring to the papal states.

All that the pope had undertaken on the basis of presumed power was a "devilish business" and had contributed to the ruin of the Christian church and the destruction of the "chief article concerning the redemption in Jesus Christ." The papal claim that no Christian could be saved unless he was obedient and subject to the pope was a "human invention" that was not commanded and was unnecessary and useless. The church had existed for at least five hundred years without a Pope and to that day the Greek church and the churches "of many other languages" had never been under the pope and still were not. The church could exist very well without such a head and actually would have done better "if such a head had not been thrown up by the devil."

In part three, the longest part of the Schmalkaldic Articles, Luther treated issues that could be discussed "with learned, reasonable individuals or among themselves." Under this rubric he discussed such issues as original sin and the law, repentence, the gospel, baptism, the Sacrament of the Altar, the keys, confession, the ban, ordination and vocation, the marriage of priests, the church, how one is justified before God and good works, monastic vows, and, finally, human traditions.* In the important and delicate article on the Lord's Supper Luther wrote:** "We hold that the bread and wine in the Supper is the true body and blood of Christ, and are not only offered to and received by the pious but also by the wicked Christians."[76]

In his conclusion to the articles Luther succinctly stated the significance of these articles for him:

> These are the articles on which I must stand and will stand, God willing, until my death. And [I] know of nothing in them to change or to yield on. If, however, someone wishes to yield something, he may do so on his own conscience.

---

*WA 50:240-53. In the 1538 publication of the Schmalkaldic Articles Luther added to the article on confession a lengthy attack on "enthusiasts . . . [who] boast having the spirit without and before the word" (WA 50:245-47). This is another indication that the original articles were directed solely against the Catholics.
**In the original dictated manuscript the word "under" was scratched out before the words "bread and wine," indicating that originally Luther had dictated "we hold that under the bread and wine . . . is the true body and blood of Christ" and had then had his secretary strike the word "under." For more on this see note 76.

Although Luther claimed in his 1538 foreword that these articles had been "unanimously" accepted by the League in its meetings in February 1537,[77] this had in fact not been the case. The formulation used in the article on the Lord's Supper had threatened to divide the Upper German cities from the other members of the League, and so an adoption of the Articles as part of the League's confession of faith had been delicately sidestepped. Luther's misunderstanding on this point was probably due to his near fatal stone attack in Schmalkalden which prevented him from participating in most of the negotiations.[78]

When 1 May 1538 finally arrived, the date set for the opening of the council in Vicenza, only one prelate was present, the exiled bishop of Upsala John Magnus. The pope had done nothing significant to prevent this miserable showing. Instead he was himself actually on the road to Nice to mediate an end to the war between Francis I and Charles V and, he hoped, to create a more favorable climate for the council. On 25 April he postponed the council for an indefinite period, citing as the reason the nonappearance of participants. Although at Nice he was able to arrange a ten-year truce between the two monarchs, he was unable to secure French approval for the council. Francis was not about to agree to a council that could only help his Habsburg rival. Accordingly, the council was postponed once more, to Easter 1539.

## On the Councils and the Church

Already before news of this latest postponement had reached him, Luther had started work on the most substantial treatise of his later years, *On the Councils and the Church*.[79] Although written in German and thus accessible to all literate Germans, this treatise is directed at a narrower audience than most of his later works. In large part it is a scholarly piece, analyzing the history of the ancient councils. It is tendentious throughout, but sustained polemical attacks on the papacy, rich with typical abuse, are largely confined to its introductory pages and to its concluding section on the nature of the church. The heart of the treatise, in which Luther analyzes the history of the ancient councils, contains much less abuse, name-calling, sarcasm, and crudity than is common in his treatises of these years; its polemics are, comparatively speaking, quite restrained. Instead Luther develops a coherent, sustained analysis and argument that is eminently persuasive more by virtue of its logic and historical examples than of its appeal to emotion and prejudice.

Luther's goal was to demonstrate, first, that the church could not depend upon the fathers and the councils to establish its faith but only on the Holy Scripture and, second, that the council had no authority to introduce anything new in matters of faith or good works but only to defend the ancient faith and the ancient good works in accordance with Scripture.

To those who sought a reformation on the basis of the fathers and councils, mainly the humanists, Luther replied that such a reformation was simply impossible.[80] First, it was apparent, he stated, that the councils were not only unequal but also contradictory. The same was true of the fathers. Attempts, like that of Gratian and Lombard, to reconcile them were doomed to failure and only made matters worse.[81]

Luther argued on the basis of a close examination of several pronouncements of the Apostles' Council and the Council of Nicaea, the first two "universal" councils of the church, that several of their decrees—on eating blood and strangled animals, on the readmittance of apostates, on the rebaptism of heretics, and on the propriety of Christians participating in war—had fallen into disuse or contradicted the church's later pronouncements. Additionally, there was no council or church father in which one could find the whole of Christian doctrine.[82]

In the second part of his treatise, Luther subjected the Apostles' Council described in Acts and the first four "ecumenical" councils—Nicaea, Constantinople, Ephesus, and Chalcedon—to careful historical scrutiny. He concluded that none of these councils had established new articles of faith. Instead they had confirmed and defended articles of faith that were even more amply and powerfully formulated in the Scripture itself. To reach this conclusion, Luther had laid out a very compelling analysis and argument based on the best historical sources then available. For instance, in discussing the Council of Nicaea he drew heavily on the *Historia Tripartita* by Cassiodorus Senator with occasional assistance from Eusebius's *Ecclesiastical History* in Rufinus' translation and with Rufinus's two additional chapters, and also from the Canon Law, and from the recently published (1538) two volumes by the Franciscan Peter Crabbe on the general councils.[83]

Luther concluded the second part of the treatise with the principal question that had prompted him to write the treatise in the first place: what is a council and what is its task? If it was not to establish new articles of faith, as Luther had just finished demonstrating, what was it supposed to do? First, Luther said, it had no power to establish new articles of faith, even if the Holy Spirit were present in it. Second, a council did have the power as well as the responsibility to suppress and condemn new articles of faith in accordance with Holy Scripture and the ancient faith. Third, a council had no power to command new good works, nor could it do so since all good works were already more than abundantly commanded in the Holy Scripture. Fourth, a council had the power and the responsibility to condemn evil works that opposed love in accordance with Holy Scripture and the ancient ways of the church and to punish persons guilty of such works.[84] Fifth, a council did not have the power to impose on Christians new ceremonies to be observed on pain of mortal sin or at peril to the conscience. Sixth, a council had the power and responsibility to condemn such ceremonies in accordance with Scripture, for they were unchristian and caused a new idolatry or worship which was not commanded by God but rather forbidden. Seventh, a council did not have the power to meddle in secular law and government. Eighth, a council had the power and responsibility to condemn such arbitrary ways or new laws in accordance with Holy Scripture. Ninth, a council did not have the power to make such statutes or decretals that sought nothing more than tyranny, that is, how the bishops should have authority and power to command what they wished and everyone had to tremble and be obedient. On the contrary, it had the power and the responsibility to condemn such things in accordance with Holy Scripture. Tenth, a council had the power to establish some ceremonies with this difference, first, that they did not strengthen the tyranny of the bishops, and second, that they were necessary and useful for the people and imparted a fine, orderly discipline and manner.[85]

A council, according to Luther, was "nothing but a consistory, a supreme court, a chamber [*Consistorium, Hofegericht, Camergericht*], or the like in which the judges pass judgment after hearing the parties. Thus a council, as Luther saw it, did not condemn even a heretic according to its own discretion "but according to the law of the empire, that is, according to Holy Scripture, which they confess to be the law of the holy church."[86] For Luther, the council performed the same function as did pastors and school teachers, although on a grander (but also more temporary) scale. It judged, anathematized, and preserved the church.*

In the third and final part of his treatise Luther turned from his discussion of the council to a discussion of the church. Although this

---

*WA 50:617. Moreover, a council, as he saw it, "should only deal with matters of faith and [then only] when faith was in great danger, for one can condemn at home public evil works through secular lordship, pastors, [and] parents and manage the good [works]." But false good works also belonged to matters of faith since they spoiled the true faith and thus also belonged in a council if the individual pastors were too weak to deal with them (WA 50:618f.).

section contains considerable substantive arguments and analysis, it also contains much more antipapal abuse and name-calling than the previous two sections. Moreover, it could stand on its own as a statement of the Protestant conception of the church and as a reasoned as well as polemical attack on the opposing Roman Catholic conception.[87]

Luther defined the "holy Christian church" as the "holy Christian people." He explained that an *ecclesia* was nothing but an assembly of people.[88] He then listed and discussed how to recognize the "holy Christian people." Among the signs of the church he listed were the presence of the word of God,[89] baptism and the Supper,[90] the proper use of the keys in disciplining offenses and the proper calling of ministers,[91] the life of prayer, [92] and the bearing of the cross.[93]

### The Historical Argument

By 1539 Luther had perfected another means of attacking and discrediting his opponents. Of the eighteen separate publications dealing with the proposed papal council that Luther issued from 1532 to 1539, nine reproduced and commented on historical documents, four more reproduced and commented on immediately contemporary documents, and three more used historical arguments extensively. Only two of the writings—one disputation and the satirical letter from Beelzebub (which may not have actually been written by Luther)—lack a significant historical dimension. Luther had learned to used history and historical documents to reinforce arguments from Scripture and from reason. He had gone beyond the younger Luther and acquired an impressively wide-ranging knowledge of church history. This new knowledge enriched and enlarged both his polemical arsenal and his theology. The polemics of the older Luther may be occasionally more violent, abusive, and vulgar than those of the younger man. They also can be richer and more sophisticated, for they have gained a historical dimension.

## CHAPTER FIVE

# Apocalyptic Expectations:
# The Scourge of God

In general Luther viewed the history of his own time as the realization of the apocalyptic predictions of Daniel and Revelation. The events of his age, he was convinced, were certain signs that the End Time was at hand. The 1530 foreword to his translation of Daniel makes clear how firmly set this conviction was. Following traditional exegesis, Luther identified Daniel's "kingdom of iron" with the Roman Empire, which, through its transference to the Germans, had survived into Luther's own time and would persist until the Last Day. The papacy was the antichrist alluded to in the eleventh chapter of Daniel, and the Turk was the small horn that replaced three horns of the beast in the seventh chapter. The appearance of the papal antichrist and the success of the Turk left no doubt in Luther's mind that the apocalyptic drama was in its final act.[1]

This apocalyptic vision plays a major role in many of the polemics of the older Luther. In subsequent chapters it will be seen how this vision, reinforced by disappointment over the reception of the Gospel in Germany and by concern for widespread indifference and even blasphemy, helped shape his polemical writings against Catholics, "fanatics," and Jews. This chapter examines another aspect of this apocalyptic vision: Luther's identification of the Turk as the "little horn" of Daniel and as the Gog of Ezekiel and Revelation. Moreover, since Luther's writings against the Turk fall slightly before the beginning of the period under consideration (1528-1530) and then towards the end of Luther's life (1541-1543), one is able to assess the alteration of the apocalyptic strain in the intervening decade.

## Earlier Attacks on the Turks

In 1521, after a hiatus of forty years, the "scourge of God," the Ottoman Turks, had once again descended upon Western Europe. Led by Suleiman the Magnificent, the Turks had taken Belgrade in 1521 and the island of Rhodes in 1522. Four years later, in 1526, Suleiman and his army had met the Hungarians and King Louis II at Mohacs and inflicted a disastrous defeat, crushing the Hungarian army and killing King Louis.

With Louis's death the dynasty of the Jagellons had come to an end and the Habsburg rule of Hungary had had its feeble beginnings. In 1521 Ferdinand of Austria had married Anna of Hungary and King Louis had married Mary of Habsburg. According to their marriage contract, Ferdinand was to succeed to the Hungarian throne if Louis died without a male heir. After the debacle at Mohacs, the majority of the Hungarian nobility had supported Ferdinand's claim to the throne, seeing in the Habsburgs their only protection against the Turks. A minority, however, had elected as king the Prince of Transylvania, John Zapolya. Negotiations between the two claimants had come to nothing. In 1527 Constantinople had recognized as Hungary's legitimate king the weaker of the two, Zapolya. Ferdinand had attacked, and Zapolya had suffered a clear defeat in the fall of 1527. But the Turks had continued to supply Zapolya with assistance, and in 1529 Suleiman had personally led his armies into Central Europe. Buda had fallen and Zapolya had been formally installed as King of Hungary. In the fall of 1529 Vienna had been besieged though not taken. All of Germany was shaken by this close call.

Luther had identified the Turks as the "scourge of God" as early as 1518. In his *Explanation of the Ninety-Five Theses,* he had stated that if the pope were able to remit God's punishments as he claimed, then he should halt the advance of the Turks, who were clearly "scourges and the rod of God [*flagella et virgam dei*]."[2] In the bull *Exsurge, Domine* the papacy had declared heretical the allegedly Lutheran proposition that "to fight against the Turks is to oppose God's visitation on our iniquities."[3] Luther had replied in his *M. Luther's Assertion of All the Articles Recently Condemned by the Bull of Leo X* that war against the Turks was futile as long as the papacy was allowed to prosper.[4] For the rest of his life this remained Luther's central conviction regarding the Turks. They were God's punishment on a sinful Christendom that, among other sins, tolerated the papal abomination.

In 1528-1529 Luther elaborated on his view of the Turks and their place in history in three treatises. The first, *On War Against the Turks,* was written in the fall of 1528 and published in January 1529.[5]

It was meant to instruct consciences how to defend themselves against the Turks. The second treatise, *Army Sermon Against the Turks,* was written at the time of the siege of Vienna and its aftermath, and indicates how these events heightened Luther's apocalyptic expectations.[6] In late 1529 he had also prepared for publication a Latin treatise on the rituals and customs of the Turks, *Booklet on the Rites and Customs of the Turks,* written in the second half of the fifteenth century by a Dominican who had spent some twenty years in Turkish captivity.* This last treatise appeared in 1530.[7]

Of these three treatises the *Army Sermon* most clearly reveals Luther's apocalyptic vision of his time and his own sense of prophetic vocation within the apocalyptic context. To be sure, in *On War Against the Turks,* Luther once again identified the papacy as the antichrist and the Turk as the very devil incarnate. Christ's return was not far off, he stated. The world was coming to its end, the Roman Empire was almost finished, just as the Jewish kingdom had been before Christ's birth. Just as Herod and the Jews had been enemies and yet had joined forces against Christ, the Turks and the papacy were enemies and yet supported each other against Christ and his kingdom. But the most interesting thrust of this treatise was Luther's insistence that to advocate a Christian crusade against the Turks was to mix the spiritual with the secular. Such actions would draw God's wrath and insure the success of the Turks. The Turk was to be fought spiritually by Christians with repentance, the amendment of one's life, and prayer. The Turk was to be fought physically under the command and banner of the emperor—and then only in self-defense and with humility and fear of God. Such physical defense was a secular matter and must remain so.[8] Luther's introduction to the *Booklet* dealt less with apocalyptic themes and more with Turkish morals and ceremonies, which he stated were superior to those of the Christians and yet which ultimately meant nothing.**

Thus a closer examination of the apocalyptic and prophetic elements in the *Army Sermon* is needed. The text for this sermon was

---

*In his foreword Luther expressed his wish for more information on the Turks and their Koran. He mentioned having read a refutation of the Koran, but expressed doubts about the reliability of its description of the Mohammedan faith. Twelve years later he was to revise this judgment (WA 30/2:205).

**Luther said that he issued the treatise to show the papists that Christianity was something other than and greater than morals and ceremonies since, as this treatise demonstrated, the Turks were superior to the Christians in morality, the observance of rituals, and the performance of good works. He also published it so that Christians who had contact with the Turks would not be induced to abandon Christ and embrace Mohammed (see note 7).

most aptly chosen for its encouragement of apocalyptic speculation. It was the seventh chapter of Daniel. This chapter relates Daniel's dream about four beasts. Each beast represents a kingdom. The last of the four beasts sports ten horns, and in Daniel's dream a new, smaller horn grows, displacing three of the previous horns. This new horn has human eyes and a mouth and speaks great things. This fourth beast harries the "saints of the most high" until an ancient man appears to sit in judgment. The beast is then slain. A "son of man" is then presented to the ancient and is given everlasting dominion.

Luther, often following traditional Christian exegesis, interpreted this fourth beast to represent the Roman Empire, which, he believed, had survived into his own day.[9] The small horn he interpreted to represent the Mohammedan kingdom, which had displaced the horns, or kingdoms, of Egypt, Greece, and Asia. The human eyes represented the Koran, which contained only human wisdom. The mouth signified the many blasphemies of the Mohammedans against the Christian faith. That the beast should harry the "saints of the most high," as was stated in Daniel, required no special interpretation, since, Luther argued, the Turks were the Christians' worst enemy. The success of the Turks was due to the Christians' sins, as Daniel had also prophesied. The advent of the Turks also signaled the approaching Last Judgment and the kingdom of the saints, since Daniel prophesied that the small horn should prosper until the ancient came and sat in judgment. But when that day would come no one knew with certainty. The Turks, however, would eventually be cast down as was prophesied in Revelation 20:8f. and Ezekiel 38:2 of Gog and Magog (Luther harbored no doubt that the Turk was the Gog of these prophecies). Although one could never be certain, Luther reckoned that the Last Judgment had to be close at hand, for the Turks had taken three kingdoms—Egypt, Greece, and Asia—and Daniel said that the small horn would replace three horns. This also indicated, as he saw it, that Germany would not fall to the Turks before the Last Judgment.

He had explained these prophecies, Luther commented, to instruct and convince the conscience of those ordered to war against the Turks. Whoever fought against them (provided the Turks had started the war) would be fighting against the enemy of God and the blasphemer of Christ, indeed, against the devil himself. Luther repeated his admonition in *On War Against the Turks* that such defensive war was a secular affair and should be fought in obedience to and under secular leadership. He then proceeded at length to exhort and to encourage the soldiers who had to fight in such a war. Those who died fighting were, as Daniel promised, "saints of the most high." And since death was a constant, daily threat, death in battle against the Turks was a far better death than most. The Turk who killed a Christian made a holy martyr out of the Christian while condemning himself to eternal flames. Luther also repeated his admonition that Christians had to first repent, improve their lives, and pray with fear and earnestness that God assist their undertaking.[10]

In the second part Luther exhorted the Germans of all conditions and estates to sacrifice their lives and goods in the defense against the Turks and warned that if the Turks prevailed, their sacrifice would be even greater. He advised that it would be best for men and women never to surrender to the Turks but rather to resist them to the death. In conscious imitation of the Prophet Jeremiah, who had written a letter to the enslaved Jews in Babylon, Luther offered advice and comfort to those Germans who had the misfortune of being carried off by the Turks. Once sold into slavery, the Christian had to obey the commandment to be obedient to one's master as saints Peter and Paul taught. Such slavery, if used properly, was useful for salvation, providing the Christian with his cross. In no case, however, should captured Christians support the Mohammedan faith or allow their masters to force them into forsaking Christ. Luther closed his printed sermon with a hopeful prediction that the Last Judgment could not be far off.[11]

At the outset of the later period, then, Luther had already clearly identified the Turk with Gog and with the "little horn" and the papacy with the antichrist. The Turk was also the "scourge of God", sent to punish Christendom for its sins, and especially for its sin of tolerating the papal abomination. Christians would have no success against the Turks until they repented of their sins and amended their own lives. But most important of all, they must first deal with the antichrist within their midst, the Roman papacy. These themes recur in Luther's later treatises.

## Admonition to Prayer Against the Turks

In fact, more than a decade passed before Luther had the opportunity actually to study the Koran, and so his promised treatise was also put off for more than ten years. In the intervening years, the Turkish threat had variously waxed and waned, but at all times had played a major role in the politics in the Holy Roman Empire and in the relations between Protestants and Catholics within the empire.[12] In the fall of 1531 Ferdinand, seeking advantage against his rival claimant Zapolya, attempted to seize the stronghold of Ofen. Unfortunately for him, he only succeeded in angering the Turks, who broke off the current peace negotiations and prepared for another attack on Hungary and Austria. Needing Protestant assistance to repel the threatened Turkish attack, Emperor Charles was forced in 1532 to make concessions to the League of Schmalkalden and agree to the Nuremberg Standstill. Suleiman did invade Hungary that year but avoided any decisive battle with the assembled Habsburg and Imperial troops. For the next few years Suleiman turned his attention toward the East and the Persians, but skirmishes along the border in Central Europe continued to keep the Turkish question in the minds of the Habsburgs and the Germans. In 1535 Charles scored a major victory over the Turkish fleet, but the gains of this victory were short-lived. In 1536 Francis and Suleiman concluded an alliance against their common Habsburg enemy. When warfare broke out between Charles and Francis that summer, Suleiman supported his ally with raids by his fleet in the western Mediterranean.

In the fall of 1537 Ferdinand ordered a punitive expedition against the Pasha of Bosnia, who was continually raiding into southern Hungary. Ferdinand's troops met with a crushing defeat, however, and Suleiman began contemplating another western offensive. In February 1538 Zapolya, who had had a falling out with Suleiman, entered into the treaty of Gosswardein with Ferdinand, agreeing to recognize Ferdinand as his successor in exchange for assistance against the Turks. War threatened in 1538 and 1539, both against the Turks and between the Protestants and Catholics. The Protestants were especially suspicious of all requests for assistance against the Turks, fearing that such levies might be turned against them. In early 1539 Luther penned an admonition to all Protestant pastors. He exhorted them to hold before their congregations the two rods God threatened them with, the Turks and the papists, and to urge their listeners to repent and mend their sinful ways.[13] This admonition remained unpublished during Luther's lifetime.

Zapolya died suddenly in 1540, and the issue of the Hungarian succession led once more to war. According to the treaty of Grosswardein, Ferdinand should have become king of Hungary. Instead, Zapolya's followers proclaimed as their king his infant son, John Sigismund. Ferdinand retaliated by invading Hungary and besieging the city of Buda. Suleiman, who supported John Sigismund's claim, responded the next year with a major invasion. In August 1541 he crushed the opposing German army, and Buda and Pest fell to his troops. John Sigismund was recognized as King of Hungary, but Suleiman appointed himself as regent until the boy reached his majority. Much of Hungary was placed under direct Turkish control.

It was under these dire circumstances, in early September 1541, that Elector Johann Friedrich wrote Luther informing him of these disasters and urging that he admonish the preachers of Electoral Saxony to led their congregations in prayer against the Turks.[14] Luther, already much exercised by the Turkish threat,[15] readily complied with his Elector's request. By mid-October his *Admonition to Prayer Against the Turks* was completed. The importance of the subject led to numerous reprints both that year and in subsequent years.[16]

In this *Admonition* Luther explicitly saw himself, and his fellow pastors, performing the same role as the prophets in the Old Testament. In it he rebuked Germany for its sins, especially its ingratitude towards God who had enlightened the Germans with the true word of God and had freed them from the "horrible abomination of the papal darkness and idolatry." He called for repentance and issued a stern and prophetic warning of what the future held for the unrepentant. Over and over again, he made explicit the parallels he saw between the age of the prophets in Israel and his own time. In all this there was a strong apocalyptic and eschatological undertone. Luther identified the Turk as the beast of Revelation, and he predicted the imminent Day of Judgment.

Luther began with Germany's shameful reception of the Gospel.

> We Germans have now for many years heard the dear word of God through which God, the father of all mercy, has enlightened us and called us from the horrible abomination of the papal darkness and idolatry into his holy light and kingdom. But even today it is horrible enough to see how gratefully and respectfully we have received and observed it. For just as if the previous sins were not enough with our angering God to the utmost (although in ignorance) with masses, purgatory, saint worship, and many other righteous works of our own and with our filling every corner with such great idolatries and with our thinking that we had done God special service with such things, we surpass ourselves and persecute the dear word, which called us to repentance from such abominations, and knowingly and willfully defend such idolatry with fire, water, noose, sword, cursing, and blaspheming, so that it would be no wonder if God allowed, or had long ago allowed, Germany to be flooded not only with Turks but with devils themselves.

It was this ingratitude, as Luther saw it, that most deserved the scourge of the Turk. But the Germans were guilty of many other sins as well. There was the rise of "incorrigibly wicked sects and heresies" such as those of Müntzer, Zwingli, the Anabaptists and many others, all exploiting the name and the cover of the Gospel. In addition, there was the "great God Mammon or avarice," which had possessed not only the peasants and burghers but also the nobility. Also, servants were up to all sorts of mischief. There was no end to theft between neighbors. Workers acted like lords. The jurists were so bad that no one wished to try a case. In the Imperial Cameral Court a "whore of the devil" was in control, as its banning of Goslar, Minden, and other cities showed as well as its assistance of "Heinz the arsonist," Duke Heinrich of Braunschweig.

> So Germany is ripe and full of all sorts of sins against God. Beyond this it wishes to defend [these sins] and defy God, so that I unfortunately have been far too true a prophet when I have often said we must be punished either by the Turks or by ourselves.[17]

There was two things the preachers should do. First, they should admonish the "bloody, blasphemous papists" to cease blaspheming God and, in the face of God's wrath, to mend their ways. Second, they should admonish the ungrateful, wanton people to improve their behavior, to honor God's word, and to call on God.*

---

*Throughout the treatise Luther self-consciously adopted a prophetic role. "It is indeed true," he explained at one point, "that we are not Joshua, who with his prayer made the sun stand still in the heaven. [We are] also not Moses, who with his heart-felt prayer divided the Red Sea. [We are] also not Elijah, who with his prayer called down fire from heaven. But we are at least the equal of those people to whom God entrusted his word and whom he inspired through His spirit to preach to us. Indeed, we are even people like Moses, Joshua, Elijah, and all the other saints, for we have the same word of God and [the same] spirit, which they had. And we are preachers, ministers, and officials of the same God that they were, although they [served Him] more grandly than we. Still, they had no higher, better God than we. They also had no better flesh and blood than we, for they were men like us, and the same creatures of God that we are. I am speaking now of us poor sinners who nevertheless hold Christ dear and seek his kingdom, not of the papists and false Christians. And God must (if I may put it this way) hear our prayer just as much as theirs, for we are members of His church, that is, His dear son's bride, which He cannot despise if it cries earnestly [to Him]. Consequently, it is no big thing for God to do as great or even greater works through us as he did through them, as we have seen and experienced to this point in the mighty and marvelous assistance he has given us against the pope's devil, which is greater than the Turks' devil, if we could conceive or believe it" (WA 51:598-99).

This comparison with the prophets led Luther at one point to reflect on his own feelings in these trying times. He had discussed what he and his fellow preachers were duty-bound to do, because he was often troubled with the thought that, since the papists' unrepentant raging and their own ingratitude had surpassed all bounds, their sins and wickedness were too great for their prayers to be answered. He had also been deeply moved by the example of the prophet Jeremiah, whom God had forbidden to pray

Having completed his advice to the pastors, Luther turned to the secular estate, admonishing its members to listen to God's word and to pray with the pastors, to establish justice in the land, to punish usury and other vices, to moderate the "ugly, accursed guzzling, playing, and extravagant living," and to receive the Sacrament. When they went into battle against the Turks, they should be certain in their own minds that they were not fighting against flesh and blood.

> Otherwise, I prophesy, one Turk will slaughter many Christians. Instead, be certain that you are battling against a great army of devils, for the army of the Turks is essentially the army of the devil. Therefore do not rely on your pike, sword, gun, power or numbers, for the devil pays no attention to such things. This we have learned by experience. The Turk has had nothing but good fortune and victories over us and will continue to have them as long as we shall fight as [if it were] men against men.[18]

Once they had armed themselves with prayer, they should commit themselves to God's will. If He wished to punish them and allow them to be killed, then they had died in their vocation and at God's command and for His sake, so that they would be His martyrs. On Judgment Day, they would be the judges of the Turks, pope, the world, and all the devils. There was little the devil could do them since their lives were already forfeit through Adam's sin in paradise. The devil could indeed shorten their lives, but that would only speed their preparation for the resurrection.

In his closing paragraphs Luther returned to his apocalyptic theme. There was the possibility, he remarked, that the Turk, just like the pope, would go to ruin. The pope and the Turk were the last two abominations and "God's wrath," as Revelation.15:1 and 19:20] called them. They were the "false prophet" and the "beast," which were both to be seized and cast into the "fiery pool." As he summed it up, in the papacy and under the Turks the regime [*regiment*] of home, city, and church were simply destroyed.

---

for his people, and by the example of Ezekiel 14, which stated that were even Noah, Daniel, and Job among the people of that time they could only have saved themselves with their righteousness. "But because I do not have the new command that Jeremiah had—that I should not pray—also because there are indeed some pious hearts (although few but undoubtedly more than a Moses or a Samuel or a Noah, Daniel, [and] Job) we may not in good conscience on our own authority give up in despair and cease praying. Rather we must hold to the universal and ancient command: 'Ask, seek, knock . . .' [Matthew 7:7]" (WA 51:612-13).

## The Refutation of the Koran

Following the major defeat of 1541, the German estates, both Protestant and Catholic, resolved at the early 1542 Diet of Speyers to field a massive army against the Turks. A special tax to support this effort was agreed upon. Although exempted by the elector from this tax, Luther nonetheless voluntarily assessed his property and paid his share.[19] He was extremely pessimistic, however, about the probable outcome of this campaign.

On 26 March 1542 he wrote Jacob Probst in Bremen a letter that strikingly reveals his pessimistic mood.

> Although there is not time to write much, my [dear] Jacob, for I am consumed by age and labors—old, cold, and misshapen (as they say)—nevertheless I am not allowed to rest, being so vexed daily be so many affairs and writing matters [with the result that] I know more of the fate of this age than [do] you. It is certain that the world is threatened with ruin [for] Satan rages so [and] the world has become so brutish. Only this one consolation remains: [that] that day [of judgment] will be soon at hand. And [it is certain that] after the world is sated with the word of God and has begun to disdain it, fewer false prophets will arise. For how should those who in an Epicurean fashion condemn the word produce [new] heresies? Germany has been, and always will be, as it has been. The nobles plan for sovereignty over everyone; the cities take counsel against them (and rightly). Thus the kingdom, divided among itself, must meet an army of demons raging in the Turks. Nor do we greatly care whether we have a gracious or angry Lord, since of course we shall by ourselves conquer and lord it over the Turks, demons, God, and all! So great is the most raving trust and security of the perishing Germans! But what should we do with this? In vain do we lament; in vain do we wail. It is left for us to pray 'May Your will be done,' [to pray] for the kingdom, [and to pray] for the sanctification of the name of God. If this occurs, we should let [things] go, tumble down, stand, perish, as they wish.[20]

After relating other depressing and portentous news—including the strange circumstances that reportedly surrounded Karlstadt's recent death[21]—Luther closed with the request that Probst pray that he, Luther, depart this world in good time, for he was fed up with this life "or rather this most bitter death."

In this same letter Luther informed Probst of his current efforts to translate into German a refutation of the Koran. This refutation, penned in Latin around 1300 by Ricoldus, a Florentine Dominican who had spent several years in the Middle East, had been translated into Greek in the fourteen century and then from Greek back into Latin in the fifteenth. Despite this curious translation history and the difficulties involved for a thirteenth-century Christian monk to gain a thorough, and reasonably fair, understanding of the Koran, Ricoldus's refutation, even in the version Luther worked with, showed for its time an impressive understanding of the Koran and the prevailing Islamic exegesis.[22] As Luther himself explained in his preface to his translation, he had read the *Refutation* previously but had been unable to believe that there could be reasonable men whom the devil persuaded to believe "such shameful things,"[23] In fact, in his 1530 *Booklet on the Rites and Customs of the Turks* he had expressed some doubt whether Ricoldus—or as Luther knew him, Richardus— had given a true picture of the Islamic faith.[24] But in February 1542, Luther for the first time had the opportunity to read a Latin translation, albeit a poor one, of the Koran, and was able to verify that Ricoldus had in fact depicted the Koran in reasonably true colors.[25] Luther had thereupon decided to translate the *Refutation* into German for the edification of the German populace. By the end of April 1542, his extremely free translation, accompanied by his own preface and afterword, had left the press.[26]

He had published this translation, he wrote in his preface, to show the Germans what a "shameful" faith the Mohammedan faith was so that Christians would be strengthened in their faith and not be influenced by the fact that the Saracens and Turks had for so many hundred years enjoyed repeated victories over the Christians. The Mohammedans had had such successes not because their faith was correct and the Christian faith was incorrect, but rather because that was the way God ruled His people. First, God allowed them to be punished and oppressed on account of their sins, as both Old and New Testaments amply showed. Second, Christian blood had to be shed from the beginning of the world to its end so that many martyrs might get to heaven. Christians had well earned such punishment by dividing themselves with heresy and sects and by living in ingratitude and contempt for Christ's precious blood, which had redeemed them.

At the conclusion of the *Refutation* Luther added his own brief "Refutation."[27] Referring to Ricoldus's assertion in the ninth chapter that Mohammed himself had confessed that not all of the Koran was true, that of his twelve thousand words only three thousand were true, Luther observed that here was a candid devil. He boasted in his own form and without any angels' masks that whatever he taught was but one quarter true and the remainder false. In fact, Luther charged, all of it was undoubtedly false, including the fourth part. He found it inconceivable that any reasonable man could seriously believe a book of which he knew one part, not to mention three parts, was lies but did not know which part was lies and which not. If the Turks or Saracens seriously believed the Koran, he continued, then they did not deserve to be called men, since they had lost all human reason. "If they are men and possess their reason, however, and nevertheless willingly and knowingly believe the Koran, then no one is responsible for their damnation but they themselves. Their master Mohammed, and the devil as well, have given them fair warning and have honestly excused themselves before God and the world of their damnation, because they openly confessed that they wished to teach lies." If this were the case, then the Turks and the Mohammedans had to be people who willingly bound themselves to the devil in exchange for the devil's help and advice. If the Turks were such people, then Christians would have a hard time waging war against them (especially with armor and weapons) "for to fight against the devil with iron is a lost cause." One first had to chase their father, the devil, off the field and summon God with His angels through true faith and the Lord's Prayer.[28]

Luther next scored the Mohammedans for having so many different versions of the Koran, only to add that it wasn't much better among the Christians, "for there are so many lies in our Korans, decretals, lie-gends, summae and countless books, so that no one knows where they come from, when they began, who their originators are."[29]

He was issuing this treatise, he stated, so that those who wished to live a holy life and who met the Turks could defend themselves from the Mohammedan faith, if not from the Mohammedan sword. But he completely despaired of those who wished to fight against the Turks and yet whose blaspheming, lewdness, and wantonness were worse than that of the Turks themselves. God could not give luck to such people.* Luther next attacked in the sharpest terms the Mohammedan

---

*One characteristic comment: "Now since . . . the greatest [portion of the] crowd knowingly serve Mammon, yes, the devil, in disobedience to God's command, should there be any great wonder if the Turks, who do not have God's command and word and, in addition, are drowned in mammon and such great luck, believe in publicly recognized lies or at least regard them [to be] innocuous lies since God is so near to them and honors them so highly with victory and riches, luck and whatever they wish. They do not consider how God generally gives such great goods, lordship, and honor to the very worst rogues, and also gives the whole world to the devil, whom He calls the prince of the world. Now when two such 'Turkish' armies go into the field against each other— one that is called Mohammedan, the other that calls itself Christian—how would you, my dear man, advise our lord God (if He did not already know) which Turks He should help and give luck to? I, one of the least of advisors, would advise him to give luck to the Mohammedan Turks against the 'Christian' Turks, as He has done to date

view of women, wives, and marriage. That the Mohammedans displayed greater discipline in war or in government meant nothing; the same was true with murderers and arsonists. "For the sinful flesh is willing and inclined to do evil and serve the devil [and] gladly maintains faith and obedience; but in doing good there is no progress." They also prayed frequently and sacrificed much. But what need was there to go on at length. "Where has there been heard of more prayer and divine services than among the idolatrous pagans, among the false prophets in Israel, and among the clergy in the papacy?" Luther asked. "And yet all their prayers put together are not worth a letter or a tittle in the Lord's Prayer." What did not proceed from faith was sin.[30]

"From all this," Luther continued, "we Christians can see how horrible, terrifying, and immeasurable God's wrath is towards the ungrateful world which has despised God's gospel." In the East the "Beast" of Mohammed had misled and plagued the world. In the West the "false prophets," the popes, had much more subtly cheated and tormented the world. "So that those there [in the East], who did not wish to listen to God's son, had to listen to the devil's son, Mohammed, and those here [in the West], who did not wish to obey the Holy Spirit, had to obey the wicked spirit in the pope." Still, in His limitless mercy, and in order to maintain His church, God had moderated his wrath. Mohammed could not deceive anyone who did not willingly wish to be deceived, for Mohammed's lies were so gross and tangible and his style of life so swinish and beastly that no reasonable man (not to mention a Christian) could believe or accept them. And under the papacy, God had graciously maintained the Holy Scripture and the sacraments so that the elect could eventually mend their ways and grasp God in His word and sacraments.[31]

Luther did not, however, think that Mohammed was the antichrist since he behaved so crudely and had a "childish black devil" who could deceive neither faith nor reason. Mohammed was an external persecutor, like the Romans and other pagans during the apostolic period.

---

without our advice, even in opposition to our petitions and pleas. The reason is that the Mohammedan Turks do not have God's word or preachers of the same. They are gross, filthy swine [and] do not know what they live or believe. But if they had preachers of God's word, perhaps at least some of them would be transformed from swine to men. But our Christian Turks have God's word and preachers, but nevertheless do not wish to listen, and are transformed from men to simple swine. In addition [they] slander the name of Christ by boasting of themselves as Christians and Christian and yet are worse Turks than those who boast of themselves as Mohammedans and not as Christians" (WA 53:390f.).

But for us the pope is the true antichrist who has the high, subtle, beautiful, glittering devil, who sits inside Christendom, allows the holy Scripture, baptism, Sacrament, keys, catechism, [and] marriage to remain. As St. Paul says, he sits (that is, rules) in God's temple, that is, in the church or Christendom, namely among such people that have baptism, the Sacrament, the keys, the holy Scripture and God's word. And nevertheless [he] rules so masterfully that he at the same time elevates his "decraptals," his Koran, his human teaching above God's word. As a result, baptism, Sacrament, keys, prayer, gospel and Christ himself are no longer of any use to the Christian, who must rather believe that he becomes holy through his own works—to which end all [clerical] foundations, cloisters, and all his [the pope's] regime are directed.

This devil does not deceive those who intentionally wish to be deceived, as is the case with Mohammed, but rather those who would not willingly be deceived, yes, the elect of God, Matthew 24. For he bears all these names: God, Christ, God's son, Holy Spirit, church, baptism, Sacrament, and all that the Christians believe and teach and which the Mohammedan rejects, and yet dashes the truth to the ground under such names and appearance through his Koran. . . .

Mohammed also boasts that he gave no signs, but Christ and Paul prophesied that the pope should sit in God's temple, pass himself off as God, and do many false signs and wonders. If you wish to know what these wonders are, then read the legends of the saints, the monks, the pilgrimages, the masses, and the like— then you will indeed see what false signs are and what sorts of wonders the poltergeists and pilgrimage-devils, saint worship or prayers have accomplished in all the corners of Christendom.

Mohammed destroyed marriage by taking many wives yet having none; the pope, in contrast, took no wife and nonetheless, under the pretense of chastity, took advantage of all sorts of wives. Without listing all their respective sins, Luther concluded that the pope was far worse than Mohammed.[32]

Before they could have any success against the Mohammedans, the external enemy of Christendom, they would have to cut down the internal enemy, the antichrist, through authentic repentance and reliance on Christ. Otherwise they would have the type of success they had experienced in the past. "I have done my part as a true prophet and preacher," Luther concluded. "He who does not wish to listen, may go his way. I am now excused, from this day forward and in eternity."[33]

## *Admonition to the Pastors*

The army of Protestants and Catholics that assembled in the spring of 1542 was led by the young Elector Joachim of Brandenburg. He had been chosen not because of military experience, of which he had very little, but because of his mediating position between the Protestant and Catholic parties in Germany. On 14 May 1542 Joachim wrote Melanchthon and Luther requesting their prayers for the success of the venture. The two Wittenbergers wrote back, promising their support.[34] In his letter Luther expressed once again his worried concern that Germany's great sins might preclude divine acceptance of their prayers. He exhorted Joachim to make sure that the military chaplains admonished the troops to honor God and behave themselves. Repeating the advice of his *Admonition,* he urged Joachim himself to maintain strict discipline over his troops. He should forbid and punish cursing and blasphemy, and encourage through the preachers prayer and fear of God. In another letter to Jonas about the same time, Luther expressed his severe doubts about Joachim's probable success.[35]

As it turned out, and as Luther himself expected, neither his advice nor his prayers appear to have helped much. The campaign was a complete disaster. Lacking money, supplies, arms, sufficient reserves, and, above all, adequate leadership, the army experienced one misfortune after the other and was finally forced by an outbreak of the plague to quit the field. Luther was disgusted by the outcome, and a self-exculpatory letter from Joachim failed to convince him that Catholic betrayal was not somehow responsible for the defeat.[36]

Luther continued to do what he could, however. In the fall of 1542 he was instrumental in persuading the city council of Basel to allow publication of a Latin translation of the Koran—the need for which Luther had long felt.[37] In fact, he apparently assisted and encouraged the Zurich scholar Theodor Bibliander in this project in other ways as well.[38] And, to counter concerns that such a publication might subvert the Christian religion, Luther and Melanchthon even provided brief Latin forewords to this translation. In his Luther warned particularly against the "idols" of the Jews, papists, and Mohammedans and repeated many of his now familiar arguments against the Turks.[39]

In early 1543, at the command of the elector, Luther and Bugenhagen issued a short *Admonition to the Pastors in the Superintendency of the Church at Wittenberg,*[40] exhorting the pastors to call their people to repentance and to admonish them to pray "against the rod of God, the Turks." In this admonition the two pastors gave free vent to their disgust with the handling of the recent campaign and to

*111*

their suspicions that some princes had turned the war tax to their own uses. Luther especially was of the opinion that such wickedness along with the lack of repentance and the other sins of the Germans had insured that their previous prayers for the success of the campaign had gone unanswered.

## The Turks and the Apocalypse

The Turkish threat waned during the remaining years of his life, and Luther turned his attention to other, more pressing matters. But his eschatological expectations continued unabated and colored many of the treatises of these last years.

For Luther, and for many of his contemporaries, both Catholic and Protestant, the Turks were first and foremost a religious and moral problem rather than a political or military one. They were the scourge of God inflicted on the Germans because of the Germans' many sins.[41] Luther and his fellow Protestant writers agreed with Catholic writers on the nature of many of these sins, such as drunkenness, usury, and greed. They also agreed that the split within Christendom had provoked God's wrath and punishment. Of course, Catholics laid the blame on the Protestants, and often explicitly on Luther, while Luther and the other Protestants viewed the "papal abomination" as the major cause of God's wrath.

Luther's writings, and Protestant *Türkenbüchlein* in general, dwelt more than did Catholic treatises on the apocalyptical and eschatological aspects of the conflict. For Luther the true antichrist was the pope, but the Turks were seen as the devil incarnate, Gog, and the little horn in the Book of Daniel. Their successes were seen as a prelude to the Last Judgment.

In marked contrast to Catholic authors, who generally cast the fight against the Turks in the traditional terms of the crusade, Luther insisted that it was just such mingling of the spiritual and secular realms that accounted for the Turks' repeated successes. He broke decisively with the medieval past by condemning any religious crusade. War against the Turks, or for that matter against attacking Catholics, was for him solely a secular matter, to be understood and fought within the rules for a just war. He ruled out all but a defensive war fought under the leadership of duly acknowledged secular authorities. Given these limitations, however, the war against the Turks was not only justified but a God-given duty of both rulers and subjects.

The major difference between the anti-Turkish writings of 1528-1529 and the writings of a decade later is a direct reflection of

Luther's intervening experience. In the late 1520s the Reformation movement had begun its transition from an ideological movement made up largely of committed individuals to an established institution embracing whole political entities. Luther had already experienced some of the inevitable disappointment and compromise that accompanies any attempt to translate theory into practice. He had also been challenged by the brutal realities of the Peasants' War, the findings of the first visitations, and the rending of the Protestant ranks. He was fully aware of the sinfulness of his contemporaries, and he excoriated them for their sins. Still, when he discussed the sins for which God had sent the Turkish scourge, he pointed primarily at the monstrous sin of tolerating the papal antichrist.

A decade later Luther had lived through repeated Christian defeats at the hands of the Turks. His apocalyptic view of the papal antichrist had developed and been elaborated. He could offer his readers with even greater conviction the bitter prediction that Christians would never prevail over the Turks until they had first defeated the papal antichrist in their midst through repentance and trust in Christ. Yet in the intervening decade Luther had also experienced extreme frustration and disappointment about the progress of the Reformation movement. He expressed this disappointment through searing indictments of the ingratitude with which the Germans had responded to the restored gospel. He upbraided them for their "Epicurean" indifference and, what was worse, for their open blasphemy. Alongside his attack on the papal "abomination," then, he added a condemnation of his contemporaries's response to the gospel.

This change should not be attributed to Luther's growing age or increased illness. In his grimmer moments, and in the articulations of his theology, he recognized that true Christians were rare, and that the great bulk of the population would remain fast in its sin despite the renewed preaching of the gospel. Yet at some level of his being, above or below his understanding as a theologian, he had apparently hoped for more than the actual course of events had provided. He himself had been drawn into the machinations and compromises involved in turning ideology into institutions. He had found himself entangled in political policies that rubbed painfully against religious principle. He had seen the politicians and the "silver and gold" jurists subordinate faith to the dictates of political prudence. He had seen peasants and burghers and princes respond to the preaching of the restored gospel with "business as usual." For him this was not a maintenance of the *status quo* but a willful plunge into greater wickedness and blasphemy.

*113*

Given the intractable nature of human beings and the ineluctable conflict of interests in the establishment of anything as great and as encompassing as the Reformation, it could not have reasonably been otherwise.* Luther was doomed to disappointment. And so as his hope for the progress of the gospel in this world, however faint, withered in the light of experience, he found solace in his hope for the Last Day. He had predicted its near advent in the 1528-1529 tracts. The events of the 1530s that disappointed so sorely also stood as further signs of the End Time.

The older Luther was largely done with cajoling his sinful Germans. Like the prophets of old he excoriated them for their sins and declared God's judgment on them. Words of prophetic condemnation are harsh; the more so when the prophet fully expects that his words will not be attended to. As Luther explained himself, "I have done my part as a true prophet and preacher. He who does not wish to listen, may go his way. I am now excused, from this day forward and in eternity."[42]

---

*Much of the controversy over Gerald Strauss's provocative and stimulating study, *Luther's House of Learning: Indoctrination of the Young in the German Reformation* (Baltimore, 1978), centers around how much success Luther and his coworkers actually expected in introducing the Reformation. Steven Ozment's assessment is persuasive:

> The great shortcoming of the Reformation was its naive expectation that the majority of people were capable of radical religious enlightenment and moral transformation, whether by persuasion or by coercion. Such expectation directly contradicted some of its fondest convictions and the original teaching of its founder. Having begun in protest against allegedly unnatural and unscriptural proscriptions of the medieval church and urged freedom in the place of coercion, the reformers brought a strange new burden to bear on the consciences of their followers when they instructed them to resolve the awesome problems of sin, death, and the devil by simple faith in the bible and ethical service to their neighbors. The brave new man of Protestant faith, "subject to none [yet] subject to all" in Luther's famous formulation, was expected to bear his finitude and sinfulness with anxiety resolved, secure in the knowledge of a gratuitous salvation, and fearful of neither man, God, or the devil. But how many were capable of such self-understanding? (*The Age of Reform, 1250-1550: An Intellectual and Religious History of Late Medieval and Reformation Europe* [New Haven, 1980], p. 437)

I would only add that at the onset of the 1530s Luther may have himself expected more than his teaching would suggest. Or perhaps it would be better to say that he had expected or hoped for less, for less ingratitude, less indifference, less plain sinfulness in direct response to the gospel. In this modest hope he was disappointed.

## CHAPTER SIX

# Against the Jews

The older Luther's polemics against Jews provide the greatest challenge to those who wish to view, or at least to treat, the later polemics as essentially theological tracts encumbered with some incidental, nontheological matter. For even the most stalwart advocates of this "theological approach" find it necessary in the case of the anti-Jewish treatises to acknowledge that external events shaped their argument and that they can only be properly understood within their historic context. Yet why should this be true of the anti-Jewish treatises and not of all Luther's other writings? We shall return to this question after examining the context and content of these most problematic treatises of the older Luther.[1]

## The Anti-Jewish Heritage

The rivalry between Christians and Jews, and its attendant hatred and violence, is as old as Christianity itself.[2] The earliest Christians were all Jews, as was Jesus himself. Christianity began as a sect within Judaism, a sect that claimed to be the true heir of God's promises to the people of Israel. These early Jewish Christians believed that Jesus was the messiah promised to the Jews, and that with his coming, his death, and his resurrection the old covenant between God and Israel had ended and a new covenant had begun. Most Jews remained unconvinced, and, understandably, they resented Christian claims that, if taken seriously, relegated non-Christian Judaism to the wastebasket for superseded religions. These conflicting claims led to violence and to attempts at repression. In Jerusalem a Christian Jew named Stephen was stoned for blasphemy. Later, a Jew named Saul, who had reportedly held the coats at Stephen's stoning, was on his way to Damascus to organize the imprisonment of Christians there when a vision of the resurrected Jesus converted him to Christianity. In such an atmosphere hostility grew, and Christians began drawing individuous parallels between the Israelites who had refused to accept the prophets of old and the Jews of their own day who refused to accept Jesus as the messiah. "Like fathers, like sons," Luke records Stephen to have said. "Was there ever a prophet whom your fathers did not persecute? They killed those who foretold the coming of the Righteous One; and now you have betrayed him and murdered him, you who received the Law as God's angels gave it to you, and yet have not kept it" [Acts 7:51-53]. When Matthew recorded his gospel, Christians in his circle held all Jews responsible for Jesus's execution. When Pilate washed his hands of all responsibility for Jesus's execution, the Jews are reported by Matthew to have cried out to a man: "His blood be on us, and on our children" [Matthew 27:26].

The Saul who had persecuted Christians became the Paul who brought his own version of Christianity to non-Jews, to Gentiles. Soon the Christians at Jerusalem and elsewhere were hotly divided over the question whether Gentile Christians had to observe Jewish customs as their Jewish Christian brothers and sisters did. Paul argued that they did not; Peter at first disagreed, and then, reportedly, came over to Paul's position. In letters on this issue Paul stigmatized Jewish observances as "dead law," and contrasted such "works right-eousness" with the "divine righteousness through faith in Christ."

With all their conviction that Jesus was the messiah promised in the Scripture, the early Christians were hard pressed to explain a very embarrassing fact. If Jesus was the messiah promised to the Nation Israel, why had so few of the Jews, the Nation Israel, accepted him as this promised messiah? Paul ruminates on this question in his last extant letter, his letter to the Romans. He first suggests that the Nation Israel must be understood spiritually, rather than literally. Not entirely satisfied with this solution, he invokes God's inscrutable will: "The pot has no right to say to the potter, Why did you make me this shape?" Not entirely satisfied with this solution either, Paul finally settles on a mystery:

> For there is a deep truth here, my brothers, of which I want you to take account, so that you may not be complacent about your own discernment: this partial blindness has come upon Israel only until the Gentiles have been admitted in full strength; when that has happened, the whole of Israel will be saved. . . . [Romans 11:25-26]

So by the end of the apostolic period, Jews in the eyes of Christians were adherents to a convenant that was no more, that had been replaced by a new covenant revealed by Jesus Christ. They were a rejected people, guilty of the murder of the prophets and of God's own Son. They were under God's wrath, a Christian view that was reinforced by the destruction of the Temple and Jewish Jerusalem in 70 and 135 A.D. At the end of time they would convert to Christianity. In the meanwhile they would serve as examples of God's wrath over those who forsake him.

With the end of an autonomous Jewish state, Jewish authorities lost the opportunity to harass their Christian rivals. With the beginning of the Christian empire under Constantine and his successors in the fourth century, Christian authorities gained the opportunity to persecute their Jewish rivals and every other non-Christian group. From the time of Constantine to our own twentieth century, Christians have made frequent use of this opportunity.

The medieval West was a society of corporations, of voluntary and involuntary communities bound together by mutual responsibility. The greatest corporation of them all, embracing all the West, was the church. In its midst existed only one foreign body, only one smaller corporation that failed to acknowledge the truth of its beliefs: the Jews. For the medieval theoretician the Jews were to be tolerated within the Christian community for the witness they gave by their suffering to the truth of Christian claims. They were responsible for Christ's death; they showed forth God's wrath towards his rejected people. To the common people, who heard their preachers describe the Jews in these, if not in much worse terms, the Jews were also the one body within their midst that did not fit in. Dietary observances kept Jews and Christians from sharing meals. Religious convictions and laws on both sides prevented intermarriage. The areas of life in which Jews and Christians could interact on a daily basis were few even in the early Middle Ages. With time the opportunities for interaction became ever more limited as Christian corporations, guilds and communes, forced Jews out of agriculture, out of commerce, out of industry and into some of the most disreputable occupations, such as petty moneylending and pawnbroking. Limited to such occupations, most Jews came to be seen by Christian townspeople and peasants as greedy, grasping, and immoral.

In the crusades, popular suspicion and dislike came together with religiously-based contempt and hatred. Some who marched to free the Holy Lands from the Infidel thought it only proper to deal first with the enemy in their midst. If one could kill for religion in the Holy Land, one could kill for religion in Western Europe. And so, over the protests of bishops on the scene and the pope in Rome, the crusaders began their crusade with the murder of thousands of Jews living in the Rhineland and along the route of march. About this time stories first began circulating about ritual murder of Christian children by Jews, about the poisoning of wells by Jews, about Jewish contempt for the Virgin Mary. Life, which had hardly been easy for Jews up to the eleventh century, became more difficult. Years could pass with nothing more for them to cope with than the traditional Christian contempt and insults, and then suddenly violence and death would visit a Jewish community.

And there were always the attempts by Christians to convert the Jews to the "true faith." Not infrequently the Jewish community would be hauled into the local church or cathedral to hear an impassioned sermon by a visiting bishop or mendicant friar on the truth of Christianity and the futility of Jewish beliefs. "Why has your God forsaken you?" was one of the most popular questions posed the Jews. "Why have you been in exile and suffered for so many years?" Of course, the answer the preacher gave was that the old covenant was ended, that Jesus was the promised messiah, and that the Jews suffered so because of their sin of rejecting their Christ. And then the preacher would parade a list of passages in the Old Testament that Christians believed pointed to Jesus as the Christ.

Some Jews were convinced and converted to Christianity. Some Jews were unconvinced, but were baptized anyway by force. Once baptized, they could not return to Judaism without suffering the penalties for apostasy. Most of the Jews probably left the sermon as unconvinced as they came, glad that the humiliating ordeal was over and not likely to be repeated for a while.

During the Middle Ages Jews enjoyed periods of relative peace and periods of active persecution and exploitation. In the Holy Roman Empire Jews became "imperial serfs," property of the emperor, under his protection (such as it was) in exchange for heavy payments.[3] The fifteenth century, the century before the Reformation, was a bad century for Jews both within and without the empire. In 1421 they were expelled from Austria, in 1424 from Cologne, in 1432 from Saxony, in 1435 from Speyer, in 1440 from Augsburg, and by 1499 from Würzburg, Mecklenburg, Madgeburg, Nuremburg, Esslingen, and Ulm. Beginning in 1470 they were driven out of the Archbishopric of Mainz. Bavaria began expelling its Jews in 1450, Württemberg in 1498. This list of expulsions could be easily multiplied several times over.[4]

Not only were there relatively few Jewish communities left within the empire, those that did remain were subject to severe legal restrictions, to economic exploitation by rulers, and to harassment and persecution by populace and authorities for alleged magical and demonic activities. The most extreme of these accusations, one leveled with some frequency in the late fifteenth and sixteenth centuries, was that Jews murdered Christian children for their blood to be used in the Passover celebration and in various magical activities.* An example of such an accusation illustrates one of the popular beliefs about Jews in Luther's day.

In 1503 near Freiburg in Breisgau browsing oxen uncovered the body of a young boy who had obviously bled to death. Suspicion immediately fell on the child's father, who was an accused thief. We have two accounts of what then occurred: an anonymous rhymed verse account entitled *A horrible, shocking story of an ungodfearing, insane, and desperate Christian man, who sold . . . his own flesh and blood to the soulless, godless, god-betraying Jews,*[5] and an allegedly eyewitness report by Johann Eck, Doctor of Theology at the University of Ingolstadt and Luther's most prominent Catholic opponent.[6] At first the father pleaded ignorance. When the corpse of his son was brought into his presence, however, it began to sweat blood.[7] The father then confessed that he had sold his son to two Jews for ten gulden, believing that they would only take some of the child's blood but not kill him. But the child died from the bloodletting.

At this point the anonymous author adds that the authorities decided to verify this confession. When questioned under torture, however, the father changed his account. Now he said that he himself had bled his child, hoping to sell the blood to the Jews, who, he had heard, would pay well for Christian blood. He had never made the sale, however, because after he collected the blood he realized belatedly that the Jews would believe that he was hoaxing them, that the blood came from an animal rather than a Christian child, and that he could not prove otherwise. So he threw the blood away.

Not sure which confession to believe, the authorities decided, as they usually did with charges of ritual murder, to arrest all the Jews of the territory and submit them to questioning, also under torture. The Jews, however, maintained their innocence. Unable to extract a confession, the authorities were forced to release them. The father, however, was sentenced to be drawn and quartered, as well as to be torn with red hot tongs. At the time of his execution he recanted his

---

*In 1144 the Jews of Norwich in England were accused of murdering a young Christian boy named William. This is the first of a series of such accusations made through the Middle Ages and into our own times. See Baron, *A Social and Religious History*, 11: 146-57.

earlier confession, and returned to his claim that it was the Jews who had murdered his child, not himself.

Eck now picks up the narrative once more. He claims to have seen the murdered child himself and to have touched the child's stab wounds with his own fingers. He also saw the father executed and heard his dying confession that the Jews had stabbed his son to death.

Eck harbors no doubts about the authenticity of this ritual murder. The anonymous author, although he relates information that should have given him pause, is also convinced of the Jews' guilt. He attributes the father's second confession, that he himself had murdered his child, to the influence of the devil.[8] He is further convinced that the father, since he returned to his original claim that the Jews had committed the murder, died a Christian bound for ultimate salvation.[9]

This incredible story is only one of several alleged ritual murders related in the anonymous account and in Eck's treatise. It illustrates well, however, the improbability of the charge of ritual murder, while at the same time it shows that even highly educated men such as Johann Eck firmly believed such libels. Eck's whole treatise, *Refutation of a Jew-book in Which a Christian, to the Dishonor of All Christendom, Claims That Injustice is Done the Jews in the Accusation That They Murder Christian Children*, published a year before Luther's most infamous treatises, is dedicated to proving, in reply to a Lutheran skeptic, that Jews did murder Christian children for their rituals; that they did desecrate the eucharistic host; and that they did do such things as poison wells and bewitch animals and ruin crops.* These were the convictions of a scholar, writing in this case for a popular audience.[10]

Such, then, were the conditions when, in 1513, Martin Luther began lecturing on the Psalms at the University of Wittenberg. There

---

*In 1540 the Jews of Tittingen and the surrounding area were accused of murdering a young peasant boy (Stern, *Josel*, pp. 180-83). While hearings were taking place at the court of the Bishop of Eichstätt, two Jews from Sulzbach presented the Episcopal Counselors with an anonymous treatise defending Jews against the accusation of ritual murder. Its author was probably Andreas Osiander of Nuremberg (Moritz Stern, ed., *Andreas Osianders Schrift über die Blutbeschuldigung* [Kiel, 1893]). Eck was then commissioned by Albrecht of Leonrod, one of the councilors of the Bishop of Eichstätt (*Verlegung*, pp. Aii(v)-Aiii), to issue a written Refutation to this treatise. The resulting publication was some 189 pages, and dealt at length with Osiander's arguments, citing in the process numerous alleged ritual murders, even explaining the use to which the blood was put, and detailing other sinister practices of the Jews. Eck was aware that the author of the treatise was a Lutheran, and expressed the hope that princes, lords, and cities would come to recognize the bad tree that could produce such bad fruit (*Verlegung*, p. Aiii). He even suggested at one point that Osiander was the author (*Verlegung*, p. Div).

were Jews left in the empire, clinging to survival in small territories often controlled by a bishop or abbot. The large territories and most of the imperial cities had expelled their Jews some years earlier. Only on rare occasions did Luther encounter Jews; he never lived in close proximity to them, but he inherited a tradition, both theological and popular, of hostility toward them. He lived within a larger community, Western Christendom, which saw the Jews as a rejected people, guilty of the murder of Christ, and capable of murdering Christian children for their own evil purposes. And he lived within a local community that had expelled its Jews some ninety years earlier. Despite this heritage of suspicion and hostility, Luther's first treatise on the Jews advocated that they be treated in a friendly manner and denounced the treatment they were currently subjected to.

## That Jesus Christ Was Born a Jew

Before the 1538 publication of *Against the Sabbatarians* Luther had published only one treatise concerning the Jews, his 1523 treatise, *That Jesus Christ Was Born a Jew*. The treatise was occasioned by the report that Duke Ferdinand had charged that Luther denied Mary's virginity before and after Christ's birth. However, the treatise went beyond a simple refutation of these charges to explain the reasons from Scripture that induced Luther "to believe that Christ was a Jew born of a virgin." With this Luther had hoped that he might "entice some Jews to the Christian faith."

> For our fools, the popes, bishops, sophists, and monks—the gross asses' heads—have treated the Jews to date in such fashion that he who would be a good Christian might almost have to become a Jew. And if I had been a Jew and had seen such oafs and numbskulls governing and teaching the Christian faith, I would have rather become a sow than a Christian.
>
> For they have dealt with the Jews as if they were dogs and not men. They were able to do nothing but curse them and take their goods. When they were baptized, no Christian teaching or life was demonstrated to them, rather they were only subjected to papistry and monkery. When they then saw that Judaism had such strong scriptural support and that Christianity was nothing but twaddle without any scriptural support, how could they quiet their hearts and become true good Christians? I myself have heard from pious baptized Jews that if they had not in our time heard the gospel, they would have remained life-long Jews under their Christian exterior. For they confess that they never yet have heard anything about Christ from their baptizers and masters.

It was his hope, Luther had continued, that if the Jews were dealt with in a friendly fashion and were instructed carefully from the Holy Scripture, "many of them would become true Christians and would return to the faith of their fathers, the prophets and patriarchs." To reject their beliefs so absolutely, allowing nothing to remain, and to treat them solely with arrogance and scorn, frightened them away from true Christianity.*

In the first part of the treatise Luther had laid out at some length the scriptural basis for his belief that Mary was perpetually virgin and that Christ, as the seed of Abraham, was a true Jew.[11] Next, out of an expressed desire to "serve the Jews so that some of them might be brought to their own true faith which their fathers had had," Luther had offered to the Jews and to those who dealt with the Jews some scripturally based arguments to show that Jesus was the Jews' awaited messiah.[12] Somewhat surprisingly, Luther had argued that at first it was enough to convince the Jews that Jesus was the true messiah. Later they could learn how he was also true God.[13]

Luther had closed with an appeal to his fellow Christians:

> Therefore, I would request and advise that one manage them decently and instruct them from the Scripture so that some of them might be brought along. But since we now drive them with force and slander them, accuse them of having Christian blood if they don't stink, and who knows what other foolishness, so that they are regarded just as dogs—what good can we expect to accomplish with them? Similarly, that we forbid them to work, do business, and have other human association with us, so that we drive them to usury—how does that help them?
>
> If we wish to help them, we must practice on them not the papal law but rather the Christian law of love, and accept them in a friendly fashion, allowing them to work and make a living, so that they gain the reason and opportunity to be with and among us [and] to see and to hear our Christian teaching and life.
>
> If some are obstinate, what does it matter? After all, we too are not all good Christians. Here I will let matters rest until I see what I have accomplished.

---

*As the apostles, who were Jews, had treated the pagans in a brotherly fashion, so the Christians should treat the Jews in a similarly brotherly fashion "so that we might convert some." After all, Luther had reminded his readers, we are the pagans and they are the blood relatives of Christ (WA 11:314-15).

The missionary tendency of this treatise is apparent from the citations quoted. Luther had obviously hoped that at least some and perhaps an appreciable number of Jews might convert to Christianity once they were exposed to the Protestant faith. While the renewed gospel was given time to do its work, patience and tolerance was to be shown the Jews. This very patience and tolerance was meant to further this missionary goal.*

## Josel of Rosheim

Although Luther had relatively little to say about the Jews during the late 1520s and the early 1530s, there is evidence that sometime before 1536 three learned Jews had visited him and, on the basis of their rabbinic tradition, had taken issue with the interpretation Luther placed on various messianic passages in the Old Testament. Already disappointed about the meager success of his missionary efforts, Luther was so frustrated by this conversation that he vowed not to enter into such a dialog again.[14] But this issue, the proper interpretation of messianic passages in the Old Testament, remained much on his mind during his final years. From the beginning of the Genesis lectures in 1535 Luther took great pains not only to insist on the Christological interpretation of the Old Testament,** but specifically to

---

*It is unlikely that Luther had abandoned his *theological* conviction that any conversions stood not in man's power but in God's. But he had already experienced the incredible successes of the heady early years of the Reformation. He thought of himself as an instrument of God's to reveal the purified gospel. While faith was always in God's power, not in man's, God used men to bring other men to faith. Perhaps He would use Luther to bring some of the Jews, perhaps even many of them, to their true messiah. The relative optimism of this position was, however, short lived. When the rush of Jewish converts did not occur, he returned to his theologically based pessimism. The Jews were under God's wrath. Their punishment made them even more stiff-necked. Some might yet find their true messiah, but they would be few. The rest were the devil's children, enemies of the true church of God.

**To summarize briefly: Luther believed that the true church of God had been established even before the Fall when God commanded Adam to eat from every tree except the tree of the knowledge of good and evil. When Satan had tempted Adam and Eve, and they had fallen, God had immediately announced the promise of the blessed seed that would crush the head of the serpent. The saints of the Old Testament lived and taught this faith in the promise of the seed of the woman. "They gave the exact same sermons that we in our time present to the church and community of God, except that they taught about the future Christ who was yet to come, but we say of him: 'Christ has come,' while they said: 'He will come.'" [WA 44:635]. For this reason Luther interpreted the Old Testament Christologically and saw all promises by God in the Old Testament as referring to Christ. Hence the saintly Jews of the Old Testament were part of the true church, living by faith in God's promise. But the New Testament revealed how

insist that the Old Testament testified to the trinity and to the incarnation. In this he adopted as his own the arguments of the Old Testament exegetes of the late Middle Ages and especially those of Nicholas of Lyra, Paul of Burgos, and Matthew Döring. He continued his debate with rabbinic exegesis in his 1538 *Three Symbols* and in his "Schmalkaldic Articles." In these publications he once again claimed Old Testament passages as witnesses to the trinity and to the incarnation. In these same treatises his anger began to show through. His tone is shrill, and abusive remarks about the Jews are more pervasive.[15]

On 6 August 1536 Elector Johann Friedrich, for reasons that cannot now be ascertained, issued a mandate forbidding Jews to settle or do business in Electoral Saxony or even to travel through electoral lands.[16] Although there is no evidence that Luther had instigated this mandate, his subsequent refusal to intervene in behalf of the Jews indicates that he approved of it.[17]

In early summer 1537 Luther remarked at table that he had received a letter from a certain Jew who had requested that Luther secure a safe-conduct allowing him to enter Electoral Saxony.[18] This Jew was none other than Josel of Rosheim (ca 1478-1554), the officially designated spokesman for the Jews within the empire.[19] It was in his capacity as a representative of his people that Josel wished to enter Electoral Saxony to confer with Luther and Elector Johann Friedrich about the recent mandate against the Jews. He brought with him very favorable letters of recommendation, one from Wolfgang Capito to Luther himself, the other from the magistrates of Strasbourg to Elector Johann Friedrich.[20] These recommendations notwithstanding, Luther remained true to his earlier resolve not to enter into further dialogue with the Jews. He refused to intercede for Josel. To his table companions he exclaimed, "Why should these rascals, who

---

most Jews had rejected their promised messiah, crucified him, and persecuted his followers. With these actions they had drawn down upon themselves God's wrath. The history of postbiblical Jewry was for Luther the history of God's implacable wrath over a rejected and forsaken people. Their life of suffering was a continuous witness to the judgment and power of God. Their conversion lay in God's power, not in man's. Some might yet accept the true messiah, Jesus Christ. But God's wrath and their suffering actually made the majority worse and more obstinate.

For a description of how this view develops, see, among others, Scott Hendrix, *Ecclesia in Via. Ecclesiological Developments in the Medieval Psalms Exegesis and the Dictata Super Psalterium of Martin Luther* (Leiden, 1974); James Samuel Preus, *From Shadow to Promise: Old Testament Interpretations from Augustine to the Young Luther* (Cambridge, MA, 1969); Jaroslav Pelikan, *Luther the Expositor* (St. Louis, 1959); Heinrich Bornkamm, *Luther und das Alte Testament* (Tübingen, 1948).

injure people in goods and body and who estrange many Christians [from Christianity] with their superstitions, be given permission? For in Moravia they have circumcised many Christians and called them by the new name of Sabbatarians. So it goes in those regions where Protestant preachers are expelled . . . I'll write this Jew not to return."[21] In his letter to Josel Luther spelled out briefly his position toward the Jews.[22] He claimed that just as his 1523 treatise *That Jesus Christ Was Born a Jew* had greatly served all Jewry, he would have very gladly interceded with the elector on Josel's behalf. But since the Jews so shamefully misused such service of his and undertook things which were intolerable to Christians, they had themselves deprived Luther of all influence that he might have had with the princes and lords. In his heart he had always felt, and still did, that the Jews should be treated in a friendly fashion so that God might look graciously upon them and bring them to their messiah, but not so that they should become worse and strengthened in their error through Luther's favor and influence.*

Some of this letter seems to harken back to the position expressed in *That Jesus Christ Was Born a Jew*. He is still advocating friendly treatment of the Jews, and he appears not to have abandoned entirely his hope for Jewish converts, although he expects their numbers to be small. At the same time there is a harshness in this letter not found in the 1523 treatise. And he refused to help Josel. Apparently, Josel was no more successful with others and had to return home without having an audience with the elector and without having the mandate against the Jews modified or lifted.[23]

## Against the Sabbatarians

Luther's first major attack on the Jews, made in his last years, was an open letter entitled *Against the Sabbatarians*[24] and addressed to a good friend. It was first published in March 1538. The "good friend" was Count Wolfgang Schlick zu Falkenau. The count had sent Luther word that Jews had been proselytizing in Bohemia and Moravia and had convinced some Christians that they should be circumcized, that the messiah had not yet come, that the Jewish law was

---

*Luther had not fully abandoned his missionary hopes, for he announced in this letter that if God granted him the opportunity, he intended to write a booklet about this to see if he couldn't win a few from Josel's paternal tribe of holy patriarchs and prophets and bring them to their promised messiah. This promised treatise may be his *Against the Sabbatarians* (See WABr 8:91n4).

eternally valid, and that it should be observed by Gentiles. Until he had time for a lengthier reply, Luther intended with this open letter to explain how these arguments of the Jews should be refuted with Holy Scripture.

The letter began by saying that the Jews had been made very stubborn by their rabbis so that they were very hard to win over. For when one developed a convincing argument on the basis of Scripture, they retreated from Scripture to their rabbis and said that they had to believe their rabbis just as Christians believed their pope and decretals. This, Luther said, was his own personal experience with them. Accordingly, in order to strengthen Christians in their faith the "good friend" should produce the old and irrefutable argument that Nicholas of Lyra and others had utilized.

Jews should be asked what was the sin for which God was so horribly punishing them. For there was God's promise (as the Jews themselves boasted) that their law should endure forever, that Jerusalem should be God's own residence, and that both the princes of the house of David and the priests of the tribe of Levi should always remain before God. Yet this and other promises had remained unfulfilled for fifteen hundred years. Now since it made no sense to accuse God of not keeping his promise and of having lied for fifteen hundred years, the Jews had to be asked what was wrong. They would have to answer that their sins were responsible.

Whatever sin the Jews might point to, it would not help their case. For in Jeremiah 31 God announced that he wished to make a new covenant or law, unlike the covenant or law of Moses, and that he would not be hindered in this by their sins.* In fact, it was precisely because they had not kept the old covenant that He wished to make a new covenant which they could keep.

This showed that the Jews were lying when they claimed that the advent of the messiah was delayed by their sins. God's promises were not contingent upon the Jews' behavior. The conclusion seemed inescapable to Luther:

---

*"Behold, the time is coming, says God, when I shall make a new covenant with the house of Israel and with the house of Judah, not like the covenant which I made with their fathers when I took them by the hand and led them out of Egypt, [the covenant] which they did not observe and I had to force them [to observe]. But this shall be the covenant that I shall make with the children of Israel after this time, says the Lord: I will put my law into their hearts and write it in their minds, and they shall be my people, and I will be their God. And no one shall teach and say to his brother or to another: 'See, know the Lord,' for they shall all know me, both the great and the small, says the Lord. For I will forgive them their misdeeds and will no longer think of their sins" [Translated from Luther's German].

Now since it is clear and obvious that the Jews cannot name any sin for which God should so long delay his promise and thus make Himself a liar, and even if they were able to name one or more [sins], nevertheless God's word made them liars, for He assured them that He did not wish on account of their sins to abandon His promise to send the messiah and to maintain the throne of David for ever and ever, it follows inescapably that one of two things must be true: either the messiah must have come fifteen hundred years ago or God must have lied (God forgive me for speaking so shamefully) and not kept His promise.[25]

God's promise had been kept and the messiah had come in the person of Jesus of Nazareth. The promised new covenant was fulfilled in Christ. The sin of the Jews for which they were suffering such a long and horrible punishment was their rejection of Christ as the promised messiah.

In the second part of the letter Luther examined the reported boast of the Jews that their law was eternal and should be observed by the Gentiles. He said that the coming of the messiah some fifteen hundred years earlier had marked the end of the old law. Moreover, for fifteen hundred years the Jews themselves had been unable to keep the law in its entirety because of the destruction of the temple and their exile from Jerusalem.

When Jesus stated that he had not come to abolish the law, Luther continued, he had not the ceremonial law in mind but rather the Ten Commandments. But the essence of the Ten Commandments had spread throughout the world well before Moses, Abraham, and all the patriarchs. This was especially true of the first commandment. All the pagans bore witness in their writings to the universal validity of the Ten Commandments. Only the commandment concerning the seventh day or Sabbath was a temporally limited addition, suited to the Jews at that time and, like other specifically Jewish, temporally bound laws, had long since fallen into disuse.

Each of these arguments was drawn out and buttressed with careful examination of the appropriate texts from Scripture. Luther was uncompromising in his insistence on the error of the Jews, but his language is still, for the most part, temperate and restrained. His hope, he told his "good friend," was that he had provided sufficient material to allow the friend to defend himself against the Sabbatarians. If the friend were unable to convert the Jews, then he should consider that he was no better than the prophets, who were always killed and persecuted by the Jews. It appeared to Luther that God had truly forsaken the Jews and that they were no longer God's chosen people.

## The Attacks of 1543

In 1543 Luther published three treatises against the Jews and Jewish exegesis: *On the Jews and Their Lies, On the Ineffable Name and on Christ's Lineage,* and *On the Last Words of David.*[26] These three treatises are best understood as three parts of one major statement. The first treatise, *On the Jews and Their Lies,* was written in response to a letter from Count Schlick of Moravia. In May 1542, the count had sent Luther a treatise (now apparently lost) in which a Jew, in dialogue with a Christian, attacked Jesus, the Virgin Mary, and Christian exegesis of the Old Testament,[27] and the count had requested that Luther refute this Jewish treatise. Luther's second treatise, *On the Ineffable Name and on Christ's Lineage,* was announced in the first treatise, while the third treatise, *On the Last Words of David,* was announced in the second. In fact, these last two treatises are more addenda to the first than independent treatises in their own right. All three draw upon the same sources, especially the writings of Nicholas of Lyra, Paul of Burgos, Raymund Martin, and Salvagus Porchetus. Together these treatises make up Luther's last testament against the Jews and the Jewish interpretation of the Old Testament.[28]

Luther introduced *On the Jews and Their Lies* with the confession that he had intended to write nothing more about or against the Jews. But because he had learned that Jews were still enticing Christians to become Jews, he had issued this book so that he might be numbered among those who had resisted the Jews and had warned Christians against them. It was not his intention, he wrote, to quarrel with the Jews or to learn from them their exegesis of Scripture, which he already knew well. Much less was it his intention to convert the Jews, for that, he claimed, was impossible. Nicholas of Lyra and Paul of Burgos had already faithfully described and powerfully refuted the Jews' filthy interpretation of the passages in question. In any case, their efforts had not helped the Jews at all, who had become progressively worse.[29]

After briefly rehearsing the argument he had developed at length in *Against the Sabbatarians,*[30] Luther took up several claims and boasts allegedly made by the Jews. First, he said, the Jews gloried in their claim of physical descent from the noblest people on earth, Abraham, Sarah, Isaac, Rebecca, Jacob, the twelve patriarchs, and the holy people of Israel. Further, they boasted and thanked God that they were created human beings rather than animals, Israelites rather than Goyim (Gentiles), and men rather than women. But, Luther replied, women were also human beings and made in the image of God. Furthermore, in Genesis 17, when God instituted circumcision, he damned all flesh regardless of lineage. As far as physical birth was concerned, Esau or Edom was as noble as Jacob, Ishmael as noble as Isaac, but what good did physical descent do them? All Gentiles were descendants of Noah through Japheth as the Jews were through Shem, and thus had equal claim to honor, nobility, and glory. In any case, all people, Jew and Gentile, were conceived and born in sin, and were accordingly born under God's wrath and condemnation and could not be God's children simply on account of nature or birth.[31]

Second, he continued, the Jews claimed superiority over others and despised them because of the covenant of circumcision. But circumcision in itself contained no holiness or power. Moreover, in Genesis 17 Moses stated that Abraham was ordered to circumcise all males in his house including sons and servants and even slaves. This meant that as far as physical circumcision was concerned, Ishmael and his descendants, among other descendants of Abraham and his household, had as much right to boast as the Jews. Circumcision did not make the Jews God's chosen people. According to Moses [Deut. 4 and 12; Leviticus 26] and Jeremiah [chapters 4 and 9], true circumcision was of the heart, not of the flesh. Furthermore, the Old Testament was full of individuals such as Job and people such as the Ninevites who were converted yet remained uncircumcised. As St. Paul taught, circumcision as a work in itself could not save. It was given as a sign, covenant, or sacrament so that those circumcised should hear and obey God's promise and word. Apart from the word of God, it was nothing. Their perversion of circumcision was like the papists' perversion of the sacraments. The papists like the Jews had fallen into works righteousness.[32]

Third, the Jews were greatly conceited because God had spoken with them and given them the Law of Moses on Mount Sinai. Indeed, they had entered into a marriage with God through the Law and had become His bride. But it was apparent from the Old Testament histories that they had become a besmirched bride, an incorrigible whore and wicked slut with whom God continually had to scuffle, tussle, and fight. This applied not only to the wicked Jews of the past but also to the Jews of Luther's own day, since their fifteen-hundred-year exile and suffering proved that they were one with the whoring Jews described in the Old Testament and not God's people. To have God's word meant nothing. The devils in hell had God's word. At issue was the fact that the Jews failed to keep God's word. Outward obedience to the Law of Moses, apart from obedience to the Ten Commandments, meant nothing. Moses himself was aware that no one could keep God's commandments except those whose sins God forgave. This required a man who bore our sins for us. It was of this man that Christians spoke and taught. It was of such a man that the prophets and apostles spoke and taught.[33]

Fourth, the Jews boasted that God had given them the land of Canaan, the city of Jerusalem, and the Temple. But God had dashed this conceit through the king of Babylon, the king of Assyria, and the Romans. The Jews failed to recognize that all this had been given them that they might obey His commandments. They wished to be God's people by reason of their deeds, works, and external condition and not out of sheer grace and mercy as all prophets and the true children of Israel had to be. They were like the papists, Turks, and fanatics, who all claimed to be the church on the basis of their own notions and without respect for the one true faith and obedience to the divine command. By their own deeds they wished to become God's people.[34]

Relying heavily on Nicholas of Lyra and Paul of Burgos, Luther in the second, and lengthiest, part of the treatise examined the conflicting interpretations of various prophetic texts in the Old Testament. These texts were interpreted by Christians as referring to the messiah and as showing this messiah to be Jesus of Nazareth. Luther gave greatest attention to the prophecy concerning "Shiloh" in Genesis 40; the "last words of David" concerning an "everlasting covenant" in 2 Samuel 23; the "consolation of the Gentiles" prophesied in Haggai 2; and the "seventy weeks of years" discussed in Daniel 9. The Jews, Luther wrote, were so convinced that the messiah had not yet come that even if all the angels and God Himself said otherwise, the Jews would not believe them. Much less were they willing to listen to Christian exegetes and even former Jews, although these exegetes had so mightily overcome the arguments of the Jews. "But their accursed rabbis, who know better indeed, so wantonly poison their poor youth and common people and turn them from the truth. For I believe that if such writings were read by the common man and the youth, they would stone all their rabbis and hate them worse than we Christians do."[35] Judgments similar to this were sprinkled throughout this section. Luther had little use for Jewish exegesis and considered the rabbis to be knowingly and wantonly misinterpreting the Scripture.* Despite these asides, most of this second section was devoted to serious, although often unoriginal, exegesis. Luther added his own

---

*At one point he related how he had personally debated such passages with three learned Jews. These Jews, Luther claimed, when they were unable to refute Luther's exegesis of the texts, had fallen back on the authority of their rabbis. For this reason, and on account of their blasphemies, Luther wished to have nothing further to do with them (WA 53:461-62).

distinctive theological perspective when he repeatedly insisted that these messianic promises, these promises of grace, were unconditional, that they were dependent not on the actions of men as some Jewish exegetes argued but solely on divine truth and grace.

In the third section Luther dealt with alleged Jewish slanders against the Virgin Mary and her son, Jesus. He accused the Jews of claiming that Jesus was a magician and instrument of the devil and that he worked his miracles by the power of the "ineffable name" (*Shem Hamphoras*). Using cabalistic numerology, the Jews changed Jesus' name into an insult and perverted the conventional Jewish greeting into a curse on Christians. They called Jesus a whore's son and Mary a whore, although they knew better. They claimed that Mary had conceived while menstruating, which meant that her offspring, Jesus, was insane or a demon's child, and they perverted Mary's name into the word for manure pile. Luther recounted, without unequivocally accepting as true, some of the crudest charges traditionally lodged against the Jews: that they poisoned wells, and that they kidnapped children, pierced them with nails, and hacked them into pieces. He believed them guilty in thought and deed of shedding the blood of the messiah and his Christians.

The Jews' claim that they were held captive by the Christians was a "thick, fat lie." They were free to leave Germany; their departure would be a blessing, for their presence was a plague on Germany. They had been expelled, Luther pointed out, from numerous countries and cities: France, Spain, Bohemia, Regensburg, Magdeburg, and other places. It was in fact the Christians who were held captive to the Jews' usury. The Christians held the Jews captive as he, Luther, held captive his kidney stone and other afflictions.

From this list of indictments Luther swung immediately into a series of harsh recommendations to secular authorities on how to deal with the Jews. Their synagogues and schools should be burned and whatever would not burn should be buried. Their homes should be destroyed. All their prayer books and Talmudic writing should be taken from them. Their rabbis should be forbidden to teach. Their safe-conducts on highways should be revoked. Their usury should be forbidden and their money taken from them.* They should be put to work in the fields so that they earned their living by the sweat of their brows. Better yet, they should be expelled after a portion of their wealth had been confiscated. Luther rejected angrily the argument that the Jews were an indispensable financial resource to governments.

---

*Some amount could be returned to converts to Christianity so that they might support themselves.

The benefit failed to outweigh the blasphemy and harm done by the Jews. It was the duty of the secular authorities, Luther insisted, to implement these recommendations. It was the duty of the ecclesiastical authorities to warn and instruct their congregations about the Jews and their lies.

In the closing section of the treatise, Luther ridiculed the Jews' hope for a messiah who would give them a worldly kingdom but not redeem them from death. He would prefer to be a sow, who had no terror of death, he said, than to have such a messiah. He juxtaposed unfavorably the spiritual kingdom of the Christian messiah to the worldly kingdom sought, he claimed, by the Jews. In the final paragraphs he rehearsed the miracles that bore witness to the truth of the Christian faith, and he repeated his arguments concerning Old Testament passages he believed referred to Jesus Christ.

In March 1543, Luther published what amounted to an appendix to *On the Jews and Their Lies.* Entitled *On the Ineffable Name and On Christ's Lineage*, this treatise was composed of two unrelated sections. In the first section Luther translated into German and discussed what Salvagus Porchetus had written in his *Victory Against the Impious Hebrews* about the power of the "Ineffable Name" (*Shem Hamphoras*). In the second part Luther reconciled the lineages of Christ given in Matthew and Luke and discussed the various Old Testament texts that he believed referred to the virgin birth of the messiah.*

The combined treatise was written, Luther said, to expose to German Christians the devilish lies of the Jews and especially the lies of the rabbinic exegetes and, further, to show those Christians who were considering becoming Jews what fine articles of Jewish faith they would have to believe. The treatise was not directed at the Jews themselves since Luther had given up all hope of their conversion. A few of their number might yet be saved, he wrote, but the great majority of the Jews were so stubborn that to convert them would be like converting the devil into an angel, hell into heaven, death into life, and sin into holiness.[36]

Luther began section one with a translation of the eleventh chapter from part one of Porchetus' treatise. In this chapter Porchetus claimed that the Jews were so hostile toward the miracles of Christ that, out of their wickedness, they had fabricated a mendacious book about Christ. In this book they claimed that Jesus had performed all his

---

*The Jewish treatise that had prompted Luther's *On the Jews and Their Lies* had apparently also maintained that it could not be proved that Jesus was of the tribe of Judah since Matthew traced the genealogy of the tribe of Judah to Joseph rather than to Mary. It was to refute this claim that Luther composed the second section.

miracles through the power of the "ineffable name" which he had obtained through trickery. In short, Jesus was no more than an evil magician.

After reproducing this legend from Porchetus, Luther spent the rest of section one ridiculing the legend and the Jews who, he claimed, believed such superstitions. It was "shit" like this, he said, that the Jews were taught by their rabbis and had to "kiss, gobble down, guzzle, and worship." With frequent vulgar asides, Luther explained the cabalistic reasoning that he alleged was behind this legend, asserted that contemporary Jews still believed such shameful lies and blasphemies, and charged that, in fact, the Jews were the worst of blasphemers and idolaters, in attributing divine power to mere letters. The devil had possessed the Jews and made them his captive. That was why they believed such foolishness, lies, and blasphemy. It would not have been surprising, he wrote, if God's wrath had long ago consigned the Christians to the abyss of hell along with the Jews for tolerating in their midst such accursed, manifest blasphemers of God. The only possible excuse was that they had not known of the Jews' horrible deeds. "But from now on," Luther warned, "you dear princes and lords who protect and tolerate Jews among you, be aware of what you're doing. I do not wish to be responsible for the consequences!"[37]

In contrast to Luther's other writings against the Jews, section one of this treatise is singularly devoid of any edifying theological, exegetical, or historical comments. Even by Luther's standards the vulgarity is excessive and unusually humorless. Offering his standard apology to critics of his polemics, Luther replied to the "merciful saints among us Christians who think that I am being too coarse and tasteless towards the poor wretched Jews in dealing with them so disdainfully and sarcastically" that the devil was the Jews' master.

In contrast to the first section, the second section of the treatise, although containing various characterizations of rabbinic exegesis as "Judas' piss," "Jewish sweat," and other excrementa, is relatively restrained in its vulgarity. More important, it contains extensive discussion of Christian and rabbinic exegesis of crucial passages in the Old Testament. Luther's aim was to show that various Old Testament passages had predicted that a New Testament would succeed and fulfill the Old. He also offered a thoughtful explanation of how the genealogies in Matthew and Luke could be reconciled with each other. He discussed in some detail what he believed to be the proper exegesis of various Old Testament passages traditionally interpreted by Christians to refer to the virgin birth. Although sarcastic and abusive asides are scattered throughout the text, the discussion is for the most part substantial and designed to refute rabbinic exegesis of the same passages.

In contrast to the first section, this section can be rightly characterized as an exegetical and theological work rather than an anti-Semitic tract.

*On the Last Words of David,*[38] published in the late summer of 1543, was even less an anti-Jewish treatise than was the second section of *On the Ineffable Name and On Christ's Lineage.* In fact, the few critical asides in the treatise are aimed at rabbinic exegesis and not at contemporary Jews in general. This does not mean that Luther had changed his mind as to the threat he thought the Jews posed or as to the harsh treatment he thought they should receive. On the contrary, the intense antagonism Luther bore the Jews continued to the end of his life and even found violent expression in his last public sermon.[39] *On the Last Words of David* just happens not be be a polemical treatise. Instead, it is a detailed discussion of those passages in the Old Testament that he believed attested unequivocally to the Christian Trinity and to the incarnation of the Word in Jesus Christ. As such, it is a fascinating example of Luther's theologically based hermeneutics and Christocentric interpretation of the Old Testament. It is also a rich source for his understanding of the Trinity and of the incarnation including the communication of idioms between the divine and human natures of Christ. But it is not, properly speaking, a polemic and thus need not detain us further.

The reaction of contemporaries to Luther's anti-Jewish writings indicates fairly clearly that his readers saw a significant difference between the early and the later treatises. *That Jesus Christ Was Born a Jew* appears to have been received with favor among Protestants, Jews, and Jewish converts (Marranos). Some Marranos in the Netherlands may even have translated the work into Spanish and sent copies to their brethren in Spain. The treatise may have even reached Palestine.[40] It may also have encouraged several South Germans to work for the amelioration of the treatment of the Jews.[41] On the other hand, it may have lent some support to the Catholic charge, aired, for instance, at the Diet of Augsburg in 1530, that the Protestants had learned their doctrine from the Jews.[42]

The later tracts met with more criticism. Catholics, not surprisingly, were sharply critical. For instance, at the 1545 Diet of Worms several Catholic deputies reportedly characterized *On the Ineffable Name* as a "hateful book, as cruel as if it had been written in blood," and argued that it incited the rabble to violence.[43] Understandably, Jewish reaction was also unfavorable. Josel of Rosheim twice petitioned the Strasbourg magistrates concerning these tracts. The magistrates agreed to forbid a second printing within their jurisdiction of *On the Jews and Their Lies,* apparently out of concern for the violence it might engender. They also agreed to urge the ministers "not to preach turmoil from the pulpit"; this in response to the report that the pastor of Hochfelden had attempted to incite his congregation against the Jews.[44]

Protestant reaction was mixed. Melanchthon sent a copy of *On the Jews and Their Lies* to Landgrave Philipp of Hesse with the mild recommendation that the book contained "much useful teaching."[45] When he sent a copy of *On the Ineffable Name*, however, he failed to add a similar recommendation.[46] It is hard to say whether this indicates disapproval; generally speaking, Melanchthon was uncomfortable with the violent tone of many of the writings of the older Luther.[47] Andreas Osiander of Nuremberg appears to have been critical of the work, although unwilling to confront Luther with his objections.[48] Luther's Zurich opponents, the authors of the 1545 *True Confession*, branded Luther's *On the Ineffable Name* as "swinish" and "filthy," and remarked that had it been written by a swineherd and not by a famous shepherd of souls, there might have been some although little excuse for it.[49]

This last criticism is interesting since it appears to focus on Luther's language rather than on his arguments or recommendations. It would be informative to know what their judgment would have been on such works as the anonymous *A Horrible, Shocking Story* and Eck's *Refutation of a Jew-Book*, which employed more moderate language to express their attacks on Jews but which in their substance were more hostile and, from our perspective at least, more libelous than Luther's works.[50] Martin Bucer, together with a group of Hessian theologians, published a memorandum in 1539, addressed to Landgrave Philipp, that offered recommendations for the treatment of Jews in Hesse that were more moderate in language but still very harsh in their effect.[51] There is no guarantee that the Zurich theologians would have shared Bucer's views, but the presumption seems reasonable that on this point Bucer and the Zurichers would not have been far apart.[52] In fact, few treatises were produced in this period that had much favorable to say about the contemporary Jews. Even Andreas Osiander's memorandum arguing against the charge that Jews committed the ritual murder of Christian children was published anonymously, perhaps for fear of criticism such "moderation" and "reasonableness" might provoke.[53]

Fortunately, no Protestant prince attempted to put all Luther's recommendations into practice. Several did, however, take some measures against the Jews as a result of Luther's writings. In May 1543 Elector Johann Friedrich revoked some concessions he had made to the Jews in 1539. He cited as his reason for doing so Luther's recent treatises, which had opened his eyes to Jewish proselytizing and to their attacks on Christianity.[54] Johann of Küstrin, Margrave of Neumark, similarly revoked the safe-conduct of Jews under his jurisdiction.[55] And Landgrave Philipp added several new restrictions to his *Order Concerning the Jews* of 1539.[56]

If publishing statistics are any guide, then the 1523 treatise had a broader appeal, both quantitatively and geographically, than did any of the four later treatises.[57] *That Jesus Christ Was Born a Jew* saw thirteen editions, ten in German and three in Latin translation.[58] Four of these editions were issued in Wittenberg, two in Augsburg, two in Basel, two in Strasbourg, and one in Speyer. In contrast, the four later treatises saw a combined total of only fifteen editions, eleven of which were published in Wittenberg, three in Frankfurt, and one in Augsburg. *On the Ineffable Name* was reprinted most, with seven German editions, five published in Wittenberg and two in Frankfurt. It is unclear why this treatise should have been the one most reprinted of the four later treatises; perhaps its sensational first half, recounting Porchetus's tale of Christ the magician, appealed to the curious.[59] *On the Last Words of David* saw only two printings, while *Against the Sabbatarians* and *On the Jews and Their Lies* saw three printings each.

In general Luther's polemics were reprinted less frequently during these later years than in the earlier stages of the Reformation. Nonetheless, these statistics suggest that even among the polemics of his last years, the anti-Jewish treatises may have been less "popular" and "sought after" than the other major polemics of his late years.[60] To give a standard for comparison: *Against Hanswurst* saw four printings,[61] *Against the Papacy at Rome* saw six,[62] *Admonition to Prayer Against the Turks* saw ten,[63] and *Short Confession on the Supper* saw six.[64] In terms of reprintings, then, only *On the Ineffable Name and on Christ's Lineage* exceeded these other polemics of Luther's old age.

## Theology and History

In recent years some scholars have insisted that Luther's attitude toward the Jews can be understood *exclusively* from the presuppositions of his theology. Wilhelm Maurer is foremost among advocates of this view, both for the strength of his argument and for the care with which he examines all of Luther's pronouncements on the Jews.[65] According to Maurer, *That Jesus Christ Was Born a Jew* was not a missionary tract, and *Against the Sabbatarians* and the three treatises of 1543 were not simply anti-Jewish libels. He believes that the 1523 treatise may be best described as a "Christological study of the human nature of Christ" with an "apologetic missionary tendency." And he describes *Against the Sabbatarians* as the beginning of a theological discussion concerning the Christian understanding of the Old Testament that is continued in the interrelated anti-Jewish treatises of 1543. These late treatises were "theological treatises" and "belong first and foremost to the history of theology."[66]

Undergirding these "theological" treatises, Maurer argues, were four basic theological principles or presuppositions that remained constant through Luther's career, from the Psalms lectures of 1513-15 to the last sermon of 1546.* These principles or presuppositions derived from Luther's theology of justification by faith alone with its distinction between law and gospel, judgment and faith. The principles were (1) that the Jews were a people suffering under the

---

*In recent reviews of the literature this general line of argument is given the title "change and continuity": meaning that Luther's practical recommendations concerning the Jews change while his theological view of their status remains constant throughout his career [Meier, "Zur Interpretation von Luthers Judenschriften."; Brosseder, *Luthers Stellung zu den Juden*, pp. 35-36 and *passim* ; Sucher, *Luthers Stellung zu den Juden*, pp. 125-69]. The weight of scholarly opinion now seems to favor this view.

The main competing interpretation, identified first with Reinhold Lewin's *Luthers Stellung zu den Juden* (Berlin, 1911), argues that there are one or two changes in Luther's attitude towards the Jews, changes manifested in his interest in converting them, in the treatment he advocated towards them, and, perhaps, even in some theological issues concerning their status within divine history and in relation to Christianity. Lewin identified two changes: in the period to about 1521 Luther was indifferent toward the Jews or hostile only on a theological level; then for a time, reaching its high point in the 1523 *That Jesus Christ Was Born a Jew*, he was sympathetic toward the Jews and harbored optimistic hopes for their conversion; finally, in the latter part of his life, he became actively hostile on both a theological and practical level. The grounds offered for these changes are normally psychological, particularly Luther's disappointment that his 1523 treatise largely failed in its missionary attempt.

One attraction of this interpretation, quite apart from its merits in dealing with the evidence, is that it allows its proponents to choose which is Luther's "true" position: the relatively tolerant and sympathetic attitude of 1523 or the hostile position of the older Luther.

Although neither interpretation was immune from misuse in the service of Nazi anti-Semitism [Meier, "Zur Interpretation von Luthers Judenschriften," pp. 235-40; Brosseder, *Luthers Stellung zu den Juden,* p. 259], the great majority of such propagandistic uses favored the view of change put forward by Lewin [Brosseder, *Luthers Stellung zu den Juden,* p. 259]. But whereas Lewin applauded the statements of the early 1520s, the Nazi propagandists argued that the statements of the old Luther represented his authentic position. For these propagandists it was convenient to depict Luther as a man who was originally friendly toward Jews but, learning from bitter experience, became one of the greatest anti-Semites of all time [see Brosseder, *Luthers Stellung zu den Juden*, esp. pp. 156ff.].

wrath of God; (2) that without divine intervention they were incorrigible and impossible to convert by human effort; (3) that their religion remained perpetually hostile to Christianity and could not cease blaspheming God and Christ; and (4) that there existed a "solidarity of guilt" between Christians and Jews: a common suffering under God's wrath, a common resistance to Christ, a common attempt to gain one's own righteousness and salvation apart from Christ, a common need for grace.

What changed over Luther's career, Maurer contends, was not these theological principles or presuppositions but rather the practical and legal conclusions Luther drew from them. Maurer, following historians before him, suggests a number of political and religious matters, perceived by Luther in a new light or to which he attached new importance, that may collectively account for this change of mind. Although always concerned over the problem of usury, for example, Luther became even more concerned over *Jewish* usury in his later years. He also appears to have shared his society's suspicions that the Jews favored the Turks and were assisting them against the Christians. Direct personal experiences may have played a role: for example, problems with Jewish converts and a frustrating debate in the early 1530s with three learned Jews over certain messianic passages in the Old Testament. Reports of Jewish proselytizing, of Judaizing sects within Christianity, of messianic movements among the Jews may have fed his ire and increased his concern over the effect Jews had on society. Most important of all, of course, was his determined effort to preserve the Christological interpretation of the Old Testament from the historicizing exegesis of the rabbis and the Christian Hebraicists who followed the rabbinic lead.[67]

Maurer places the harsh recommendations themselves in their theological context. At issue was the matter of blasphemy. For Luther a Protestant territory was Christian not to the extent that its inhabitants were Christian but to the extent that it refused to tolerate anti-Christian teaching in public. By the mid-1530s Luther had abandoned his belief that Jewish blasphemy against Christ and God was confined to the privacy of the synagogue. Having encountered Jewish propaganda and received report of active Jewish proselytizing, Luther became convinced that the Jews and their blasphemy were a threat to the public good. His demands—that the synagogues be burned and buried, that Jewish prayer books and the Talmud be destroyed, that rabbis be forbidden to teach, and that Jewish worship be forbidden—stem from his belief that Jewish teaching and preaching contained blasphemy.[68]

These harsh recommendations were for Luther an expression of "rough mercy" [*scharfe Barmherzigkeit*] that might save a few Jews from the flames of hell,[69] while "soft mercy" (such as that expressed in his 1523 treatise) only made the Jews worse and worse.[70] "Rough mercy" was the paradoxical action of God in judgment and grace. The Christian preacher was to proclaim this from the pulpit; the Christian authorities were to carry it into practice.[71]

The central concern of the late treatises was not, however, these political and economic expressions of "rough mercy." Luther's late anti-Jewish writings were attempts to defend and maintain theologically and exegetically the Christian sense of the Old Testament and to refute competing Jewish exegesis. Maurer argues at length that Luther was attempting to found a new school of exegesis that would direct the research efforts of the Christian humanist Hebraists. In these treatises Luther was concerned fundamentally with the perpetual problem of the relation between the Old and the New Testaments.[72]

The attractiveness of this "theological" explanation of Luther's attitude toward the Jews obviously goes beyond its ability to account for Luther's beliefs and behavior. For one thing, it makes clearer the inappropriateness of *racial* anti-Semites claiming Luther as a patron of their cause. Luther identified a Jew by his religious beliefs, not by his race. (Identification of a Jew by his race is, in any case, a concept foreign to the sixteenth century.) If a Jew converted to Christianity, he became a fellow brother or sister in Christ. For racial anti-Semitism religious belief is largely irrelevant. For example, under National Socialism a person was considered Jewish if either of his grandparents were Jewish, whatever his religious convictions. Scholars who point this out are not condoning religious anti-Semitism. They are only pointing out that the logic of religious anti-Semitism leads to attempts at conversion, not to genocide.

A "theological" explanation as presented by Maurer also allows the modern scholar to conclude that the theology itself does not necessarily lead to the political and economic recommendations Luther actually recommended to the rulers of his day. For example, Maurer characterizes Luther's harsh recommendations as an "anachronism," "utopian but also hopelessly reactionary," an "unrealizable remnant of medieval tradition."[73] Luther's attempt to separate Christians from Jews is judged "a mistaken decision that was deeply grounded in the social reality of his time and that, furthermore, reveals a deficiency in his understanding of history."[74] For Maurer, Luther's *theological* considerations remain valid to this day,[75] while in the social and political realm, he was fighting a "losing battle."[76] In short, this distinction allows contemporary theologians to embrace Luther's theology without also having to embrace his anti-Semitic practices.*

---

*Not all theologians are comfortable with this approach. Aarne Siirala writes: "Is not the structure of the Lutheran consensus presented above the structure of a rationaliza-

Maurer is certainly right to insist that the primary subject of the later treatises, whether viewed quantitatively or qualitatively, was the proper exegesis of the Old Testament. He is also right to insist that, when doing critical theology, one must distinguish between the essential assertions of Luther's theology and their specific application, which may have been conditioned by the circumstances of the sixteenth century. As Maurer realizes, Luther's theology of justification, and the conclusions one draws from it, remain of central importance for the Jewish-Christian dialogue of today.[77] In this dialogue it would not do to confuse "accidents" with "essence."

From an historical perspective, however, this "theological" evaluation of Luther's attitude toward the Jews is unsatisfactory. Sixteenth-century readers of Luther's treatises, and even Luther himself, could not have distinguished between what Maurer termed the "essential theology" of the tracts and the "remnants of medieval tradition" that they also contained. For Luther and for his contemporaries the "remnants" of prejudice and discriminatory treatment were in logic and in practice tied to the theological description of the Jews as a God-forsaken people suffering under divine wrath. Theology and practice reinforced each other. So twentieth-century scholars may conclude that for the purposes of twentieth-century theology those aspects of Luther's theology that twentieth-century theologians deem essential need not entail the practical recommendations that Luther made. But the historian must insist that *Luther* saw a clear relationship between the two. To be sure, the historian may also conclude that Luther was illogical or that he was using his theology to rationalize beliefs and prejudices that he and his society shared. Nevertheless, for the historian the distinction between "essential theology" and "medieval remnants" tells more about the twentieth than about the sixteenth century.

Neither the vulgarity nor the violence nor the charges of satanic motivation nor the sarcastic mocking is unique to these treatises. If any-

---

tion? It may be understandable as a reaction against those interpretations in which Luther has been blamed for modern anti-Semitism or made a scapegoat for the holocausts of our generation. But the attempt both to find a scapegoat and an interpretation of history in terms of a rationalization, in which a certain present position is defended by repressing and avoiding certain facts of history, is a sign of an escape from facing one's own loyalties and disloyalties in the present. To characterize Luther's attitude toward the Jews as 'religious,' 'biblical' or 'theological' does not clarify this complex issue. Even the Inquisition, for example, claims to be all that, but in that case we are ready to see in it a pathological element in the perversions of the generations in question" (Aarne Siirala, "Luther and the Jews," *Lutheran World* [1964]:356).

thing, Luther's 1541 *Against Hanswurst* and his 1545 *Against the Papacy at Rome, Founded by the Devil* contain more scatology, more sallies against the devil, more heavy sarcasm, and more violence of language and recommendations. The polemics of the older Luther against Turks and Protestant opponents are only slightly more restrained. Against each of these opponents—Catholics, Turks, other Protestants, and Jews—he occasionally passed on libelous tales and gave credence to improbable charges. In all these respects Luther treated the Jews no differently than he treated his other opponents.[78]

With many of these other polemics the vulgarity and harshness may have been a deliberate rhetorical tactic. The language was consistent with the general tenor of the polemical contest. But can the same be said of the anti-Jewish treatises? Ostensibly, Luther was replying to a Jewish treatise that defamed Christ, the Virgin Mary, and Christianity in general. Unfortunately, this treatise is now lost, so that it is not possible to evaluate its rhetoric and style of argumentation. There were some anti-Christian Jewish writings produced in this period, but not enough to allow us to locate Luther's work within a polemical contest between Christians and Jews, even assuming there was such a contest.[79] In any case, this is not really necessary since the treatises were explicitly aimed not at Jews but at fellow Protestants. In this respect his anti-Jewish writings have more in common with his attacks on Protestant opponents that with his attacks on Catholics and Turks.

For Luther the Catholics and Turks were *external* threats, coming from outside the Reformation movement itself. Also they were threats closely bound up in politics. This can be seen from the fact that the treatises against Turks and Catholics were almost all written at the request of Elector Johann Friedrich and reflect the political interests of the elector and his fellow members of the League of Schmalkalden. In contrast, in his attacks on Sacramentarians and Jews he was worried primarily about *internal* subversion, about the threat these opponents posed from within the movement. The Sacramentarians claimed to be fellow Christians and to be in essential agreement with Luther, and yet they denied the real presence in the Lord's Supper. The internal threat they posed is obvious.[80]

Significantly, Luther also viewed the Jews, or rather Jewish exegesis, as more an internal than an external threat.* It was, after all, to counter Jewish efforts to proselytize Christians (or to counter Judaizing sects

---

*Maurer argues that from the late 1520s on the Jews are seen by Luther as no longer having any connection with adherents to the gospel. They are now seen as part of a common front comprising papists (including heretics), unbelieving Jews, and Turks

within Protestantism) that Luther wrote his *Against the Sabbatarians*. Of greater threat, however, was the challenge posed by Jewish exegesis of the Old Testament. Luther believed his Christological interpretation of the Old Testament and his Christian interpretation of various messianic Old Testament passages to be of vital importance to his theology. Jewish exegetes challenged both. And, increasingly, Protestant theologians and translators were adopting the exegetical opinions of the Jewish exegetes.[81]

In the later anti-Jewish treatises Luther attempted to dissuade fellow Protestants from employing rabbinic exegesis. He attacked the exegesis itself, using historical, scriptural, and theological arguments. But he also employed his rhetorical skills to attack its source: the Jews themselves. To discredit the message it helps also to discredit the messenger.

There is another significant dimension to Luther's anti-Jewish treatises that links them with the other polemics of his later years. Heiko Oberman has recently pointed out that Luther's anti-Jewish polemics cannot be understood properly apart from his apocalyptic beliefs. Luther believed that he was living on the eve of the Last Judgment, that with the establishment of the Reformation and exposure of the papal antichrist within the church the devil had unleashed his last, most violent attack on the true church. The devil's servants in this final assault were the papists, the fanatics, the Turks, and the Jews. Luther saw it as his duty in this apocalyptic struggle to attack the devil with all the vehemence at his command and to defend the church against all the devil's thrusts. His attacks on the Jews, Oberman insists rightly, cannot be understood properly apart from this apocalyptic context.[82]

To insist on the importance of context for a proper understanding of Luther's anti-Jewish treatises is not merely good history. It also makes it more difficult for modern anti-Semites to exploit the authority of Luther's name to support their racist beliefs. This is all to the good. But we cannot have it both ways. If the anti-Jewish treatises cannot be divorced from their context without serious distortion, then the same should be true for his other writings. It is not intellectually honest to pick and choose.

---

(Maurer, "Die Zeit der Reformation," p. 395). Although this is true for the Jews themselves, Jewish exegesis is seen as a threat from within the Reformation movement.

## CHAPTER SEVEN

# One Among Many: The Example of *Against Hanswurst*

When scholars discuss the "coarseness" of the polemics of the older Luther, they often point to *Against Hanswurst* as a prime example.[1] In the early twentieth century this coarseness was sharply criticized, especially by Catholic scholars, and defended by Protestants.[2] Commonly, the apologists conceded the violence and coarseness in some of Luther's treatises such as *Against Hanswurst*, but argued that such coarseness was common in the sixteenth century. Luther's opponents—Prierias, Alveld, Eck, Emser, Cochlaeus, Karlstadt, Zwingli, and so on—were no more delicate than he.[3] Eric Gritsch, editor and translator of *Against Hanswurst* for *Luther's Works*, American Edition, expressed the common wisdom when he argued that Luther's language in *Against Hanswurst* was as violent as that of Duke Heinrich in the *Duplicae* and that such violence was not uncommon in the polemical literature of the sixteenth century.[4] But is the common wisdom correct? And even if harsh and violent polemics were common, was Luther's own abusiveness a deliberate rhetorical tactic, calculated to fit the larger rhetorical context? To provide some perspective on Luther's abusiveness, and to explore the question of its calculated nature, this chapter examines a number of publications that preceded, accompanied, and followed *Against Hanswurst*.

## Early Stages of the Controversy

*Against Hanswurst* was but one salvo in a war of placards and treatises waged for several years between Duke Heinrich of Braunschweig-Wolfenbüttel on one side and Landgrave Philipp and Elector Johann Friedrich on the other.[5] The exchange of charges and

insults began first in 1539 but had its roots in much earlier developments. From the early years of the Reformation Duke Heinrich had
stood among the movement's most determined opponents, less out of
personal religious conviction than out of loyalty to Emperor Charles
V. Dependent upon Charles's favor for the retention of recently
acquired territory, Heinrich had dutifully followed the emperor's lead
in both political and religious affairs. So once Charles had pronounced against the Protestants in the 1521 Diet of Worms, Heinrich
had zealously made attempts to execute the decree in his own lands.

Heinrich was reinforced in his opposition to the Reformation by the
Peasants' War of 1525, which he laid to the Reformation's account.
The Reformation also became entangled in his long-standing feud
with the cities of Braunschweig and Goslar, which both embraced the
Lutheran Reformation in the late 1520s. Although a territorial city,
Braunschweig had managed over the years to gain considerable
independence from the duke. And Goslar, a free imperial city, had
been locked for years in an struggle with the duke over mining and
forest rights. With the entrance of these two cities into the League of
Schmalkalden in the 1530s, Heinrich found himself confronting not
simply two small cities but the whole Protestant League. To counter
this threat, he joined in June 1538 with Emperor Charles, King Ferdinand, Cardinal Albrecht of Mainz, the dukes of Bavaria, and others
to form the Catholic League. Heinrich was made the League leader
for northern Germany. Given the passionate convictions and high
stakes on both sides, it took little to set off the controversy between
Heinrich, leader of the Catholic League in northern Germany, and
Landgrave Philipp and Elector Johann Friedrich, leaders of the
League of Schmalkalden.

When in the spring of 1538 the League of Schmalkalden decided,
somewhat provocatively, to hold its meeting in the city of Braunschweig, Duke Heinrich refused to grant either Landgrave Philipp or
Elector Johann Friedrich safe-conduct through his territories. When
despite this the landgrave paraded by the fortress of Wolfenbüttel with
a heavily armed escort, he was fired upon. Then it was Duke
Heinrich's turn. While crossing Electoral Saxony with a large escort
provided by Duke Georg, he nearly clashed with a number of the
elector's men. Finally, towards the end of the year, the landgrave
detained a ducal secretary carrying letters to Cardinal Albrecht and to
Imperial Vice-chancellor Held that the landgrave read as revealing the
covert hostile intentions of the Catholic League toward the Protestants.

These incidents gave each side considerable cause to criticize the
other. Duke Heinrich saw the League's meeting in Braunschweig,

and, even more so, the inclusion of the cities of Braunschweig and Goslar in the League of Schmalkalden, as direct challenges to his claims of sovereignty over these cities. Landgrave Philipp and Elector Johann Friedrich viewed the refusal of safe-conduct as a hostile, illegal act. Duke Heinrich believed that Elector Johann Friedrich had meant to ambush him when he had crossed Electoral Saxony, and that only the escort given him by Duke Georg had forestalled the elector's criminal intentions. The duke also viewed the seizure of his secretary and the opening of his letters as clearly illegal and hostile. These incidents were discussed at exhausting length in the subsequent polemics.

It was the Protestants who first took to the printing press in this quarrel, but only after several preliminaries. To excuse his confiscation of the letters of another imperial prince, and to indicate the hostile intentions of the Catholic League, the landgrave had sent a manuscript explanation and copies of the seized letters to various princes. Duke Heinrich had replied, sending a letter to the landgrave and a more detailed manuscript attack and justification to the same princes to whom the landgrave had written. Then in late 1539, at the urging of the landgrave's father-in-law, Duke Georg,[6] the landgrave and the elector decided to commit the Protestant case to print. First they published their *True and Thorough Report*, in which they reproduced the documents they had previously circulated in manuscript along with Duke Heinrich's reply to Landgrave Philipp and their reply to him.[7] They also issued a separate printed reply to the lengthy letter that Duke Heinrich had sent to various princes in response to the landgrave's first communication.[8] Hence their reply was published before Duke Heinrich's original letter.

Duke Heinrich responded in early 1540 by publishing a collection of three letters: Duke Georg's original letter to Landgrave Philipp, urging him to publish an explanation for his behavior but also expressing considerable reservation about the propriety of seizing the secretary; Duke Wilhelm of Bavaria's disapproving response to the landgrave's initial account of the affair; and Duke Heinrich's own letter that he had sent to the various princes in response to the landgrave's first communication.[9] At this point, each side was accusing the other of numerous illegalities, treachery, mendacity, dishonorable conduct, and malicious slander.

As the year 1540 passed the treatises multiplied and the rhetoric escalated. Even in the titles, the princely authors competed with each other for rhetorical advantage. Duke Heinrich published his *Second Steadfast, Well-Grounded, and True Answer to the Elector of Saxony's and the Landgrave of Hesse's Newly Published Slanderous,*

*Defamatory, Notorious, Fabricated, Mendacious, and False Libel.* [10]
Landgrave Philipp and Elector Johann Friedrich replied separately.
The landgrave's *Apology or Second True, Honorable, Steadfast,
Christian Reply to All the Fabricated, False Allegations . . . by Duke
Heinrich the Younger of Braunschweig Presented in his Latest Fabri-
cated, Wicked, Ignoble Publication* appeared in Latin and German
editions. [11] The elector issued a very lengthy (over two hundred pages)
*Second Treatise [Abdruck]: True, Steadfast, and Well-Grounded
Replies to Duke Heinrich of Braunschweig's . . . Defamatory, Fabri-
cated, and Mendacious Notorious Libel, Slanderous Treatise, and Pub-
lication.* [12] Duke Heinrich responded to the landgrave's *Apology* with
his *Third Steadfast, True, Upright, Godly, and Well-Established,
Irrefutable Answer to the Landgrave's Recently Published Ungodly,
Unchristian, Dishonorable, Mendacious, Fabricated, and Baseless Libel
Against His Princely Grace.* [13] Against Elector Johann Friedrich's
*Second Treatise* he issued his *Well-Grounded, Steadfast, Grave, True,
Godly, Christian, Nobly-Inclined Duplicae Against the Elector of
Saxony's Second Defamatory, Baseless, Fickle, Fabricated, Ungodly,
Unchristian, Drunken, God-Detested Treatise.* [14] It was to the *Duplicae*
that Luther was to respond.* Other parties also became involved in
the public quarrel. On Duke Heinrich's side, there appeared three
treatises attacking the city of Braunschweig and its involvement with
the League of Schmalkalden. [15] From the opposing camp, Duke Ernst
of Braunschweig and Lüneburg issued a treatise disputing Duke
Heinrich's claims regarding Braunschweig; the city council of Braunschweig issued a treatise in its own behalf; and Hans Koch, a former
official of Duke Heinrich's, published an apology in which he also
attacked Duke Heinrich. [16]

Each of the principal treatises offered point-by-point refutations of
the most recent publication of the opponent. For the most part they
dealt with questions of fact and law—for example, whether Duke
Heinrich had actually refused the requested safe-conduct and what his
legal obligations were in this regard. But as the titles also indicate,
from the very outset each side impugned the intentions, honor, and
veracity of its opponent. And each claimed to have God on its side.

By the end of 1540 the accusations had also become intimately personal. Although many of the charges were without foundation, there
were sufficient failings on both sides to provide considerable ammuni-
tion to opponents. The elector was the hardest to slander, although

---

*Whereas the princes wrote treatises with titles that were miniature essays in them-
selves, Luther contented himself with a two-word title: *Against Hanswurst.* In general
Luther's titles were much shorter than those of other authors during this period.

even his supporters admitted that he occasionally drank too much. The landgrave, with his bigamous marriage contracted in early 1540, was an easier target.[17] Duke Heinrich's reputation for sexual morality was hardly better, however. His mistress, Eva von Trott, had borne him three children before her apparent death, which had been marked with full ecclesiastical ceremonies including vigils and masses for the dead.[18] It later came out that her death was a hoax, that Heinrich had hidden her at one of his castles, and that their secret relationship had produced several more children. Heinrich also had to answer for the long imprisonment of his brother Wilhelm, who had contested their father's will that stipulated inheritance of the territory by the rule of primogeniture and thus deprived Wilhelm of a share of the territory. Finally, in 1540 a rash of arson had broken out in the Protestant territories, and many suspected that Catholics were responsible. When under torture several suspected arsonists "confessed" that they had been hired by the duke's men, the Protestants had all the proof they needed to include arson among the duke's other alleged crimes.

During 1541 thirty or more publications were added to the controversy. The Imperial Diet in Regensburg, meeting from April through July, was flooded with treatises from both sides. And as was so often the case, the Protestants appear to have managed this propaganda attack more effectively than did the Catholics. The elector and landgrave carefully considered and coordinated their publications.[19] For example, the *Duplicae* had appeared at the end of 1540 or early 1541, and called for a response. The electoral court first thought to have Luther pen the official reply to this treatise.[20] But Luther decided to issue the attack under his own name so that he would have more leeway in developing his argument.[21] And so the official reply was left once again to the elector and his councilors. It was entitled *True, Steadfast, Well-Grounded, Christian, and Sincere Reply to the Shameless, Calphurnic Book of Infamy and Lies by the Godless, Accursed, Execrable Defamer, Evil-Working Barabbas, Also Whore-Addicted Holophernes of Braunschweig, Who Calls Himself Duke Heinrich the Younger.* [22] The elector circulated three hundred copies of this treatise at the Imperial Diet and even had it translated into French for presentation to the emperor.[23] *Against Hanswurst*, which was available at least a month before the Diet, was also circulated there and found, according to Melanchthon, an avid readership. It went through three editions.[24] The third prong in this three-prong response was penned by Georg Spalatin, who defended the House of Saxony and its lineage against slurs made by Duke Heinrich.[25] His treatise was written in close consultation with the electoral court.[26] Also prepared in time for the Diet and printed in Wittenberg was a

*147*

*Supplication* to the emperor concerning the recent outbreak of arson and attributing responsibility for this arson to several of Duke Heinrich's officials.[27] When the duke published a reply to the *Supplication*, the League of Schmalkalden published a rejoinder.[28] Also about this time there was published in Wittenberg a copy of the agreement between Duke Heinrich and his brother Wilhelm, which did not present the duke in a charitable light.[29] The landgrave also published in Latin and German his *Third True Reply*.[30] Duke Ernst of Branschweig and Lüneburg and Hans Koch each published another attack, and the city council of Braunschweig issued two additional treatises.[31] The Protestants also benefitted from a supplication to the emperor from the von Trott family, asking for an investigation concerning the fate of Eva von Trott. This supplication, Duke Heinrich's reply, and the family's rejoinder were later printed as one treatise.[32]

The duke was kept busy replying to all these attacks. He issued his *Fourth . . . Answer* against the landgrave, and against the elector his *Grave, Well-Grounded, True, Godly, and Christian Quadruplicae, Against the Godless, Insane, Obstinate, Apostatized Church-Robber and Accursed, Wicked Antiochus, Novatianus, Severianus, and Pimp of Saxony's . . . Fabricated, Lying, and Shameless Libel*.[33] He or his supporters also replied to Duke Ernst, to the city council of Braunschweig, and to the Protestants' *Supplication* regarding arson.[34] The duke also published his own *Supplication*, to which both the landgrave and the elector replied.[35]

It was also during the first half of 1541 that the first anonymous satires appeared. From the duke's camp there appeared in early February an *Evangelical, Fraternal, Faithful Instruction* addressed to the landgrave and purportedly written by one "Master Justinus Warsager, executioner at Warheitsbrun," or, in English, "Master Justinus Truthsayer, executioner at Truthspring."[36] This satire dealt, among other matters, with the landgrave's bigamy. In response, the landgrave encouraged Johann Lening, a Hessian pastor, to publish an anonymous *Expostulation and Letter of Rebuke from Satan, Prince of this World, to Duke Heintz of Braunschweig, His Sworn Servant and Faithful Vassal*. Not to be outdone, the ducal party countered with a *Dialogus* against the *Expostulation*.[37] Three other satires also emerged from the Protestant camp: *Recent News: Two Open Letters Written to Hans Wurst in Wolfenbüttel, the First from Lucifer, the Second from the Executioner at Wolfenbüttel*; *Three New and Humorous Conversations: How the Wolf, Recently a Man (Although Not For Long) Named Heinz Wolfenbüttel, Was Damned to the Depths of Hell*; and *Recent News From Rome: Where Does the Arson Come From?*[38] There may have also appeared that year or early the next Nicholas von Amsdorf's anonymous *A Poem Indicating How Pious Duke Heinrich of Braunschweig Is and How Wicked the Lutherans Are*, and the Catholic rejoinder *Contrarium Against a Lying Libelous Poem, Which Was Recently Printed Against Duke Heinrich of Braunschweig and the Roman Catholic Church*.[39]

The list of titles need not end at this point. In 1542 at least another thirty publications appeared, and by 1546 the controversy had generated nearly a hundred. Among these publications were not only treatises but also rhymed verse, songs, and satires.[40] But this recital has gone on long enough; *Against Hanswurst* must be placed within this context.

The immediate predecessor to *Against Hanswurst*, and the coarsest treatise to appear in the controversy thus far, was Duke Heinrich's *Duplicae*. It was a point-by-point refutation of Elector Johann Friedrich's *Second Treatise* of 1540. As such, it was lengthy and repetitious. The bulk of the treatise dealt, repeatedly, with the central issues of the dispute: the denial of safe-conduct for the League meetings in Braunschweig, the duke's claims to Braunschweig, the seizure of the duke's secretary, the near-clash when the duke had crossed Electoral Saxony, and so on. The discussion of these substantive issues was liberally peppered with insults, name-calling, and abuse. Since we are interested in comparing the coarseness and abusiveness of this treatise with *Against Hanswurst*, we shall focus on the "seasoning" rather than the substance of the treatise. But it should be remembered that most of the treatise concerned matters of fact, law, politics, and aristocratic honor.

In analogous fashion, it should be kept in mind that much of *Against Hanswurst* also dealt with substantive issues, specifically, with the nature of the true church, the certainty of doctrine, and the distinction between office and the person who held it. The section on the characteristics of the true and false church was of sufficient independent value that it was separately reprinted in 1543 along with the Schmalkaldic Articles.[41] Still, a goodly portion of *Against Hanswurst* was devoted to a point-by-point reply to the *Duplicae*. The treatise as a whole was also liberally seasoned with personal and partisan abuse. As with the *Duplicae*, we shall focus narrowly on this aspect of the treatise.

Throughout the *Duplicae* Duke Heinrich repeatedly characterized Elector Johann Friedrich as a monstrously fat and clumsy drunkard who had maliciously and dishonorably published numerous slurs against the duke. For example, quite early in the treatise the duke opined "that if the monster or marvelous beast, the wicked, drunken Nabal of Saxony had not been drunk on beer or wine at the time he

149

wrote his untruthful and baseless would-be reply, he would perhaps have refrained from such clumsy, fickle, untruthful, defamatory, and impudent writings."[42] The elector was "nature's marvelous beast, [a] malicious, wine-addicted, drunken, accursed, senseless, lying man."[43] He was likened to various biblical villains such as Nabal, Ben-Hadad, and Moab. His lineage was disparaged by the Welf duke, and he was accused of conceit.[44] In reply to the elector's accusations of military incompetence and even cowardice, the duke asked sarcastically, "But who is the Nabal of Saxony, a would-be warrior, to talk much about manliness, since he has never in his whole life drawn a sword in earnest or seen a war or battle order unless depicted for him on the table by his Order Master, Hans Dolschtz, using the mugs, cups, and glasses he had guzzled dry?"[45] Above all the elector's veracity and probity were impugned. As the duke offered his refutation one-by-one for the arguments the elector had employed in his *Second Treatise*, the duke branded each charge a shameless lie and a malicious, dishonorable fabrication and labeled the elector accordingly.

While Duke Heinrich characterized the elector as a fat, malicious, and lying drunkard, and likened him to Nabal, Ben-Hadad, and Moab, Luther characterized the duke as a devil, likened him to an "archprostitute" and "harem guard", and charged him with adultery, arson, cowardice, murder, and demonic possession. The public reasons Luther gave for his entry into the fray was a need, first, to defend the essence of the faith against the duke's attack and, second, to refute reference in Heinrich's *Duplicae* to the elector as one "whom Martin Luther, his dear, devoted [subject], has called 'Hanswurst'."[46] Hanswurst was a clown who wore a wurst or sausage around his neck and was found in many of the comedies and farces of Luther's day. At the outset Luther denied that he had ever called his prince or any other specific person "Hanswurst." The proper reply to such charges was "Devil, you lie!" He then proceeded to attack the devil, who, he charged, had possessed Duke Heinrich.

> Indeed, since you and your Heintz are such gross bumpkins that you think such foul and lame gossip should harm me in this issue or do you honor, you are both the real Hanswursts, bumpkins, louts, and boors. And I would answer you both with this, that both of you, father and son, are incorrigible, honorless, perjured rogues when you say that I have called my gracious lord "Hanswurst." No further answer is needed for such wurst-tricks. Perhaps some suppose that you regard my gracious lord as Hanswurst because, by the grace of God (whose enemy you are), he is strong, fat, and of solid body. But suppose what you will, so do it in your pants and hang it around your neck and make a

sausage of it for yourself and gobble it down, you gross asses and sows![47]

To Heinrich's other charges, that the elector was a heretic, an apostate, a rebel, a monster, a Nabal, a Cain, and the like, Luther replied that Heinrich was simply lying like an "arch-prostitute" who called an honorable virgin a whore without cause and knowing better and thus made herself more hated and the virgin more esteemed. All the papists and their adherents, as befitted devils and their servants, lied shamelessly in their books and talk, but their curses and slander came to nothing.[48] On occasion Luther combined his charges into a devastatingly abusive and *ad hominem* portrait: "For although Nero also set fire to Rome," he remarked at one point,

> he nonetheless did so publicly and risked as a man what might come of it. . . . But this faint-hearted wretch and fearful sissy [Duke Heinrich] does everything treacherously. He would be better as a harem guard; he should do nothing but stand like a eunuch, that is, a harem guard, in a fool's cap with a fly swatter and guard the women and that on account of which they are called women (as the gross Germans put it).[49]

Above all, Luther repeatedly attacked the devil Heintz rather than the man Heinrich.

In the *Duplicae* the duke had also branded the elector a heretic and had charged that he was disobedient to both church and empire. "He talks alot about the word of God," the duke wrote, "and yet he is a public persecutor of the universal holy Christian church and the word of God, hates discipline and virtue, and loves boozing and drunkenness, and carries wickedness in his heart and duplicity on his tongue."[50] Since the elector refused to be in the obedience of the universal Christian church, he could remain eternally in the disobedience of the devil's church. Once the duke even suggested that the elector was either the evil spirit itself or at least its faithful follower.[51] It should be noted, however, that this charge of satanic motivation is rarely explicit in the *Duplicae*. In his concluding remarks the duke nicely summarized his characterization of the elector: he was "a drunken Ben-Hadad, and a despiser of the word of God, and an apostate from his beatific word and the universal Chirstian church, an obstinate heretic . . . a persecutor of the right and true God and His beatific word, [one] of unchristian belief and unpeaceful temperament, and a sower of all disobedience and awaker of all discord, a profaner of God's name and word."[52]

Luther, too, had a great deal to say about the religious convictions of his opponent. From the beginning of the world to its end, Luther explained, there were two churches, the true and the false, or as St. Augustine called them, Abel and Cain. The Protestants had remained faithful to the "true ancient church" while the Catholics, including Duke Heinrich, had apostatized from the ancient church.[53]

Although Luther willingly conceded that the Catholics had the same baptism, Sacrament of the Altar, keys, creed, and gospels as the ancient church and the Protestants, he argued that they had fallen away from them. Drawing on Hosea and Ezekiel [chapter 23], he likened the papal church to a young virgin bride who takes to whoring.

> For it is such a whore that I have in mind when I rebuke you as a apostate, straying whore—you who in your childhood were baptized in the dear Lord as true Christians [and] lived several years like the ancient church. Subsequently, when you became grown and reached the age of reason (as I myself with many others also did), you saw and heard the beautiful ceremonies of the papal church as well as its glittering income, honor, and power, yes, the splendid holiness and great worship services and fabled kingdom of heaven. Then you forgot your Christian faith, baptism, and Sacrament [of the Altar] [and] became the zealous pupils and young little whores (as the comedies say) of the procuresses and archwhores until you old whores once again make young little whores, and thus the pope's, indeed, the devil's church increased and continually made many of the true virgins of Christ, who were born in baptism, into archwhores.[54]

It was within the terms of this larger struggle between the true and false churches that Luther placed the controversy with Duke Heinrich. Moreover, he fully believed that the struggle was reaching its climax in his own time.[55] As with his other polemics against Catholics, "fanatics," Turks, and Jews, this conviction allowed him to direct his attack more against the devil allegedly motivating the opponent than against the man himself.

In his *Duplicae* Duke Heinrich defended himself against the charges of arson and of faking his mistress's death by taking the offensive. He categorically and vehemently denied that he or his officials had hired any arsonists and alleged that the elector and landgrave had fabricated the charges to frame him. When the elector and the landgrave caught arsonists, they tortured them into confessing falsely that the duke or his officials had suborned them.[56] With regard to the rumors about the deceased Eva von Trott, the duke replied that either the elector had dreamed them up or, as was his custom, had mendaciously fabricated them while in his cups. Although the duke confessed himself a sinner, he was done, he claimed, a gross injustice and injury by this story.[57] He then turned to the "plank" in his opponent's eye: the landgrave's bigamous marriage. In his *Third Answer* of 1540, he had passed on the rumor that the landgrave had contracted a bigamous marriage.[58] In the *Duplicae* he presented more details, including the allegation that the scholars at Wittenberg had assisted with the bigamy.[59] The duke also charged that the landgrave had seduced and made pregnant the daughter of a citizen of the city of Braunschweig during the League's meetings there.[60]

Luther, too, favored offense over defense when it came to the failings within his own camp. While conceding that Johann Friedrich occasionally drank too much—a practice common in Germany which he could not condone—he denied that these occasional excesses in any way affected Johann Friedrich's highly competent rule of his territories.[61] Heinrich's characterization of Landgrave Philipp as a bigamist and an Anabaptist* was given much briefer treatment. Luther contented himself with *ad hominem* attacks on Heinrich and a very vague comment about the landgrave: "In Hesse I know a landgravine, who is and should be called wife and mother in Hesse, [and there] will probably be no other to bear and suckle young landgraves—I mean the duchess, daughter of Duke Georg of Saxony."[62] Having said this, Luther immediately went over to the offensive.

> But from the beginning no one has more blasphemously dishonored marriage then Heintz of Wolfenbüttel—that holy, temperate man who glosses over and conceals his shameful, impenitent, obstinate adultery under the horrible judgment and wrath of God (namely death which consumes all men so that the son of God himself had to help us) with divine services, masses, and vigils. Thus he made blinders, even a fool's cap, out of God and the Christian faith, as if death, resurrection, and eternal life were a joke and a confidence game.[63]

In defending the elector against the charge of drunkenness, he had pushed the counterattack even more strongly:

> For you know that all the world knows how you treat your laudable princess—not only like a soused and crazy rowdy and drunkard but also like a senseless raving tyrant, who daily and hourly

---

*Because the landgrave was relatively tolerant of Anabaptists, Duke Heinrich called him the elector's "Münsterite brother," refering to the Anabaptist kingdom of Münster.

gorges and guzzles himself full, not of wine, but of devils, as Judas did in the Last Supper. For you spew forth nothing but devils from your whole body in all you do and are, with blasphemy of God, cursing, lying, adultery, raging, excoriating, murdering, arson, and so on, so that your equal is found in no history. . . . In addition you are unable to carry out your shameful fornication, your adultery, without slandering and abusing God's name, and concealing the poor wench, as if dead, with your holy divine services, masses, and vigils.[64]

The vehemence of these two passages is not atypical for long stretches of the treatise.

There are some forms of abuse in *Against Hanswurst* that are little used in the *Duplicae* : scatological language and sexual slurs. As we have seen, Luther told Duke Heinrich and the devil to do it in their pants and gobble it down.[65] He remarked that he, too, had once been "stuck in the behind of the hellish whore, the pope's new church."[66] He likened Duke Heinrich and the papacy to "archwhores" and stated that the duke would make a good harem guard or eunuch.[67] "You should not write a book until you have heard an old sow fart," he wrote,

Then you should gape in wonder and say, "Thank you, beautiful nightingale, there I hear a text for me!" Hey boy, Rüdem [Duke Heinrich's publisher], that would be good to print in a book, nowhere else but in Wolfenbüttel, against writers and the elector. Oh, they shall hold their noses at it, and [they] will have to confess that Heintz Haremguard has also become a writer.[68]

With all the insults in the *Duplicae*, the language never reaches this point.

When the two treatises are compared as we have just done, it becomes difficult to escape the impression that *Against Hanswurst* represented an escalation in the coarseness and abusiveness of the controversy. The range of insults has been enlarged and the rhetoric intensified. In part this must be attributed to Luther's vastly superior rhetorical skills. The treatises by Elector Johann Friedrich, Landgrave Philipp, and Duke Heinrich are wooden and plodding in comparison. In part this must also be attributed to Luther's intense conviction that he was engaged in the climactic battle between the true and false church, that the real opponents were not men but devils, and the stakes were salvation and eternal life. It should be noted that the vehemence of *Against Hanswurst* received little comment from Protestants. Heinrich Bullinger of Zurich, not exactly one of Luther's promoters, did characterize it in a later letter to Bucer as "unbecoming, completely immodest, entirely scurrilous, and frivolous," but his evaluation remained private.[69] Melanchthon, who generally disapproved of Luther's more passionate efforts, had nothing but praise for the work. As for Luther himself, he wrote Melanchthon that, upon rereading the treatise, he wondered what had happened to him that he had written so moderately against the duke. He ascribed this "moderation" to the difficulties—a severe middle ear infection— he was having with his head at this time.[70] This odd remark, perfectly in keeping with his earlier description of the treatise as a "short and gentle booklet,"[71] may be another case of Luther's drier humor. Or, on the other hand, he may have actually believed that he had been unreasonably restrained in attacking what he believed was simply another of the devil's minions. The devil, of course, deserved all the abuse that could be heaped upon him.

## Some Later Publications

Elector Johann Friedrich's *True Reply* to Duke Heinrich's *Duplicae* was written with a specific audience in mind: the princes and officials assembled at the Imperial Diet at Regensburg. He distributed three hundred copies at the Diet, and gave a French translation to the emperor.[72] The landgrave's *Third True Reply* was aimed at this same audience of counselors and rulers. And the landgrave did not content himself with distributing copies at the Diet but also sent copies to other rulers such as the Strasbourg city council.[73] Given this select audience, and given the goal of discrediting Duke Heinrich in the eyes of his fellow rulers, it is not surprising that these treatises were very much like their predecessors in the dispute. They devoted most of their pages to the disputed questions of fact and law that divided Duke Heinrich from the League of Schmalkalden. At the same time, however, these treatises contained more *ad hominem* abuse than their predecessors.

In the *True Reply*, for example, the elector went beyond his previous practice of likening Duke Heinrich to a variety of biblical villains such as Antiochus Epiphanes, Judas Iscariot, Nabal, Cain, Holophernes, Barabbas, and Doeg (although he still made these attributions)[74] to upbraid the duke repeatedly for his "dissolute and shameless whoring and knavish life" and specifically for his "Stauffenburg adultery," by which he meant the affair with Eva von Trott, "the dead and yet still living wench," whom the duke had hidden at his Stauffenburg residence.[75] The duke was "Satan himself and the devil incarnate," a clown and a jester's dummy, a ugly drunk who could not control his temper when intoxicated, an "inhuman murderer," and an arsonist.[76]

There is probably no one explanation for this increase in *ad hominem* abuse. With each exchange of treatises, the accusations had become more personal and abusive. So the *True Reply* may simply reflect the natural dynamics of such a polemical contest. The *Duplicae* was the most abusive treatise to appear to date. Perhaps the elector may have felt the need to match and even exceed it. The abusiveness of the *True Reply* may also reflect greater information about the details about Eva von Trott's alleged death, which first began circulating about this time.[77] It is also possible that the *True Reply* may have owed some of its greater abusiveness to Luther's *Against Hanswurst*, which the elector had read before writing his own treatise.[78] In any case, as an example of powerful and sophisticated rhetoric, the *True Reply* falls far short of *Against Hanswurst*. Moreover, it lacks the apocalyptic framework of Luther's treatise as well as the occasional scatological remark. As an exercise in *ad hominem* abuse, however, it does approach Luther's own contribution.

As is to be expected, Duke Heinrich did not take kindly to the elector's *True Reply* or Luther's *Against Hanswurst*. In his *Quadruplicae* of 31 May 1541 he replied to the elector's various accusations, matching argument for argument and insult for insult. The litany of abuse becomes almost hypnotic. Within the first three pages of the 157-page treatise, the elector is called, among other things, "the desperate, lying, wine-addicted, drunken, honorless and shameless Hans of Saxony," "the unwashed, gross, callow, and unlearned boor of Saxony," "the perjured, mendacious, honorless and soulless donkey-beast, Hans Wurst of Saxony, . . . a manifest liar, breaker of the peace, and a foresworn, apostatized, and godless man," "a manifest and intentional blasphemer, despiser, destroyer, and plunderer of God and His true church," a "wine-addicted, conceited, drunken, and beer-guzzling Nabal."[79] Hardly a sentence in the whole treatise is free of abusive comments. Some of the more imaginative later epithets include: "apostate, honorless, perjured, rebellious heretic," "bloodthirsty, murderous, conscienceless, perjurer of Saxony," "senseless, callow, Thersites, Cyclops, and Polyphemus," "foolish, asinine, drunken Ben-Hadad with his long jutting ears," "lying, whore-addicted, apostatized heretic, Severian, Saducee, Novatian, and persecutor of the clerical estate," and "pimp at Torgau."[80] To the elector's accusation that he had engaged in a drunken brawl at the 1530 Diet of Augsburg, the duke replied that "the one who was drunken, soused, foolish, and dissolute was none other than the drunkard of Saxony, who was accustomed to becoming soused with the wine stewards and wine servers as well as with the cooks and scullery boys. So it is that this drunkard yearns greatly to befoul himself in wine and beer just like a pig in the muck and manure."[81]

The *Quadruplicae* was directed against the elector's *True Reply*, and very little notice was taken of Luther's attack. But the duke was unwilling to ignore it completely. In one paragraph he denied that he had given Luther cause to attack him in print, and he charged instead that the "desperate villain of Saxony," Elector Johann Friedrich, had put Luther up to it. "All Christian pious hearts" testified that the "godless monk" had accomplished nothing more with his treatise than to expose "his own shame [and his] godless, conceited, unjust, unchristian, jealous, hateful and biased cast of mind." Many now recognized that "in such a godless monk there is no consideration or promotion of theology or God's honor but rather all self-seeking, wicked, godless, jealous, underhanded dealings, and that he did not intend or seek peace [and] unity but rather antipathy, disunity, and bloodshed." He would be repaid with the loss of his salvation by his father, the devil, "to whom the faithless apostate was born by means of an incubus, as can be proved."[82]

When it first appeared, *Against Hanswurst* appears to have represented an escalation in the level of abuse. But several of its characteristics that distinguished it originally from the other contributions to the controversy can be found in subsequent treatises. To be sure, it remained the only publication in the dispute with extensive theological content. But its abusiveness, if not the elegance of its insults, was surpassed by later publications. The *Quadruplicae*, for example, contained more insults, and *Three New and Humorous Conversations* more violence. The *Expostulation, Recent News,* and *Three New and Humorous Conversations* relied for their humor on the premise that Duke Heinrich was a minion of Satan.[83] Since Luther's treatise assumed an apocalyptic context, the climax of the struggle between the true and false church, it offered a consistent orientation that allowed Luther almost automatically to reduce, or elevate, his opponents to the status of a devil or Satan himself. The other treatises of this controversy largely lacked this encompassing world view. Although Luther was the first to employ scatological abuse, he was not the last. In the *Three New and Humorous Conversations*, for example, Duke Heinrich is condemned to various punishments in hell for his misdeeds, including a three-year sentence in which "he must daily kiss Pope Joan precisely where she passes wind as many times, if that is possible, as he had honored with his kiss the feet of the three popes Leo and Clement and Paul, called the Third."[84] Within this larger context, the coarseness of *Against*

*Hanswurst* still seems notable but not unique.

The pamphlet war continued through 1541 into 1542, with Luther content to observe from the sidelines.[85] New literary forms were employed to reach a wider audience: satires, rhymed verse, poems, songs set to familiar melodies, and even graffiti.[86] In a remarkably short time, the opposing governments had become skilled propagandists exploiting a wide range of techniques that the new medium of printing afforded.[87]

## The Seizure of Braunschweig-Wolfenbüttel

It was only time before the pamphlet war became a fighting war as well. The spark was provided by Heinrich's continued harassment of the cities of Goslar and Braunschweig. In the late 1530s Goslar had torn down several cloisters outside its walls that could have been used by Heinrich as bases from which to attack the city. Heinrich, in turn, managed in 1540 to have the city placed under the imperial ban for its actions, and this gave him the legal right to attack the city. The League of Schmalkalden raised strenuous objections and the ban was lifted. Heinrich proceeded with his plans anyway. Even King Ferdinand failed to dissuade him. In response Elector Johann Friedrich and Landgrave Philipp, as the leaders of the League of Schmalkalden of which both Goslar and Braunschweig were members, warned King Ferdinand first on 10 May 1542 and then again on 25 June that they would be forced to defend the two cities. In a letter dated 29 June the elector informed the Wittenberg theologians of the League's plans and requested Melanchthon to translate into Latin for publication their declaration of war and its justification.[88] On 13 July they formally declared war. Faced by an overwhelmingly superior force, Duke Heinrich quickly stocked his strongest fortresses and then fled his territories to seek support from his Catholic allies. But help was not forthcoming. Without hardly striking a blow, the forces of the League of Schmalkalden occupied Braunschweig.

For Luther the victory was a gift of God, granted without regard for the Protestants' sins and unworthiness, and he warned the Protestants against becoming proud or boastful on its account.[89] To Anton Lauterbach, pastor in Pirna, he wrote that it was God who had done everything. "It is not human things that are happening today," he explained, "so there is the certain hope that all [these things] are the precursors and harbingers of that holy day of our redemption, Amen!"[90]

One of the first acts of Braunschweig's new rulers was to impose the Reformation.[91] A commission was established under the leadership of Johann Bugenhagen (who fourteen years earlier had provided a church order for the city of Braunschweig), a visitation was rapidly undertaken, and a new church order was established. These efforts were seriously undermined, however, by the conduct of the occupying soldiers and princes, who were busily exploiting the populace. Matters soon became so bad that, as Luther remarked anxiously to Justas Jonas, the population might well, given better conditions, prefer Duke Heinrich to the present plundering. For Luther this was another sign that the end was on its way.[92]

Although thwarted in his quest for military assistance, Duke Heinrich of Braunschweig-Wolfenbüttel was able to raise diplomatic support for his position. The emperor intervened, and there was talk of returning the land to the duke or to his son or, until the dispute could be resolved, to some third party appointed by the emperor. On 2 December 1543 the elector wrote Luther, Bugenhagen, and Melanchthon that he and the other League members feared that if they complied with the emperor's proposals they would be returning the "poor people of the territory" to the papacy. If they rejected the emperor's proposals, on the other hand, they risked war. What would the theologians advise?[93]

In their reply the Wittenbergers made an important, but difficult distinction. If the League believed that it had just cause for its seizure of Braunschweig, that it could rule it conscientiously and well, and that it had the capacity, with God's help, to defend it, then it was proper and necessary not only not to pass over the religious question in the negotiations but also, in the case the Catholics resorted to force, to defend the churches in the land as if they were their own churches. If, however, such defense was an "impossibility," then the Gospel counseled passive suffering of the Catholic persecution. They left it to the elector, the landgrave, and the rest of the League to decide which condition applied in the case of Braunschweig.[94]

The elector's counselors disagreed sharply with the Wittenbergers,[95] and managed to persuade him to take a bolder course. Although most of the south German cities who were members of the League took a position similar to that of the Wittenberg theologians, the city of Constance also recommended against surrendering Braunschweig under any circumstances. The Wittenbergers were accordingly forced to defend their original advice. Given a choice between turning Braunschweig over to third parties appointed by the emperor or waging war, what should a preacher advise? "Should he recommend a war in the fatherland for which no one could see a beginning, a middle, or an end?" They felt not. Fortunately from their standpoint, this choice did not have to be made, for the emperor, who needed the Protestants' support for his wars, was unwilling to push too hard. The negotiations in 1543 and 1544 came to nothing.

## Concerning the Captured Heinrich of Braunschweig

With the Peace of Crepy in September 1544 between Emperor Charles and King Francis, the emperor was finally able to turn his full attention—and full might—to affairs in Germany.[96] Conscious of the emperor's stronger position, the League finally reached an agreement with him in Worms in July 1545 to turn Braunschweig over to him. Duke Heinrich, who had participated in these negotiations, refused to sign the agreement, however, fearing with some reason that it might well lead to the loss of his lands to the Habsburgs. In the fall of 1545, with the assistance of French money, he assembled a large army. In September 1545 he reoccupied his dukedom. The Reformation was suppressed, the Protestant clergy expelled, and children baptized under the Protestant ritual were rebaptized. Although taken by surprise by the duke's swift reoccupation of his territory, the elector and the landgrave quickly armed and, supported by a contingent led by Duke Moritz of Albertine Saxony, marched into Braunschweig. On 21 October 1545 Duke Heinrich and his eldest son Karl Victor were taken captive by Landgrave Philipp without a fight. The exact circumstances of this capture remain unclear to this day, and, at least for a time, both the electoral court and Luther were uncertain about what had happened.[97]

At first Luther feared that this sudden surrender indicated collusion between Heinrich and the League. A letter from Cornelius Cordatus to Melanchthon, however, convinced him that God had directly terrified the League's opponents and had delivered Duke Heinrich and his son into the League's hands.[98] Soon afterwards, the elector, who in all likelihood feared that the landgrave might yield to the entreaties of the emperor and release Duke Heinrich and his son, requested Luther to write a treatise urging that Duke Heinrich not be released. Although Luther was quite willing to satisfy his elector's request, he balked at a suggestion by Chancellor Brück that he change a passage that might offend the emperor.* Despite later concern about this one problematic passage, Chancellor Brück was greatly impressed by Luther's efforts.

---

*The passage dealt with the raising of troops in the Netherlands for use in Germany against the Protestants (WA 54:402).

"It is an excellent, magnificient writing given directly to the man by the Holy Spirit," he wrote the elector, "for the histories and the sayings from Scripture that he cites are to be taken to heart and not despised." Luther's open letter *To the Elector of Saxony and the Landgrave of Hesse Concerning the Captured Heinrich of Braunschweig* came off the press at the end of December 1545.[99] As Brück also noted, the treatise was moderate in tone and word. There is a striking contrast between it and *Against Hanswurst* written four years earlier.

He had been admonished and implored by many great people, Luther began, to write the elector and the landgrave, asking them not to release Heinrich of Braunschweig "since God Himself had for once remarkably and wonderfully put an end to [Heinrich's] immeasurable tyranny and raging." These people were also concerned that if he were released, matters would be worse than before. He realized that the elector and the landgrave were aware of these considerations. But, given the likelihood that they would be besieged with impressive, forceful requests for his release from his "powerful and laudable relatives," others had persuaded him that a "faithful, submissive admonition" would not be despised.[100]

Such advice did not proceed from want of mercy, Luther insisted.[101] Even so, he could not recommend Heinrich's release. Heinrich had lost all trust. "Since God had now undertaken his punishment, who will be so bold as to release him before the proper repentance and true improvement occurs and trust is planted and [it] is truly recognized that God is placated?" That would be to tempt God, which was inadvisable.[102]

Drawing on Old Testament history, Luther warned the princes not to follow the example of King Ahab who released Ben-hadad after God had delivered him into his hands and so fell under God's wrath. "It is indeed a pitiful thing on earth," he observed, "that often a pious man must perish not on account of his own sins but on account of the sins of others in which he becomes a participant through great forbearance and kindness and all too indulgent compassion."[103] He then discussed the various "malicious ruses" undertaken by the Catholics against the Protestants from the time of the Diet of Worms in 1521 onward. Among other things, he disputed Catholic claims that the Catholic League was purely defensive. To release Heinrich would be to give comfort and encouragement to all of the papacy. They would argue that God had forced Heinrich's release.[104]

To the Catholic charge that the Protestants were unmerciful and lacked compassion Luther offered a two-fold reply. As for "secular or bodily mercy," the elector and the landgrave were demonstrating great mercy by capturing Duke Heinrich and not releasing him. They showed mercy to the duke by checking his "tyranny, blasphemy of God, and evil deeds," which was good for him; and they thereby rescued and protected pious and innocent people from the duke. As for "spiritual mercy," Luther urged Duke Heinrich to humble himself before God and demonstrate true repentance. The loss of his territory was but a mild penance in comparison to what his sins deserved. God would graciously accept true repentance, and it was even possible, as had happened to David in the Old Testament, that he would be returned to his rule.[105]

In the second part of his open letter Luther urged his Protestant readers not to boast or exalt themselves. It was God who had given them the victory against the papacy, not the Protestants' strength or piety.[106] Although one should honor God for the victory, this did not mean that arming should be neglected; only that reliance should not be placed on one's own arms but only on God. God could have defeated the papists without the Protestants' arms but he had allowed their arms to be his "masks" [*larven*] under which he took away the Catholic's courage and destroyed them with terror. To refuse to arm would be to tempt God. God would tolerate neither those who tempted him nor those who were presumptuous.[107] Luther closed the treatise with Psalms 64 and 76, directed against the Catholics.[108]

Both *Against Hanswurst* and the later open letter were published in support of electoral policy toward Duke Heinrich of Braunschweig-Wolfenbüttel. Although both treatises contained theological material, they served primarily political and propagandistic ends. Each was rhetorically well-suited to its particular task. *Against Hanswurst* was a contribution to a highly vituperative debate, which had already produced a succession of increasingly abusive treatises. Although *Against Hanswurst* represented an escalation in the level of vituperation, it was not greatly out of line in the controversy's trend toward greater abusiveness and was soon joined by equally if not more abusive treatises.

The open letter served a different end. While *Against Hanswurst* was written *against* Duke Heinrich, the open letter was written *to* Landgrave Philipp and his supporters. It aimed to persuade rather than abuse, so its rhetoric was different from *Against Hanswurst*, although the same Duke Heinrich was its subject.

The open letter is at best a minor work within Luther's corpus. But it does show that four years after writing *Against Hanswurst*, Luther could write a moderate, well-reasoned polemic against Duke Heinrich, if political circumstances made it advisable. This suggests that the abuse and coarseness found in the early treatise was a deliberate polemical tactic. When Luther was harsh and abusive, it was by choice.

## CHAPTER EIGHT

# Politics and Polemics:
# The Last Years

The last major polemic of Luther's life, his *Against the Papacy at Rome, Founded by the Devil*, was written at the request of his prince, Elector Johann Friedrich of Saxony. It was intended to inform Protestants of the true horror of the papal antichrist and to discredit the council convened at Trent. Its effect was to strengthen the resolve of the members of the League of Schmalkalden on the eve of the outbreak of the Schmalkaldic War.[1] At the 1544 Diet of Speyer the emperor had made significant religious concessions to the Protestants in exchange for their active support of his war against France and the Turks.[2] When the pope took the emperor to task for these concessions, the elector decided that Luther should respond.[3] It is clear from correspondence between the elector and Chancellor Brück that it was Luther's polemical talents rather than his theological acumen that the politicians hoped to employ. Indeed Brück remarked to the elector, once the papal council was proceeding, that it would be appropriate for Luther to "hew away with the ax, for which he has, by God's grace, a greater talent than other men."[4] This talent was amply displayed in the resulting treatise and its accompanying cartoons. Without question it is the most intentionally violent and vulgar writing to come from Luther's pen. It was also superb for rallying the faithful on the eve of battle.

Not surprisingly, Landgrave Philipp of Hesse, Elector Johann Friedrich's coleader of the League, was highly pleased by the treatise.[5] Others were more critical. The electoral delegates at the Diet of Worms (1545) reported that some at the Diet were offended by Luther's efforts. They felt that Luther had done more injury to himself through his harshness than had been suffered by his adversaries. This comment prompted the elector to come to Luther's defense. On

26 May 1545 he wrote the councilors that he could well imagine the emperor and others taking offense at the "bad words" [*bösen Wort*]. But Luther, he explained,

> has a special spirit that does not allow him to be moderate in this matter or otherwise [and] that without doubt [he] would not have used these bad words without special reasons. For this reason, too, he was specially awakened against the papacy to cast it to the ground. It is also not his intention to convert the papacy, which is also not possible; therefore for him good words are not necessary. It is his fixed intention to so display the papacy that everyone becomes aware of the abomination of the papacy and knows how to defend himself against it.[6]

When the councilors reported that the title page, which depicted the pope enthroned in the jaws of hell (Plate 1), was particularly offensive, the elector replied that Luther was endowed with a "singular spirit." For this reason, not he, Elector Johann Friedrich, nor his uncle, Elector Friedrich, nor his father, Elector Johann, were able to dictate what Luther wrote or did. Luther had a way of looking at things that would not occur to others, and therefore he, the elector, could not help it if there were those who took offense.

The elector's remarks about his lack of control over Luther's "singular spirit" were a bit disingenuous. It is true that he and Landgrave Philipp and the other leaders of the League could not dictate what Luther would publish. It is also true that Luther occasionally published treatises that the League may have found embarrassing.[7] On the other hand, as *Against the Papacy at Rome* proved, the elector and the landgrave had often in the preceding years counted on Luther's "singular spirit" to produce emotionally powerful treatises. In their polemical effect, if not in all their explicit arguments, these treatises supported the elector's and the League's policies and encouraged the members of the League.

Earlier chapters have examined other occasions where Elector Johann Friedrich or Landgrave Philipp of Hesse encouraged Luther to publish on matters of concern to the princes: on resistance to the emperor, on refusal of a papal invitation to a General Council, and on the quarrel with Duke Heinrich of Braunschweig-Wolfenbüttel. This chapter focuses on three additional publications that, whatever Luther's intention, served political interests: *Against the Bishop of Magdeburg, Cardinal Albrecht* (1539), *An Example How to Consecrate a Proper Bishop* (1542), and *Against the Papacy of Rome, Founded by the Devil* (1545).

## *Against the Bishop of Magdeburg, Cardinal Albrecht*

Luther's first direct contact with young Albrecht of Brandenburg, of the house of Hohenzollern, archbishop of Magdeburg and Mainz, administrator of Halberstadt, elector of the empire, and, from 1518, cardinal of the church, came with the famous letter of 31 October 1517 that called on Albrecht to restrain his indulgence preachers and sent him the Ninety-Five Theses on Indulgences.[8] From this inauspicious beginning the relations between the Primate of Germany and Martin Luther showed curious ups and downs. For instance, in 1521 while on the Wartburg Luther penned an attack on Albrecht and his relic collection at Halle with its associated indulgence. The treatise was held up by Georg Spalatin. But Luther's private letter to the cardinal, admonishing him to cease the sale of indulgences at Halle and threatening a published attack if he failed to so so, did reach the cardinal. It elicited a truly surprising reply. The cardinal assured Luther that the matter that had prompted Luther's letter had long been taken care of, described himself as a "poor sinful man" and a "useless, stinking clot" in need of God's grace, and expressed his willingness to suffer brotherly and Christian chastisement.[9] This humble letter appears to have had the desired effect: Luther was so mollified and impressed that he refrained from public attacks on the cardinal for the next six years. Four years later at the time of Luther's wedding, Albrecht, who as German's primate should have disapproved, instead sent the Luthers a spectacular wedding gift of twenty gulden. Luther refused to accept the gift, but Kathie, without informing her husband, put it quietly to good use. In 1526, at the instigation of his friend Johann Rühel, who was in Albrecht's service, Luther addressed an open letter to Albrecht, urging him to marry and to turn his bishopric into a secular princedom.[10] And in 1527, when Georg Winkler, Protestant preacher in Halle, was murdered, Luther attributed responsibility not to Albrecht but to the cathedral chapter at Mainz.[11]

As late as 1530 the cardinal was still enjoying a reputation for moderation among the Protestants, who hoped he might play a mediating role at the Diet of Augsburg. Luther himself entertained this hope and, to help it along, published in mid-1530 an open letter to the cardinal urging him to work among the Catholics to see that they maintained the peace and left the Protestants in their "true faith."[12]

But Luther was rapidly disabused of even his limited hopes for the cardinal. At the end of March 1531 Albrecht personally returned to Halle and began immediately to exert pressure on the Protestant-inclined citizens to return to Catholicism.[13] In his *Against the* ₍*Character*₎ *Assassin at Dresden*, which appeared in early May 1531, Luther used Albrecht's treatment of the Halle Protestants as an example of Catholic attempts to execute the hostile recess of the Diet of Augsburg. He even prepared notes for an open attack on Albrecht, but was dissuaded from carrying out his resolve by entreaties from Brück and Rühel and by the press of other work.[14]

During the next few years Luther occasionally made unfavorable comments about Albrecht and his religious policy, but it was a secular issue, the so-called Schönitz affair, rather than a directly religious one, that finally impelled Luther to publish in 1539 his last attack on Cardinal Albrecht.

Luther described his *Against the Bishop of Magdeburg, Cardinal Albrecht* (1539) as a matter of Christian duty.[15] In it he sought to vindicate the reputation of one Hans Schönitz of Halle, executed in 1535 by order of Cardinal Albrecht, and to indict the cardinal for a gross and deliberate miscarriage of justice. It was, as Luther himself put it, a "hard, sharp little book of reproach."[16] But in comparison to his other polemics in these later years, it is a moderate and restrained work. To be sure, there are antipapal asides and some abusive sections, but for the most part Luther's appeal is to reason and to a sense of justice, not to emotion and anticlerical sentiment. He obviously was holding back deliberately, for his two private letters to the cardinal on this issue were far harsher than this published rebuke.[17] Moreover, Luther published this treatise despite considerable pressure not to do so from influential relatives and supporters of the cardinal. All these factors have led a recent investigator to conclude—rightly I believe—that this treatise represents a fairly pure expression of Luther's ethical concerns.[18]

Its political significance lies, therefore, not in Luther's motivation in issuing the treatise, but in how the treatise fits into a larger dispute between Elector Johann Friedrich and Cardinal Albrecht. This dispute had been going on since 1534, and, in turn, was part of the much older contest between the houses of Wettin and Hohenzollern for leadership in central and northern Germany.[19] In this broader context Luther's attack on the cardinal's brand of justice served more than Luther's ethical concerns, although that may be all that *he* intended to do. A brief survey of the "Schönitz Affair" and its relation to the "Halle Matter," and a consideration of the timing of Luther's attack, should illumine the wider significance of this polemic.

In early 1534 Cardinal Albrecht exiled from the city of Halle a number of Protestant city council members. These exiles turned to Elector Johann Friedrich for succor, and Luther seconded their petition with a letter of his own.[20] This appeal allowed Johann Friedrich not only to come to the aid of coreligionists but also to renew a long-standing claim of his family. Among other titles he and his predecessors claimed the rights of burgrave [*Burggrafenrechte*] of Magdeburg. This office, he believed, gave him jurisdictional rights over the city of Halle including the right to exile subjects. The exiles from Halle encouraged him in this (probably exaggerated) notion of his authority over Halle.[21] Once Elector Johann Friedrich attempted to assert these alleged rights, and the authorities in Halle referred the matter to Cardinal Albrecht, the two electors began a lengthy attempt to resolve the conflicting claims through mediation. In the summer of of 1535 these negotiations were complicated by the addition of the so-called "Schönitz Affair," and Luther himself was drawn into the matter.

Hans Schönitz and his brother Anton were leading merchants in Halle.[22] Hans had been entrusted for years with various of the cardinal's public and private money matters. In 1531 he had become one of the cardinal's privy counselors with particular responsibility for Albrecht's public and private finances and for the luxurious building plans the cardinal had for Halle. In this capacity he was instrumental in inducing the estates of Magdeburg and Halberstadt to approve a tax to be used to cover both Albrecht's private and public debts. In the process, he employed all sorts of questionable tactics to squeeze as much money out of the estates as possible. When, in 1534, the cardinal made a request for new taxes, the estates countered with a demand for an accounting of the uses of the earlier tax, thereby placing the cardinal in a potentially embarrassing situation. On 6 September Hans Schönitz was suddenly arrested. Under torture he confessed to a variety of crimes involving the misuse of the cardinal's funds. This confession was presented to a court, which, without giving Schönitz the benefit of defense counsel, condemned him to be hanged. The execution followed immediately without the public or even Schönitz's family present. Right before his execution Schönitz recanted his confession and insisted on his innocence. This haste seemed all the more suspicious since Schönitz's family and friends had offered to make good any losses sustained by the cardinal on account of Schönitz's alleged misappropriations and had posted surety in an amount substantially greater than the alleged misappropriations. They had also petitioned the Imperial Chamber Tribunal to hear the case, which the Tribunal had offered to do. Of course Schönitz's execution made this appeal moot.

Schönitz was probably guilty of some of the charges against him, but one cannot easily escape the conclusion that Cardinal Albrecht had encouraged him in his questionable tactics and had then, when faced with the demand for an audit, sacrificed his trusted counselor in order to deflect certain criticism from himself. With Hans's execution, brother Anton no longer felt safe in Halle and fled, taking with him Hans's records. Another financial official in difficulties with the cardinal, Ludwig Rabe, also took flight.

Luther first became involved in the affair in the summer of 1535 when Anton asked him to request from the elector sanctuary and protection for himself. He indicated his willingness to submit to legal proceedings in his dispute with Albrecht.[23] The elector, seeing perhaps an opportunity to act on his claim of jurisdictional rights over Halle, immediately fulfilled the request.*

About this same time Ludwig Rabe, who had found sanctuary in Luther's own house, received a threatening letter from the cardinal informing him that if he did not desist from making statements about the executed Hans Schönitz, the cardinal would hold him responsible and see that he was punished.[24] Luther immediately sprang to Rabe's defense and, on 31 July, fired off a blistering letter to the cardinal.[25] He was writing, he explained, not because he harbored any hope of accomplishing anything useful but rather to satisfy his conscience before God and the world. He did not wish to be charged with supporting a wicked cause by his silence. He denied that Rabe was spreading rumors about the Schönitz affair and accused the cardinal of using the affair as a pretext for attacking him rather than Rabe. In no uncertain terms he requested the cardinal to leave him and his house guests alone and to desist from attempts to censure the private thoughts and words of others.[26]

But this was not the end of the affair. As Luther became more familiar with the details of the case, his anger grew. Finally, in early February 1536 he wrote the cardinal a furious letter full of specific accusations, many to be repeated later, and announced his intention to publish a treatise on the whole affair.[27]

At this point in 1536, however, an attack on Cardinal Albrecht would have caused difficulties not only for the cardinal but also for Elector Johann Friedrich, who harbored some hopes for a satisfactory settlement of his claims in Halle. And so, although preliminary negotiations in February and March were disappointing to the elector, he did take steps in mid-May, through Chancellor Brück, to prevent the publication of Luther's threatened attack.[28] Cardinal Albrecht also moved to head Luther off. First, he had Duke Georg of Anhalt attempt to placate Luther, but to no avail.[29] He also tried to employ the family connections of the Hohenzollerns. Various family members

---

*WABr 7:205. Shortly thereafter Luther also assisted with the task of authenticating the records Anton had brought with him and which he intended to publish in defense of his brother (WABr 7:277-79, 298).

asked Elector Johann Friedrich to forbid the publication of the treatise. Margrave Joachim II of Brandenburg spoke personally with Luther.[30] Duke Albrecht of Prussia sent his chancellor, Johann von Kreytzen, to discuss the matter with Luther, and the reformer and the duke exchanged several letters on the subject.[31] For the duke an attack on Albrecht was tantamount to an attack on the house of Brandenburg, and he warned that such an attack might hinder the progress of the Reformation.[32] This warning had to be taken seriously since Margrave Joachim II of Brandenburg was at this very time contemplating the introduction of the Reformation into his territories.

The Hohenzollern approach to Elector Johann Friedrich met with a certain amount of success. Johann Friedrich sent Chancellor Brück to Luther to convey the concern of the Brandenburg elector and his family, and probably Johann Friedrich's concern as well.[33] Certainly, as the elector's major representative and advocate in the negotiations, Brück was aware of the elector's interests in Halle and his desire not to alienate the cardinal at this juncture.[34] Luther did not back down in his reply to Brück,[35] but the treatise remained unwritten and unpublished.

Negotiations between the two sides dragged on into 1538. In February of that year the mediators reached an agreement that, on balance, was favorable to Elector Johann Friedrich. But when the required ratification of this agreement was not forthcoming from Cardinal Albrecht and various other obstacles arose, Elector Johann Friedrich began to suspect duplicity by Albrecht. Accordingly, by the summer of 1538 his hostility toward Albrecht and the Hohenzollerns generally had grown considerably.[36]

Meanwhile in Wittenberg that spring a young humanist and poet named Simon Lemnius had offered for sale a collection of Latin epigrams that, on the one hand, depicted several Wittenberg citizens in unflattering terms and, on the other hand, praised Cardinal Albrecht extravagantly. On 16 June Luther took to the pulpit to denounce Lemnius's work and to attack Cardinal Albrecht as a "shit-bishop, a false, lying man." He also announced his intention to publish a more elaborate attack on the cardinal.[37] Once again the Hohenzollern family rallied to the defense of the cardinal. The cardinal's nephew, Joachim I of Brandenburg, sent sharp complaints to Johann Friedrich, Landgrave Philipp, Johann of Küstrin, and the three princes of Anhalt, Johann, Georg, and Joachim.[38]

This time, however, Elector Johann Friedrich was considerably less inclined to inhibit Luther's pen.[39] The elector was so angry with what he considered to be the cardinal's duplicity relating to the February agreement that he even entertained the idea of employing force to resolve the matter.[40] In any case, during the negotiations of that fall and winter the elector hardened and increased his demands.[41] And even a last minute attempt by Georg of Anhalt failed to dissuade Luther from his resolve. In mid-December he took pen in hand and rapidly composed his promised attack. *Against the Bishop of Magdeburg, Cardinal Albrecht* appeared early in the new year.[42]

In the treatise Luther confronted explicitly Duke Albrecht of Prussia's insistence that an attack on Cardinal Albrecht would be an attack on the entire Hohenzollern family. He humbly requested all of the cardinal's many relatives not to interpret what he wrote as an attack on the whole family. He knew that there were many eminently pious, Christian, and praiseworthy princes in the family. After all, what could an emperor, a king, and all the world do about the fact than occasionally "a degenerate child and a prodigal son" came out of a praiseworthy family?*

For much of the rest of the treatise, Luther discussed the specifics of the Schönitz affair. The essence of his position, expressed at the outset and clearly repeated throughout the treatise, he summarized as follows:

> According to the divine prohibition of Job 31, the bishop should not have been nor was he permitted to be [Schönitz's] judge [since he was a party to the dispute, and] therefore his whole case is condemned as clearly invalid by divine law and judgment. Second, even if he were judge, still by God's prohibition he was not permitted to resort to torture since public law was not only offered to him but he was also summoned to it by his proper [superior] authority [the emperor through the Imperial Cameral Tribunal] whom he was obliged to follow according to God's word. And, in addition, he unnecessarily resorted to [this] dangerous, obscure [*finstern*] law, thereby tempting God and condemning himself, [and], beyond this, (as [is] reasonable [to assume]) throttling out a false confession, for he who tempts God

---

*Citing examples from history and Scripture, he asked how his contemporaries could expect to fare better than "such great holy people." "Listen, dear princes and lords, you must not place us wretched preachers in the position that if we chastise a rogue of your family, you would get angry about it and assert [that] we had slandered the whole family. Otherwise we would finally be forced to say to you in response that you should not turn your laudable, honorable lineage into a cover for ignominy, strengthening or defending blasphemy and vice under it. In such a case your reputation and honor would be disgraced on account of a prodigal son and [you] yourselves would become complicitous. One should not defame great princes and lords—that [I] say to them so that they do not defame themselves with unprincely crimes. For me it is easily said [Mir ists bald gesagt]: I cannot defame anyone if I speak the real truth . . ." (WA 50:399).

should justly fail and break his neck. Third, contrary to God's decree to accept the light, [he has] fled and kept to the darkness, thereby acknowledging by God's decree that he has an unjust, evil case and his opponent a just case because the latter sought and requested the light. Fourth, . . . he, as a single man, in the absence of the other man [Schönitz], speaks what he wishes contrary to God's command and decree: "No one ought to die on account of one [person] giving testimony against him." Thus [he] is condemned on all sides by God's four different decrees, and Hans Schönitz is redeemed and pronounced free.[43]

Each point of this four-count indictment—God's judgment on Cardinal Albrecht, Luther claimed, not his own—was discussed separately with evidence cited to prove Luther's contention.*

In his concluding paragraphs Luther once more justified his speaking out in the Schönitz affair. He had done so, he explained, first to fulfill his obligation before God. Second, he hoped with this statement that he might move the cardinal's conscience to repentance.

For Luther this treatise was clearly a matter of conscience, and the pressure that the various princes had put on him not to publish had caused him considerable distress [*Anfechtung*]. But, echoing Genesis, Luther insisted that he had had to speak, for Schönitz's blood cried out.[44]

For Elector Johann Friedrich, however, this treatise may have had other significance. The elector claimed rights of legal jurisdiction over Halle. The Schönitz Affair revealed how Cardinal Albrecht was capable of misusing his legal jurisdiction. Nevertheless, in 1536 and 1537, when negotiations between the cardinal and the Saxon elector still looked promising, Johann Friedrich was willing to discourage Luther from publishing his promised attack. In late 1538 Johann Friedrich

---

*Of more general interest in this lengthy discussion are Luther's pronouncements on the use of juridical torture, a practice abhorrent to us but common and accepted in his day (for the following, see WA 50:410-14). In the sixteenth century torture was considered a conscionable juridical means for ascertaining the truth, since it was believed that God would grant an innocent person the strength to endure the torture. As Luther saw it, however, torture was a questionable judicial procedure and should not be used unnecessarily. Some people, he explained, were of such a nature that they could not endure torture and would accordingly confess to crimes they had not committed so as to escape the torture. Luther then cited examples of people who were wrongly executed or punished on account of such forced confessions. He concluded that when there was recourse to public proceedings then such secret, exceptional proceedings should be avoided, for they tempted God, which was forbidden on pain of God's wrath and displeasure. This position hardly seems liberal today, since Luther did not rule out the use of torture in all cases, but for that time it was a step in the right direction.

*171*

saw considerably less reason to intervene on behalf of the cardinal or
the cardinal's relatives. There is no guarantee, of course, that Luther
would have listened to his prince, had the elector asked him not to
publish. The Lemnius Affair may have been the straw that finally
broke Luther's long-standing forbearance. It may be no more than
coincidence that the hardening of the elector's bargaining position
coincided with Luther's attack. But whatever Luther may have
intended to accomplish with this treatise, for Elector Johann Friedrich
it seems to have served as one more bargaining chip in his contest
with the house of Hohenzollern.*

## An Example How to Consecrate a Proper Bishop

On 6 January 1541 the absentee bishop of Naumberg died, setting
the stage for another confrontation between the old and new faiths.
The bishopric of Naumburg for the most part abutted on the territory
of Electoral Saxony. Although technically it was still directly under
the emperor [*reichsunmittelbar*], it had in the course of the fifteenth
century become increasingly tied to Saxony. In the treaty of 1485,
which divided Saxony into Albertine and Ernestine Saxony, the right
of secular protection over Naumburg [*Schutzvogteirechte*] was granted
to Ernestine Saxony. Throughout the early sixteenth century the

---

*The conflict over Halle between Cardinal Albrecht and Elector Johann Friedrich con-
tinued after 1539, and Luther found it necessary at one point to dissuade his elector
both from seizing Halle by force and from selling it outright to Cardinal Albrecht. For
a fine analysis of Luther's involvement in this later affair, see Eike Wolgast, *Die Wittenberger Theologie und die Politik der evangelischen Stände*, pp. 253-62.

With the Reformation thus secure in Halle, Cardinal Albrecht decided to move his
extensive relic collection from Halle to Mainz. Luther took this opportunity to publish
an anonymous satire on the collection and its transfer. This *New News from the Rhine*,
a two-page pamphlet, purported to be an announcement of the translation of the relics
from Halle to Mainz and a list of new acquisitions including "two feathers and an egg
from the Holy Spirit" and "half a wing from St. Gabriel, the Archangel." It also reported that the cardinal intended to bequeath to the collection "a whole fifth of his faithful,
pious heart" and "a whole half ounce of his truthful tongue" and that the pope had already promised forgiveness of all previous sins and all future sins for ten years to those
who honored these relics with a gulden (WA 53: 404-5). This little pamphlet was published in Halle by the printer Hans Frischmut. When he was then imprisoned for printing a "notorious libel," Luther wrote a letter to Jonas in Halle acknowledging his authorship of the pamphlet and threatening a major public attack on "the bride at
Mainz," Cardinal Albrecht (WABr 10:172-77). This threat was never carried out, however, for fear of causing the imprisoned Frischmut additional difficulties. Soon after-
ward Cardinal Albrecht died, as Luther viewed it, unrepentant to the end (WABr
10:225-26).

electors of Saxony had as one of their goals the incorporation of the bishopric into their territory; the bishop and chapter of Naumburg sought to prevent this. With the introduction of the Reformation into Electoral Saxony, issues of religion became intertwined with these political concerns. The chapter at Naumburg remained staunchly loyal to Catholicism while the electors encouraged the Protestant sympathies of the citizens of the city of Naumburg. By the mid-1530s Elector Johann Friedrich had decided that when the current bishop of Naumburg died, the chapter would not be allowed to elect a new bishop without the elector's knowledge and prior approval. The chapter, of course, harbored other plans. Once the bishop died, conflict between chapter and elector was inevitable.[45]

In Luther's house on the evening of 22 January 1541, Chancellor Brück told Luther, Jonas, and Bugenhagen that the elector, bothered by his conscience, wondered if he did not have the responsibility to reform the bishopric of the papal "abominations" whether or not the bishop had died.[46] On the one hand, he was considering attempting to induce the chapter, without the use of force, to select a bishop acceptable to him. On the other hand, he was also considering imposing, with force if necessary, the practice of previous centuries where the Christian community elected its bishop.

The three Wittenbergers addressed both these options in their written opinion. If the elector and his predecessors had a long-standing and firm right to insist that no bishop be elected without their knowledge and approval—the theologians claimed not to know exactly what the elector's rights were and Chancellor Brück had some doubts that this was a long-standing right—then he should exercise this right and force the chapter to elect a bishop capable of carrying out his duties in a Christian fashion. If he lacked a firm, long-standing right, or did not wish to exercise it, the elector should make a request, even a forceful request [*preces potentes oder armatae*], that they consider a person acceptable to him. If, however, the canons would not accede to this request but instead continued with their election, it was advisable that the elector patiently wait for another occasion, which God would certainly grant. Having framed this opinion, the Wittenbergers learned the next day that the chapter had gone ahead and elected a new bishop without waiting for the elector's consent.

In the Naumburg chapter's two notes to the elector informing him of their action they failed even to mention whom they had elected. In fact they had elected Julius von Pflug, provost of the chapter at Zeitz, a learned humanist from a respected Saxon noble family. Pflug belonged to the reforming party within Catholicism and was the probable author of the Meissen Book. Although desirous of reaching a reconciliation with the Protestants, he was unwilling to compromise what he recognized as the substance of the Catholic faith. Of all the possible candidates for the position of Catholic bishop of Naumburg, he was the most likely to cause the elector considerable trouble. But for the time being he did not accept the chapter's election, requesting instead time to consider its call. For a year he delayed his decision.

He was not completely inactive in the meanwhile, however, nor was the elector. In July Pflug obtained an order from the emperor asserting the *Reichsunmittelbarkeit*, the independence from Saxony, of the bishopric and warning the elector not to encroach on this independence. This did not deter the elector from appointing in September a "provisional" lay administrator for the secular affairs of the bishopric. This administrator was to control the secular administration of the bishopric until a bishop was elected who was acceptable to the elector. This step represented the effective subordination of the bishopric to the territorial sovereignty of the elector. Also in September the cathedral was forcibly opened to Protestant preaching.

In October and November, 1541, the Wittenberg theologians were called upon to make recommendations concerning Naumburg. In their first opinion, written when there was still some hope that the chapter might agree to elect a person more acceptable to the elector, the theologians advised that the chapter be maintained.[47] Their detailed recommendations give the strong impression that they were worried that the elector harbored plans to secularize the bishopric and to appropriate its income for nonecclesiastical purposes.* Although they recognized that the chapter and bishopric had to be independent of the papacy, they recommended no other changes in the procedures for electing a bishop. The elector should maintain his right of "oversight" as the bishopric's patron to see that qualified people were chosen in the election of canons as well as the bishop. They did not spell out further this right of "oversight," leaving open the possibility of developments in the direction of the control of the bishop and chapter by the secular lord. There is no indication, however, that they intended such developments to occur. On the contrary, the whole opinion tends in the opposite direction.[48]

---

*This impression is reinforced by their recommendations concerning the bishop himself. They stressed that it was of the greatest importance that the chapter not elect a "youngster"—a favorite tactic of princes for seizing control of a bishopric—but rather a man who had a mind for Christian doctrine and proper ecclesiastical practice. They suggested Prince Georg of Anhalt as a well-suited candidate. As for Nicholas von Amsdorf, who apparently had been mentioned as a possible candidate, they expressed doubt whether he would accept such a call.

On 25 October it became clear that the chapter would not agree to a new election of a bishop more acceptable to the elector. Under these circumstances the elector was determined as sovereign and patron of the bishopric to appoint a Protestant bishop. To this end, he sent Chancellor Brück to Wittenberg to solicit the Wittenbergers' approval for this plan.[49] The Wittenbergers responded with an opinion, now lost, in which they apparently recommended once again that the matter of the bishop and his election be left as it was. Instead, the gradual reformation of the territory, independent of its Catholic bishop, should be continued. As for the elector's plan, they apparently argued that such a course would be extraordinarily dangerous and would lead to political complications. They recommended against it.

The elector found their opinion unacceptable and, through his counselors, suggested to the theologians in some detail how a Protestant bishop might be elected and established.[50] The theologians, however, remained unconvinced of the wisdom of this course. In their reply they stressed how the papists could use such an act—touching as it did on the bishops' estate without which, the "true and serious papists" believed, there could be no sacrament, no forgiveness of sins, no church—to induce secular rulers to take action against the elector. They also voiced some doubt that all the members of the League of Schmalkalden would support the elector in such a course. Instead they recommended once more that the issue of the bishop be allowed to continue as it was. The election of a Protestant bishop was not crucial. After all, the elector had already appointed a lay administrator and, in the ecclesiastical realm, the Catholic bishops had long ceased to carry out their offices. They also repeated their recommendations for the establishment of a proper consistory. Their fears that the elector might simply secularize the bishopric and turn its income to nonecclesiastical purposes were voiced directly. They suggested that most of the income would continue to be needed for the administration of the bishopric, for the establishment of schools, hospitals, and the consistory, and for the support of the churches. What was left over could be used for other needs. They conceded that it was important to control the income of the ministers so that they did not indulge in a "papistic" style of life. The papistic character of the bishopric should also not be maintained. On the other hand, in the long run it would also not work for the princes simply to abolish the bishopric and take its endowments and let the pastors and schools go to waste and maintain no church government, no ordination, no consistory, and no visitation. This would frighten sensible men from the ministry.[51]

Once again the elector and his counselors rejected the theologians' advice.[52] Finally, in meetings at Torgau, the Wittenberg theologians acquiesced to the elector's plan. "Since it is thought that it is advantageous that the bishopric have appointed a person who should have the episcopal name and office," the Wittenbergers began, and with this choice of words suggested perhaps their lingering doubts, then it was good for the people to know what they should believe. To this end the theologians set down what they viewed as the best justification for the proposed action and what steps should be taken in carrying out the elector's plan. First, it was true and undeniable, they argued, that the elector was obliged to prevent the people in the bishopric from being deflected from the gospel, which surely would occur if Pflug were bishop. This justified the elector's contesting Pflug's election. Now with its election of Pflug and its refusal to undertake a second election, the chapter had lost its right of election, for it was only willing to elect papists who were persecutors of true doctrine. But the church without a bishop and a territory without a government could not stand. Accordingly, the elector, as patron, should exercise his authority to see that the churches and territory be taken care of. At the same time he should not overstep his authority as patron. What he should do is assemble the city councils and the territorial nobility and propose to them a qualified person for bishop. If the elector and these assembled individuals could agree on a person, then such agreement would be a true election "for in previous times the election was accomplished by the foremost [individuals] from the populace and by the governing authority." They recommended that the bishop be publicly ordained by several preachers with a simple laying on of hands and with prayer and with no other "spectacle." Once again they stressed that the bishop must be a highly qualified individual, not conceited or disputatious. The lay administrator could continue to administer the secular affairs of the bishopric. Both the bishop and the administrator should be informed of the income they could expect for themselves and for carrying out their appropriate duties. This should be done in such a way that made clear to the estates that a proper government remained, not just the appearances of one.[53] With these last remarks the Wittenbergers once more underlined their concern that the bishopric not simply be appropriated and its resources turned to nonecclesiastical ends.

By the fall of 1541 Elector Johann Friedrich had already settled on Nicholas von Amsdorf as his candidate for Protestant bishop of Naumburg. Neither Amsdorf himself nor the Wittenberg theologians were enthusiastic about this choice, but the elector eventually had his own way.[54] Amsdorf's ordination was scheduled for 20 January 1542, the anniversary of Pflug's election. Everything came to a head at the same time. On 11 January Pflug finally informed the Naumburg chapter that he accepted its election. On 17 January a proclamation from Pflug was posted at the cathedral announcing his acceptance of the chapter's election and calling on the bishopric's inhabitants to remain faithful to their true bishop. On the 18th the elector accompanied by Luther, Amsdorf, Melanchthon, and a large following entered Naumburg. Two days later Amsdorf was consecrated bishop.

In the negotiations preceding the election of Amsdorf, the Naumburg council, while making its Protestant sympathies clear, raised a very pertinent question. Could it could properly agree to this new election seeing that it had sworn in its oath of homage to the now deceased bishop that, in the case of a vacancy, it would remain obedient to the chapter as its governing authority? Not surprisingly, the elector thought it could. When, after some negotiations on this point, the estates of the bishopric requested a three-week delay in the proceedings so that they might seek to release themselves from this oath, the elector became greatly displeased and the estates were admonished to cease their resistance. The elector informed them that he intended the next day, 20 January, to proceed with an election together with the clergy, the congregation, and those estates who supported him. At this point he also announced to the estates his choice of Amsdorf as bishop.

That evening, the nineteenth, at the elector's suggestion (and according to a plan apparently discussed with Luther),[55] the estates sought out the Wittenberg theologians for advice on this matter. Luther's attempt to settle their doubts is a fascinating theological justification of a revolutionary political (and religious) act. It illustrates most dramatically that his view of the papacy as the antichrist might, as it did in the case of resistance, allow him to modify his normal teaching concerning the obedience owed secular authority. According to Melanchthon's notes,[56] Luther argued that "if a ruling bishop persecuted the gospel in one article or more, then the chapter along with the patron, or, if the chapter refuses, the patron along with the estates are obliged to depose the same persecutor if he does not mend his ways, irrespective [of the fact] that the estates as subjects had sworn allegiance to the bishop." Now since it was obvious that obligations were not binding in this case, the same was true in relation to the chapter if it would not undertake a proper election or lent support to a persecutor. In such a case the chapter was to be held in the same regard as was the persecutor. The estates along with the patron were obliged to resist the intentions of such a chapter and to provide the churches with proper ministers and rulers, just as each authority

177

was obliged to provide its own pastors irrespective of all obligations or sovereignty [*Hoheit*]. The command to teach properly and to hold proper divine services took precedence over all other commands.

It was also clear, Luther continued, that the estates neither could nor should hinder the patron from contesting the improper election. And if the chapter had lost its right of election, then it was certain that all legitimacy for electing [*Gerechtigkeit zu wählen*] devolved upon the church, that is, upon the estates along with the patron. This was the church according to ancient law and the first institution, as was expressed in one of the canons of the council of Nicaea and in many histories.

Luther then turned to the weighty objection that although it might be that one should abandon improper teachers and depose them, one should not withdraw from secular obedience or feudal tenure to the bishop and chapter. He replied:

> This is certain, that the parochial property [*Pfarrgüter*] and legitimacy [*Gerechtigkeit*] should and must follow the service, as the gospel says, 'To the worker belongs his wage' [Luke 10:7]. Thus this property was not given for the pomp and idleness of the canons. Rather it was given for the required provision of church offices, about which the text in the Codex [of the Canon law] commands in clear words: 'He who does not perform his office should not enjoy his prebend and should be deposed.' And in this regard it appertains to [the duties] of the patron and estates to take cognizance.
>
> In addition to all this, one knows that the adversary itself wishes to have these two items undivided—their idolatry and worldly power or properties—and at bottom does not seek the maintenance of proper church government. Rather he primarily and actually [seeks] the suppression of proper doctrine and maintenance of its improper way along with its magnificence.
>
> Since they then do not allow the episcopal office to be separated from the secular [office] and we cannot allow them, as persecutors, the episcopal office, therefore others [that is, the parochial property] must also follow the proper bishop. [This was the procedure] described in the Decretals, when the Donatists were ousted from their church properties as [ones] who were no more in the proper office, and these same properties were devoted to the proper church government, as was undoubtedly the intention of the founders. Numerous such examples are to be found in the histories.[57]

In closing Luther warned the estates of the likely repercussions that would follow the election of a Protestant bishop.[58]

Ostensibly confined to the religious sphere, this argument had profound implications for the secular realm. Not only did it justify disobedience towards false teachers and advocated their removal by secular authorities, but it also justified disobedience in both spiritual and secular matters towards a class of secular rulers—the ecclesiastical prince or ecclesiastical corporation, a large group ruling a goodly portion of Germany in the sixteenth century. What is more, it advocated their removal and replacement by the estates and patron. Radical as it was in light of Luther's general advocacy of obedience by Christians in secular matters even to a nonbelieving or persecuting secular authority, it was confined to those rulers whom, Luther argued, directly possessed their goods and rule because of, and for the sake of, the church. This argument bears a resemblance to the argument developed in Luther's 1539 *Concerning the Three Hierarchies*.[59] In both arguments it appears to be the blasphemous claim by the rulers to be acting as Christians that deprives them of their claim to authority. Naturally, this argument had potentially revolutionary implications for the political relations of Catholic and Protestant in Germany.

Whatever the problematic aspects or implications of this argument, it managed to convince the Naumburg estates. The next morning, the twentieth, the council and estates indicated their approval to the elector. With this the "election" was completed. The "first ordination of a Protestant bishop on German soil"* took place on 20 January 1542.

On the morning of the ordination the Naumburg estates had requested "for the good of the common man" that the elector have published the "whole negotiations" or at least Luther's opinion on the matter.[60] The elector agreed to this request. While in Naumburg Luther was asked by the elector to pen such a treatise and he readily

---

*Spalatin's expression, cited by Brunner, *Nikolaus von Amsdorf*, p. 61n37. Luther preached "a very forceful and consoling sermon" in which, among others things, he spoke of the great burdens of the episcopal office and of how God was able to accomplish His purpose even through the "weak" individuals who filled this office. He also admonished his listeners to remain faithful to the decision that they had reached that day (WA 49:XXVII-XXXIX). It was also Luther, assisted by several of the superintendents from neighboring areas, who actually ordained Amsdorf (for a detailed analysis of the ordination and its meaning, see Brunner, *Nikolaus von Amsdorf*, pp. 60-76). The form of the ordination followed closely the form used for the ordination of ministers, indicating the essentially similar character of both offices in the ministry of the word. Following the ordination came the oath of homage, which in its studied ambiguity left open the extent of the authority of the lay administrator appointed by the elector (Brunner, *Nikolaus von Amsdorf*, pp. 76-78). It gave a foretaste of the later difficulties between Amsdorf and the lay administrator in the negotiations on the formulation of this oath.

promised to do so. The elector reminded him of this promise on 31 January and again on 20 March.[61] With this latter letter he also enclosed a recent treatise by Pflug addressed to the Imperial Diet at Speyer. Since most of his treatise was already finished, Luther was able only in the closing pages to address some of Pflug's arguments. The promised treatise, entitled *An Example How to Consecrate a Proper Christian Bishop*, appeared by the end of March.[62]

Despite the title, the treatise deals only cursorily with the actual election and ordination of Amsdorf and thus provides the reader with very little example of how a proper Christian bishop should be consecrated. Moreover, its arguments in defense of the election and ordination of a Protestant bishop in Naumburg do not go beyond or develop the arguments used on 19 January 1542 to convince the Naumburg estates and, in a significant area, fall short of the argument advanced then. Instead, it addresses, often in wandering and verbose fashion, three questions:

> . . . whether in this [matter] we had the right, in opposition to the chapter's free election (as it is called), to elect another bishop and thereby to deprive them of their free election and to drive them from their rightful possession; and whether the members and estates of the bishopric were able to pay homage and swear [allegiance] to another without violation of their oath and obligation made to the chapter in the case of a dead bishop (as they say); finally, whether it is right to accept consecration or ordination from such a damned heretic.[63]

The "damned heretic" was, of course, Martin Luther.*

To the first question, Luther asserted, reply was given by the first three commandments of the first table of the Ten Commandments, as well as by commandments in the New Testament such as "Beware of false prophets who come to you in sheep's clothing but within they are ravening wolves" [Matthew 7:15]. Man was accordingly forbidden false Gods, false use of God's name, false worship and preaching. With such a "thunderbolt of divine judgment" not only bishop and chapter of Naumburg but also the pope, cardinals, and all else in their government [regiment] were not only deposed but also eternally

---

*Luther also prefaced his discussion of these three questions with the assertion that he would leave to the jurists of ecclesiastical law their "disputations" "since I do not know anything about it and also do not desire to know [anything]." Instead, he wished to speak of the matter as a theologian "or (if they wish to have it so) as a heretic and apostate papist" (WA 53:233). In this remark we may detect a lingering echo of his disapproval of the whole affair.

damned to hell along with all who obeyed them.[64] This was the essence of Luther's argument, spun out over several pages and richly decorated with abuse and his usual attacks on the papal claims and practices.[65]

On the second point, whether the estates were forsworn, Luther argued that issue was not the oath itself but to whom the oath was sworn. Where there was no true bishop—where, in other words, the estates' oath and homage were received under false pretenses—there was no true oath and hence no possibility of being forsworn. Taunting the Catholics for the objections they would raise to this argument, Luther cited canon law, common sense, and experiences out of his own past to prove that oaths received under false pretenses were null and void.[66] The oath the estates had made was to a true bishop, and once they had elected a true bishop, this oath was once more in force. The oath and its associated obedience had not changed, only the person who was bishop.*

On the third point, whether it was right for Amsdorf to have accepted ordination from a "damned heretic," namely Luther, Luther confessed that he was like all men a sinner and what was good in him was not his own but God's and Christ's gifts. Still, he understood the holy Scripture and how to consecrate a Christian bishop much better than did the papists. In any case, their own canon law taught that a bishop was properly consecrated even if he were ordained by a simoniac or heretic. His conscience was clear, Luther announced, for not only he but also the bishops or pastors of the neighboring areas had participated in the consecration and laying on of hands, as was the practice in the ancient church and as was taught in the ancient canons. In addition, the church and the people as well as the territorial princes and protectors had also been personally present at the consecration.[67]

The seizure of the bishopric of Naumburg by Elector Johann Friedrich and the subsequent election of Nicholas von Amsdorf as its first Protestant bishop were acts carried out by political entities—the territorial sovereign and the estates—operating in an ostensibly religious capacity. The elector was acting in his capacity as patron and "emergency bishop," the estates as representatives of the Naumburg congregation. The actual congregation was also drawn into the process during

---

*WA 53:246-56. The elector, Luther explained, as the territorial sovereign and protector of the bishopric, had been forced by the chapter's behavior to act as an "emergency bishop" [*Not Bischove*] to maintain the holy gospel and the recognized truth. The elector and his brother, Duke Ernest, had promised, however, to maintain the bishopric as before and not to take anything from it.

Amsdorf's ordination when they were asked to signify their approval with a loud amen, which they reportedly did. Despite these considerations, which do possess a certain plausibility,[68] it is hard to escape the conviction that the takeover of the bishopric of Naumburg by Electoral Saxony was primarily a political act, carried out by political entities. The subsequent negligent treatment of Amsdorf by the electoral government—he was granted little real authority and wholly insufficient revenue to carry out his episcopal functions—gave graphic evidence of the elector's real priorities. The Wittenberg theologians had in their various opinions repeatedly warned against just such an exploitation of the bishopric, but in vain.

Having voiced his objections and reservations in private, Luther had then given full public support to his elector's plans. In his conversation with the Naumburg estates and in his *An Example How to Consecrate a Proper Christian Bishop*, Luther did all he could to give a theological rationale and justification for the elector's actions. Fundamental to his argument, both in his oral presentation and his *Example*, is his conviction that the papacy is the antichrist. This conviction allowed him to develop an argument before the Naumburg estates that had potentially revolutionary implications for the political relations of Catholics and Protestants in Germany. Luther himself may have had second thoughts about his argument, and in any case he retreated significantly from his earlier, oral position when he penned his *Example*. Even then the apocalyptic context is clear: the whole papal government [*regiment*] fell under the divine condemnation of the false prophets, and oath to a papal bishop, that is, a false bishop, was no oath at all.

Luther and his colleagues had been pushed by the elector into supporting his policy regarding Naumburg. His later bitterness over the handling of Naumburg was, in light of the support he had finally given the elector's project, quite understandable.[69] He had accommodated himself to the political plans of the elector and his counselors—the "silver and gold jurists" whom Luther found so repugnant—and had been subsequently burned.

## Against the Papacy at Rome

At the heart of Luther's *Against the Papacy at Rome, Founded by the Devil* lies his intense conviction that he was attacking the antichrist itself. Old age and illness may have made Luther less restrained and more verbose.* But he was still able to follow a clear outline and develop

---

*Luther himself remarked that his age may have made him verbose (WA 54:283f.).

a coherent historical, logical, and, above all, scriptural attack on the papacy. No, the explanation for this treatise is found not in his health but in his view of the world. It was his goal in this treatise to depict in the most vivid colors possible the true horrifying nature of the papacy. The pope was not and could not be the head of the Christian church, the vicar of Christ. "Rather [he] is the head of the accursed church of the very worst rascals on earth; vicar of the devil; an enemy of God; an opponent of Christ; and a destroyer of the church of Christ; a teacher of all lies, blasphemy, and idolatries; an arch-church-thief and church-robber of the keys [and] all the goods of both the church and the secular lords; a murderer of kings and inciter of all sorts of bloodshed; a brothel-keeper above all brothel-keepers and all lewdness, including that which is not to be named; an antichrist; a man of sin and child of perdition; a true werewolf."[70] Luther would avail himself of every means of driving this conclusion home: logic, historical analysis, exegesis of Scripture, and verbal abuse.

The occasion for this "last testament" against the papal antichrist was a papal letter to Emperor Charles V. In exchange for active support from the Protestants in his war against France and the Turks, the emperor at the 1544 Diet of Speyer made significant concessions in the religious sphere. In the final recess of the Diet, dated 10 June 1544, the emperor, using the Protestant formula, announced that a complete settlement of the religious division could only be accomplished in a "general, Christian, free council in the German nation." Since it was uncertain when such a council would occur, it was proposed that another imperial diet should be held in the autumn or winter. At this diet a plan for a "Christian reformation" previously drawn up by "learned, good, honorable, and peace-loving persons" would be considered. In the meanwhile the emperor renewed on his own authority the religious standstill and suspended all legal proceedings against the Protestants at the Imperial Cameral Tribunal. All holders of ecclesiastical properties "without regard for which religion they are" were guaranteed their income, which was to be used to support the "necessary ministry of the churches, parishes, and schools, as well as the alms and hospitals." All recesses against the Protestants passed by previous diets were also suspended.[71]

The papacy was understandably upset when it learned of these concessions. The pope instructed Cardinals Crescenzio, Cortese, and Pole to draft an admonitory letter to the emperor. After rejecting a first draft that took the emperor to task in unusually sharp language, the pope had a more moderate brief composed. It was dated 24 August 1544. Addressing the emperor as his "most dear son," the pope said that he was writing on account of the recess of the Diet of Speyer, prompted by the example of Eli who, by failing sufficiently to chastise his erring sons, brought God's wrath down upon himself. The pope stated that the emperor had grossly overstepped his office and encroached on authority reserved solely to the Apostolic See in presuming to consider, without even mention of the pope's name, a general council or a national council or even an imperial diet at which religious matters would be discussed and resolved by laity and even heretical teachers. Numerous examples from Scripture and church history were adduced to show how God had punished such presumption in the past. Unable to tolerate the emperor acting as "head" in such matters, the pope greatly desired the emperor's assistance as "arm." Also, as he pointed out in his own defense, he had summoned a council to Trent, but no one had appeared. Even so, he had only suspended the council, and so with peace the council could reopen. In the meanwhile the emperor had to desist from infringing on the ecclesiastical sphere, from discussing religious questions at the diet, and from disposing of ecclesiastical property. Moreover, he had to cancel all the agreements made with the Protestants. If he failed to do all this, the pope would be obliged to take sterner measures.[72] A copy of this brief, perhaps through the initiative of Imperial Chancellor Granvella, very quickly reached the Protestants and Martin Luther.*

Even more embarrassing for the papacy, a copy of the earlier, sharper draft of the letter also fell into the hands of the German Protestants, apparently forwarded to them by Protestants in Venice.[73] On 9 January 1545 Luther wrote Amsdorf that he had seen the papal bull or letter but had thought it a lampoon.

> Now I think otherwise after it has been disseminated among all the courts. I am utterly convinced that if this letter is genuine the papists are promoting some great and extraordinary monstrosity, that is, the pope would rather publicly worship the Turk and Satan himself . . . than allow himself to be brought into order or reformed. . . . I shall not be idle, however; and I shall depict that bull in its [true] colors, if my health and time permits.[74]

The letter Luther refers to here, the sharper draft, made many of the same points as were made in the letter actually sent to the emperor, only in a more threatening and harsh manner. The papal claim to supreme authority over doctrine as St. Peter's successor and Christ's

---

*WA 54:196. It would appear that even imperial councilors were not above employing Luther's polemical talents when it suited their political interests!

vicar on earth were forcefully asserted. The emperor was also reminded that the command "feed my sheep" was made not to the
emperor but to Peter and his successors. Attention was drawn to the
fact that the emperor owed his position to the translation of the
Roman Empire from the Greeks to the Germans by the pope, Christ's
vicar. The emperor was directly threatened with God's wrath if he did
not renounce the objectionable provisions of the Speyer recess. And
the pope promised the emperor the council he sought, but with a very
significant qualification:

> Do you want a council? We give you a council, and there shall
> be no delays interposed by us that keep it from occurring. Do
> you want it in Germany? We ourselves would not deny [this] pro-
> vided that it can be free and Christian there. For in order for it
> to be Christian, it is necessary that the heretics do not join there
> as if they were part of any council since they no longer are and
> have separated themselves [from the church]. But it is not for the
> emperor or anyone else to investigate and to declare who are of
> this sort [heretics] but for us, who have received this [power of]
> judgment from Christ himself.

The emperor's task, then, in order that the council might be free, was
to seek peace and to leave the controverted issues to the examination
of the council.[75]

As we have seen, Elector Johann Friedrich and Chancellor Brück
encouraged Luther to publish a reply to the papal letters.[76] Luther
needed no prodding.[77] For several months in early 1545 rumors concerning this polemic circulated widely. On 21 March Luther informed
Landgrave Philipp of the imminent publication of the treatise, and on
25 or 26 March the publication was completed.[78]

This treatise is the most violent and vulgar to issue from Luther's
pen. Yet it contains more than ranting and railing, and shows that
even at the end of his life Luther could produce a persuasive argument
using historical examples, logic, and a shrewd exegesis of Scripture.
Both his arguments and his abuse can only be suggested in the following brief summary.

In his lengthy and extraordinarily abusive introduction to the
treatise Luther attacked the pope's two letters, denounced the papal
conception of a council, explained the Protestant call for a "free
Christian council in German lands,"* and defended the emperor's

---

*His definition is worth noting: By "free" the Protestants meant that everyone, and
especially appointed delegates, should at all times be free to say, complain, and respond
to whatever served to improve the church and to root out scandals and abuses. But
the "Roman school for scoundrels and its schoolmaster" perverted the word "free" to

right to convene a council without the pope's permission.[79] Then in part one Luther examined "whether it is true that the pope at Rome is the head of Christendom, above councils, emperor, angels, and everything else as he boasts." This section is by far the lengthiest in the treatise, and also the best organized and argued. In comparison, parts two and three, dealing with whether the pope was subject to the judgment of anyone else and whether he had translated the Roman Empire to the Germans, are disproportionately short, only a few pages each in length, and rely more on polemic than persuasion. Luther appears simply to have run out of energy and time by the time he came to parts two and three.

Luther began part one with a historical argument designed to demonstrate that the first pope was Boniface III (r. 607), who was acknowledged by the regicide King Phocas to be head of all the churches. His predecessors had been no more than bishops of Rome, he claimed.[80] Next Luther attempted to prove by logic "that the papal abomination did not come from God nor did it begin in God's name, but rather through God's wrath as punishment for sins [it was] founded by the devil and came into the church in his name." First, it had not been founded by secular authority, which in any case did not have the authority to act in God's realm. The papacy itself, he pointed out, denied that it was founded by secular authority. Second, it had also not come from spiritual authority, that is, from Christendom and bishops or from councils, all of which also lacked the authority to establish it. In this regard too, he indicated, the papacy denied that it

---

mean that they would be free, that nothing would be spoken or undertaken against them, and that their life and ways would be confirmed. The princes and estates used the word "Christian" to mean a council "where one should deal with Christian matters and through Christian people in accordance with Scripture." According to "his Hellishness along with his school for scoundrels," however, "Christian" meant nothing more than "papal" and whatever they judged and concluded. The pope branded as heretics all who disputed this and barred them from participation in the council, despite the fact that these heretics included God the Father, Son, and Holy Spirit, and the Holy Church. It followed that God, and especially the Holy Spirit through whom, it was boasted, the council was assembled and all decisions were reached, could not come to Trent. St. Paul would also have to remain out of the "holy, free, Christian council of the holy Madame Pope Paula III." The pope distorted the third word "German" or "in German lands" by insisting that Emperor Charles had to provide peace and security for the council. Then by fabricating a danger where there wasn't any, he had a ready excuse for not holding the council that he could blame on the emperor and the estates. In fact, Luther concluded, the pope never wanted to hold a council in German lands. There were many excuses he could avail himself of. Twice he had used the Turks, and he could also always incite the French to harass the emperor, as he had most zealously done in the last twenty years (WA 54:210-17).

was founded by bishops or councils. But because God had ordained no estate on earth to rule, except these two, namely the spiritual and the secular, then one had to conclude, he argued, that the papal estate came not from God but from the devil.[81]

Turning from "historical" and "logical" arguments to "Scriptural" ones, Luther tackled first the papal interpretation of Matthew 16:18-19:

> You are Peter, and on this rock I will build my church, and I will give you the keys to heaven. Whatever you bind on earth shall be bound in heaven and whatever you loose on earth shall be loosed in heaven.

The Christian interpretation of Matthew 16 had to be understood on the basis of Christ's words in John 6:63, "My words are spirit and life."

> Accordingly, these words of Matthew 16 must also be spirit and life, namely, when he says, 'I will build my church on this rock.' Here 'build' must be a spiritual, living building. 'Rock' must be a living, spiritual rock. 'Church' must be a spiritual, living congregation, yes, living in such fashion that it all lives eternally. So this rock is now the son of God, Jesus Christ, alone and no one else, [and] concerning whom the Scripture is full, and we Christians know well. To build or be built on this rock cannot be accomplished with laws or works, for Christ cannot be grasped by hands or works but must come through faith and the word. Thus even the church cannot make itself spiritual or living through itself or its own works, but rather it is built through faith on this rock, and so [is] spiritual and living so long as it remains built on this rock, that is, until eternity. . . . And in summary, this text, Matthew 16, speaks of faith, that he who believes is built on this rock, as one says, he who trusts God has built well.[82]

He then supported this interpretation with corroborating passages from 1 Peter and Ephesians and with a discussion of the context in which Matthew 16:18-19 occurred, drawing freely on other scriptural passages to illustrate and reinforce his interpretation.[83]

Next Luther took up the papal interpretation of the "keys of heaven" which were promised Peter. First, he stressed, Christ was not speaking here of laws or of our works but of his works, namely, the retention and remission of sins. Second, the keys and the associated power to bind and loose sins were not given to the apostles and saints to establish their lordship over the church but solely for the good of and use of sinners. Finally, the keys were not given to St. Peter alone but to all Christians.* As far as binding and loosing was concerned, Christ, Luther said, was speaking of the binding and loosing of sins. But the pope applied it to churches, bishops, emperors, and kings and translated this into the claim that the whole world owed him obedience. Luther then enumerated some of the "great damage" that had been done by the papal interpretation of the power of the keys.[84]

Having finished with Matthew 16, Luther took up the papal interpretation of John 21:15, "Feed my sheep." On the basis of numerous scriptural citations, Luther contended that Christ had addressed this command not only to Peter but to all the apostles and disciples. He also disputed the papal reading of this passage that saw Christ giving Peter supervision over *all* the sheep. This was, he said, an unwarranted interpolation. Finally, he pointed out that the true reward for tending Christ's sheep was suffering and persecution.[85]

Having in part one established (at least to his own satisfaction) that the papacy was of the devil, Luther did not bother to develop a lengthy argument in parts two and three, but instead contented himself with a largely rhetorical attack. He asserted that the pope and the curia had no knowledge of Scripture and were unable to judge what was heretical or Christian. The pope's claim to be judge of all, superior to the church and the bishops, revealed him, Luther said, to be the antichrist. With this conclusion, Luther spelled out at passionate length how the pope should be treated by the bishops and the secular lords and forced to restore what he had stolen and done in the church.[86]

Part three was even shorter than part two. At issue was whether the pope had transferred the Roman Empire from the Greeks to the Germans. "That is truly a very crude, apparent lie indeed," Luther began, "which everyone can see and grasp." First, where did the pope get such a realm? And how should he give that which he himself did not have? Then Luther laid out the history of the relations between Charlemagne and the pope which, as he saw it, showed that the pope never

---

*To support this third contention Luther stated that Peter acted as the spokesman of the apostles and represented them all in conversations with Christ. Luther also cited various actions taken by the other apostles independently of Peter. Peter had also founded other churches, not just Rome, and had ordained other bishops, not just the bishop of Rome. There was no justification, Luther concluded, for the Roman bishop to claim precedence over these other cities and bishops. In fact, he pointed out, the bodies of Peter and Paul might not actually be in Rome despite the papacy's claims to the contrary. In any case, it was likely that someone else had founded the church in Rome well before Peter's arrival. Finally, that a city was founded by an apostle did not confer special sanctity or importance on it as the examples of Antioch, Alexandria, and Hippo proved (WA 54:249-58).

possessed an empire to give. In the concluding lines to this section, and to the treatise as a whole, Luther promised another attack. Ill health, the press of other writings and responsibilities, and, finally, death prevented Luther from fulfilling this promise.

The preceding summary suggests only partially the violence of Luther's feelings toward the papacy and the vulgarity with which he attacked it. There can be little doubt that the violence and the vulgarity was intentional and well-considered on Luther's part. He was utterly convinced that the papacy, as the antichrist, the devil's foremost minion, deserved every word of it—and worse. He was contending not against men but against powers and principalities of darkness. To fail to see this dimension of the struggle would be to misunderstand completely Luther's intention behind the treatise.

Luther even commissioned Lucas Cranach to do a series of eight cartoons to give graphic expression to his evaluation of the papacy. He provided instructions for what the cartoons were to show and penned satirical verses to accompany them. The violence and the vulgarity of the treatise carried over to the cartoons. For example, in the treatise Luther at one point urged the emperor, kings, princes, and lords to deprive the pope of Rome, the Romagna, Urbino, Bolognia, and all of his other possessions because he, the pope, was the "possessor of the worst faith" and had acquired all his possessions through "lies and deceit, blasphemy and idolatry." And he continued:

> Next one should take the pope, cardinals, and whatever servants there are of his idolatry and papal holiness, and rip out their tongues at the roots (as blasphemers of God) and nail them on the gallows in the order in which their seals hang in a row on the bulls, although all this is insignificant [punishment] in relation to their blasphemy and idolatry. Next, let them hold a council or whatever they want on the gallows or in hell among all the devils. For they did not begin the accursed papacy out of ignorance or infirmity.[87]

One of the cartoons depicts the pope and cardinals, and their tongues, being treated in just this brutal fashion (see plate 2). Another example, this one of the vulgarity with which Luther felt the papacy should be treated, came in his discussion of the keys. Because the pope had "snatched" St. Peter's keys for himself, Luther said, the papal keys should be regarded as nothing but false, painted keys. "In addition, we may in good conscience," he wrote, "take his coat-of-arms, which features the keys, and his crown to the privy and use them to relieve our needs [and] afterwards throw them into the fire (it would be better if it were the pope himself)."[88] The associated cartoon shows a

# REGNVM SATANAE ET PAPAE.
## 2. THESS. 2.

In aller Teufel namen sitzt
Alhie der Bapst: offenbart jtzt:
Das er sey der recht Widerchrist
So in der Schrifft verkündigt ist.
Mart.Luth.D.

**1545.**

1. The Kingdom of Satan and the Pope. 2 Thessalonians 2 (In the name of all devils the pope sits here, now revealed as the true antichrist as proclaimed in Scripture).

# DIGNA MERGES PAPAE SATANISSIMI ET CARDINALIVM SVORVM.

Wenn zeitlich gestrafft solt werden:
Bapst vnd Cardinel auff Erden.
Jr lesterzung verdienet hett:
Wie jr recht gemalet steht.
Mart. Luth. D.

2. Just Reward for the Most Satanic Pope and His Cardinals (If the pope and cardinals were to receive temporal punishment on earth, their blasphemous tongues would deserve what is rightly depicted here).

**Bapst hat dem reich Christi gethon**
**Wie man hie handelt seine Cron.**
**Machts jr zweifeltig: spricht der geist** Apoc
**Schenckt getrost ein: Gott ists ders heis**
**Mart: Luth: D.**

3. The Pope, God of the World, is Worshiped (The pope has treated the kingdom of Christ just as his crown is here being treated. If you have doubts about it, the [holy] spirit says [Rev. 18] pour it in with good cheer, God Himself commands it).

Hie wird geborn der Widerchrist
Megera sein Seugamme ist:
Alecto sein Kindermeidlin
Tisiphone die gengelt jn.
Mart.Luth.D.

4. Birth and Origin of the Pope (Here is born the antichrist. Megaera is his wetnurse, Allecto his nursemaid, [and] Tisiphone who walks him [Megaera, Allecto, and Tisiphone are the three furies]).

5. How the Pope, Obeying St. Peter, Honors Kings.

Was Gott selbst vom Bapstum hellt
Zeigt dis schrecklich bild hie gestellt:
Dafür jederman grawen sollt:
Wenn ers zu hertzen nemen wollt.
Mart: Luth: D.

6. The Monster of Rome, Found Dead in the Tiber, 1496 (What God Himself thinks of the papacy is shown here by this horrible picture, which should horrify all who would take it to heart).

PAPA DAT CONCILIVM IN
GERMANIA.

PAPA DOCTOR THEOLOGIE ET
MAGISTER FIDEI.

Saw du muſt dich laſſen reiten:
Und wol ſporen zu beiden ſeiten.
Du wilt han ein Concilium:
Da dafür haß dir mein merdrum

Der Bapſt kan allein außlegen
Die ſchrifft: vnd jrthum außfege
Wie der Eſel allein pfeiffen
Kan: vnd die noté recht greiffen.

M. Luther G.

1. 5. 4 5.

7. *Left*: The Pope Offers a Council in Germany (Sow, you must allow yourself to be ridden, and well spurred on both sides. You wish to have a council: for that here is my turd). *Right*: Pope, Doctor of Theology, and Master of Faith (Only the pope can interpret the scripture and sweep away error, just as only a donkey can pipe and sound the right notes.).

# PAPA AGIT GRATIAS CAESARIBVS PRO IMMENSIS BENEFICIIS.

Conradinus Conradi IIII Imperatoris filius, Siciliæ & Neapolis Rex, a Clemente IIII Papa capite truncatus.

Accipe nunc Papæ infidias, & crimine ab uno
Difce omnes.

Gros gut die Keiſer han gethan
Dem Bapſt: vnd vbel gelegt an.
Dafür jm der Bapſt gedäckt hat
Wie dis bild dir die warheit ſagt.
Mart: Luth: D.

1545.

8. The Pope Thanks the Emperor for His Immense Benefits (The emperor has done much good for the Pope and checked evil. For that the pope thanked him, as this picture truly shows you).

# HIC OSCVLA PEDIBVS PAPAE FI‹ GVNTVR.

**PAPA LOQVITVR.**
Sententiæ noſtræ etiam iniuſtæ
metuendæ ſunt.

**RESPONSIO.**
Aſpice nudatæ gens maledcttá natæ,
furioſa
Ecco qui Papa el mio bel uedere,

Nicht Bapſt:nicht ſchreck vns mit deim bañ
Vnd ſey nicht ſo zorniger man
Wir thun ſonſt ein gegen wehre
Vnd zeigen dirs Bel vedere.
Mart.Luth.D.

9. Kissing the Pope's Feet (Don't frighten us, Pope, with your ban, and don't be such a furious man. Otherwise we shall turn away and show you our rears).

These woodcuts appear in Vol. 54 of *D. Martin Luthers Werke, Kritische Gesamtausgabe* (Weimar).

peasant defecating into the papal tiara while two other peasants await their turn (see plate 3). A third cartoon shows a Pope and three cardinals being expelled from the anus of a female devil while three furies are nursing and caring for three infant popes. This cartoon was titled "origin of the pope" and was a graphic echo of Luther's assertion in his treatise that the pope had been born from the devil's behind (see plate 4).[89]

The treatise and cartoons did not lack for critics, even from among the Protestant ranks. What these critics failed to realize, Luther believed, was the true, apocalyptic gravity of the situation. On 14 April he thanked his old friend Amsdorf for his "distinguished testimony" on his book and observed that it did not please everyone equally. He then shared with Amsdorf his reaction to the critics of the treatise:

> But you know my nature, that I am not accustomed to attend to what displeases many provided that it is pious and useful and that it pleases the few good [people]. Nor do I think that those [who are displeased with it] are bad, but they either do not understand the substance, quantity, quality, and all the predicates—genera, species, properties, differentiae, and accidents—that is, all of the horrifying and horrible monstrosities of the papal abomination (for no eloquence or talent can comprehend or appraise it), or they fear the wrath of kings.[90]

And when challenged on the cartoons, Luther replied that he realized that he did not have long to live and yet he still had much that ought to be revealed about the papacy and its kingdom. For this reason he had published these pictures, which each said a whole book's worth of what ought to be written about the papacy. With them he could testify to the whole world what he thought of the pope and his "diabolical kingdom." It was, he stated, his testament. And he had placed his name on the pictures so there could be no charge that they were anonymous libels. He was prepared, he said, to offer in the presence of the whole empire a justification for their publication.[91]

If Luther's overriding concern was to issue his last testament against the papal antichrist, the political significance of this testament was not lost on the princes, even the Catholic ones. It is even reported, for instance, that King Ferdinand, after reading the treatise through, remarked that while the crudities would have to be expunged, the treatise was otherwise not badly written.[92] The strictures of the papal briefs obviously still rankled. On the Protestant side, Landgrave Philipp wrote the elector that he had read through the treatise on the previous day (29 March 1545) and that it pleased him very much. And

Elector Johann Friedrich was so pleased with the work that, according to Luther's own report, he distributed twenty florins worth of copies.[93]

## Minor Attacks

*Against the Papacy at Rome, Founded by the Devil* was the last major treatise of Luther's life, but a number of lesser works did issue from the press during his last months. In the same letter of 21 March 1545 in which he announced to Landgrave Philipp of Hesse the imminent appearance of his *Against the Papacy at Rome*, Luther also thanked the landgrave for sending him a little Italian report of his death.[94] This amusing fabrication, which Luther termed the work of a "pitiful shit-priest [*Scheispfaff*]" who wished to do well but had nothing in his belly," purported to be a report of the demonic manifestations surrounding Luther's death and burial. He intended, Luther told the landgrave, to publish the report in Italian and German with a statement that he, Martin Luther, had read it. As promised, *An Italian Lie Concerning Doctor Martin Luther's Death, Issued at Rome* was soon printed in Wittenberg to amuse partisans of the Reformation. Several south German reprints quickly followed.[95]

More serious was the publication, probably first in Strasbourg and then in Wittenberg, of excerpts from Barnes's *Lives of the Roman Popes*, freely translated into German and introduced with a preface by Luther.[96] Entitled *The Papal Fidelity of Adrian IV and Alexander III Practiced Against Emperor Friedrich Barbarossa*, the treatise offered an antipapal and proimperial (and partly spurious) account of the conflicts between Emperor Friedrich Barbarossa and Popes Adrian IV and Alexander III. The clear intent behind its publication, explicitly confirmed in Luther's preface, was to demonstrate the contempt and treachery shown secular authority by the papacy. Luther was especially incensed by the humiliating submission demanded of the emperor by the pope in which the emperor was forced to lie prostrate on the ground while Pope Alexander placed his foot on the emperor's neck and said, "It is written: 'On adders and basilisks you will walk and [you will] tread on lions and dragons.'"[97] To make this point graphically clear, and for the benefit of the illiterate as well, Luther also had issued a cartoon depicting the pope treading on the neck of the emperor (see plate 5).

Sometime before 2 May 1545 Luther also received a printed list of Latin articles formulated by the theological faculty at Louvain and confirmed and issued by the emperor.[98] Initially, Melanchthon intended to reply to these articles but other affairs intervened.[99] Finally, Luther himself undertook the task. On 9 September Melanchthon was able to send Justus Menius a copy of Luther's Latin *Against the Thirty-Two Articles of the Louvain Theologists*, a list of seventy-five countertheses to the thirty-two articles of the Louvain theologians.[100] It is unlikely that his theses would have convinced anyone not already of his persuasion, for they are too brief and consist more of assertion than persuasive argumentation. They must have appealed to the converted, however, since there appeared four Latin editions and three German translations that same year.

In closing his *Against the Thirty-Two Articles* Luther indicated that he would have more to say on the matter shortly, God willing. On 23 September he announced to Veit Dietrich that he was at work on a special treatise against the Louvain theologians but that his health and age slowed him down and the press of other business impeded his work on the treatise. Another treatise against the pope and one against the Zwinglians ought also to be written, he wrote, "but one [person] cannot do everything."[101] Two trips to his native Mansfeld to mediate between the disputing counts of Mansfeld as well as time spent composing his open letter to the elector and the landgrave concerning Duke Heinrich of Braunschweig-Wolfenbüttel also slowed his work on this polemic.

In a letter of 17 January 1546 Luther described himself as "old, decrepit, sluggish, inactive, and now one-eyed" hoping for a "well-deserved rest" but still overloaded with writing, speaking, acting, and doing. He had begun, he wrote, to work on a public treatise against the Louvain theologians. He was more enraged at "those brutes" than befit a theologian and old man, "but one must resist Satan's monsters even if one must blow at them with one's last breath!" On 19 January he wrote Amsdorf that in the Netherlands the mass priests and the monks were murmuring indignantly and impatiently against God because He had allowed Duke Heinrich of Braunschweig-Wolfenbüttel to be conquered and captured despite the fact that they had offered many thousand masses for his welfare. As for himself, he was praying for and expecting "that day of our redemption and the perdition of the world with its pomp and malice." "Let it be, let it be soon and quickly!" he exclaimed and then added, "I am occupying myself with writing against the asses of Paris and Louvain, etc. And I am fairly well for such great age, but the days are short and business delays my work."[102] Four days later, on 23 January, Luther was off on "business" once again, making his third trip to Mansfeld to mediate between the disputing counts. On

18 February he died in Eisleben. In his pocket was found the beginning pages of this projected polemic. To his last breath Martin Luther was resisting "Satan's monsters."[103]

# Epilogue

A study of the polemics of the older Luther may seem an inappropriate vantage point from which to suggest corrections to the traditional treatment of Luther. What can a study of the least attractive activity of the Reformer's career tell us about studying the other aspects of his life? Yet it is often the most problematic aspects of a subject that force a reevaluation of method. And scholars have certainly had problems in satisfactorily integrating the polemics of the older Luther into their overall view of the Reformer, so much so that they often ignore these later polemics entirely. The reason for this difficulty, I submit, is that scholars have placed too much emphasis on Luther himself and especially on his theology and have not paid enough attention to changes in the nature of the movement he initiated, to the pressures of his environment, and to the secular significance of his actions.

This is not to say that the man and his theology can be ignored. Every polemic dealt at least in passing with theological issues. Moreover, Luther's apocalyptic vision of the struggle between the true and false church is crucial for understanding his later polemics. Awareness of his world view helps us to understand why Luther treated each of his opponents with similar harshness and abusiveness. Each was a manifestation of Satan; each a part of the false church. The pope was the antichrist, Protestant opponents were false prophets and apostles, the Turks were Gog and the "little horn of the beast," the Jews were God's rejected people. Each fit into Luther's Augustinian vision of the struggle between the true and false church that began with Abel and Cain and would continue until the End Time. This vision allowed Luther to identify the devil behind each of his opponents and to address this Satanic opponent rather than the human beings who were but its mask. Heightening Luther's sense of cosmic struggle was his conviction that the End Time was nearly at hand; that with the exposure of the papal antichrist seated within the church, Satan had unleashed all his minions for one final, climactic battle. Luther's own ill health and expectation of death, combined with his disappointment about the reception of the Gospel within Germany, fed his sense of the imminence of the Apocalypse and his desire to do final battle with the devil. Luther saw his polemics as salvoes in this greater war. He was obliged as a servant of God to launch the most ferocious attacks he could against the enemy of God manifested in all these opponents of the Reformation.

He was well equipped for the battle. He possessed extraordinary rhetorical skills, and he had always had the ability to generate a towering anger against his opponents and to express this anger to good rhetorical effect. In his later years the pain of poor health and a frequently somber mood intensified the anger that he chose to unleash in his polemics.

But considerations of physical and mental health, and sensitive analysis of theological assumptions and arguments, can only explain so much. In the case of the later polemics, even stalwart advocates of the traditional concentration on theology and personality realize that within these terms the later polemics remain puzzling and disconcerting. And if a broader perspective is needed for a satisfactory understanding of the polemics, the rest of Luther's biography can probably also benefit from a wider approach.

This book has argued that more attention must be paid to challenges and constraints posed by the nature of the Reformation movement at various stages of its development. By the late 1520s and the early 1530s, the Reformation had passed from a revolutionary movement made up primarily of ideologically committed individuals to a more conservative movement led by rulers of territories and city-states. This transition was unavoidable if the Reformation was to endure, but it also affected Luther's polemics.

One result of the changed circumstances was that most of the older Luther's polemics were addressed to his own supporters. The time for proselytizing had largely passed. Now the Reformation needed to be consolidated and defended in the face of threats from Catholics, Turks, Jews and Jewish exegesis, and "fanatics." The task demanded exhortation rather than explanation. Emphasis was placed on the righteousness of the Protestant cause and on the wickedness and eventual futility of the opponents' cause. While there was still need for education in the tenets of the Protestant faith, stress now was placed on the deepening of beliefs already held. It was time to rally the troops, to whip up passions for the battles ahead. This stage in the movement's history was well served by Luther's apocalyptic vision of the climactic struggle between the true and false church, between the followers of Christ and the minions of Satan. His highly charged rhetoric and liberal abuse of opponents proved useful to the movement's leaders and reassuring to its followers. Such were the treatises circumstances called for. Such were the treatises that Luther delivered.

The later polemics also illustrate how more attention must be paid to political pressures on Luther and his fellow theologians. The Reformation movement was from the beginning religious *and* political. But, in these later years political considerations, often divorced from religious concerns, gained the upper hand. A significant milestone in this transition was the formation of the League of Schmalkalden in February 1531, despite Luther's misgivings, to defend its members against Catholic attack. Its leaders were Landgrave Philipp, who fully realized Luther's value as a publicist in support of the League, and Elector Johann, who was much more cautious about encouraging Luther's polemical talents. Another milestone came in 1532, however, when Elector Johann died and was succeeded by his son Johann Friedrich. The new elector was far more aggressive than his father or his uncle, Friedrich the Wise, in voicing his support for the Reformation. Moreover, he was willing to go on the offensive and to encourage Luther to attack in print the Reformation's opponents.

Eike Wolgast has noted how Elector Johann Friedrich was prone to solicit advice from Luther and Luther's colleagues only after policy had been set. "The original function of the Wittenberg opinion, to advise conscience," he concluded, "was increasingly transformed by Johann Friedrich into the function of relieving consciences, as a religious sanction and reassurance for otherwise autonomous and often previously made decisions of the politicians."[1] Much the same thing can be said about the polemics that Elector Johann Friedrich solicited or encouraged in support of his own policies or the policies of the League. On several occasions the elector used Luther's polemical abilities to relieve and reassure Protestant consciences and to provide sanction for what were largely autonomous political decisions. Of course, it did not take much to induce Luther to attack the opponents of the elector or the League. He was usually quite willing to attack pope and papists, and many of his published attacks in his later years were unsolicited. Nevertheless, there can be no doubt that these treatises were a support to Elector Johann Friedrich's political goals and to League policy. This was true even in cases where Luther harbored some reservations concerning the politicians' decisions. The question of whether to accept an invitation to a papally convened general council illustrates this point.

The rulers and theologians were of different minds on how best to deal with a papal invitation to a council. Rulers such as Luther's own prince, Elector Johann Friedrich, tended to view the problem as political and legal. The elector himself saw the papal invitation to a council and the papal council itself as legal snares, set to capture the Protestants. He thus thought it best to protest the papal council and refuse to participate. The elector's theologians, including Luther, disagreed. They expected nothing good from a papal council, but nonetheless they repeatedly urged their prince and the League not to refuse the invitation. Not surprisingly they lost the argument with the princes, not once but on several occasions. They then acquired the task of justifying the rulers' decision and discrediting the papal council. The numerous attacks on a papal council that flowed from Luther's pen in the 1530s and especially in the months following the League meeting of 1537 were honest expressions of Luther's critical view of a papal council. But by discrediting the papal council in his readers' eyes, he also gave tacit support to the politicians' policy of nonattendance.

Political pressures also influenced his publications on the question of resistance to a possible Catholic attack led by the emperor. Under intense pressure from politicians and jurists who were unwilling to accept the theologians' reservations concerning armed defense of the faith, Luther first "allowed" a positive law justification of resistance and finally, much assisted by his apocalyptic expectations, developed the theological argument that if the emperor attacked the Protestants on account of their faith then he would not be acting in his capacity as a superior secular authority but rather as a servant of the papal antichrist. Similarly, his publication justifying Elector Johann Friedrich's seizure of the bishopric of Naumburg represents an accommodation to the wishes of his prince despite Luther's own misgivings. His two treatises concerning Duke Heinrich of Braunschweig-Wolfenbüttel also involved him in what was largely a political affair. Even his "matter of conscience," his *Against the Bishop of Magdeburg, Cardinal Albrecht* (1539), appears to have served his prince's political interests, whatever Luther's own intentions.

In short, several of the polemics of the older Luther demonstrate that the elector used Luther's extraordinary polemical abilities as one more weapon in his own and the League of Schmalkalden's struggle with Catholic powers. Luther's task was to exhort Protestants to stand fast in the face of Catholic, and also Turkish threats, and to reassure them that God and right was on their side. The elector encouraged and commended the vehemence and even vulgarity that Luther employed in accomplishing this task, and his encouragement was given not only for works that he himself had commissioned but also for works such as Luther's attacks on the Jews and on the Sacramentarians, which Luther himself had initiated. Although more prominent in the later years, this political dimension is present from very early in the history of the Reformation movement and should be given greater consideration.

The meaning of Luther's publications, and his acts generally, is not exhausted by a statement of his intentions, much less a statement of his *theological* rationale. The historian must also evaluate the meanings the polemics had for Luther's contemporaries, for Protestant and Catholic rulers, for his coworkers and for opposing publicists, and for Protestant and Catholic readers in general. And such an evaluation must include a consideration of the rhetorical force of Luther's treatises as well as their explicit content. As is seen, for example, in the case of resistance, whatever the theological content (and its consistency with Luther's earlier pronouncements on the two realms), the rhetorical force of Luther's treatises led both Protestants and Catholics to conclude that Luther had done an about-face and that he was now encouraging Protestants to resist even an imperially-led Catholic attack.

In general, the inflammatory rhetoric in which Luther couched his attacks on Jews, Catholics, and "fanatics" conveyed its own message to his readers, apart from any theological arguments. On occasion, such as in the question of resistance, the rhetoric and the theology may even have worked at cross-purposes. His contribution to such developments as the Wittenberg disturbances of 1521-1522, the Peasants' War of 1524-1525, and the gradual formation of the Lutheran territorial church [*landesherrliche Kirchenregiment*] must be reassessed in these broader terms. If it is correct to say that the radicals in Wittenberg, the peasants in the uprising, and the Lutheran princes misunderstood or misconstrued Luther's theology or some aspect of it; if it is correct to say that Luther never intended to encourage the disorders in Wittenberg, the uprising of the peasants, or the formation of an institutional church fully subordinated to secular control, then some effects must also be pointed out. Luther's forceful attacks on papal practices encouraged others to put a drastic end to these practices; his frequent pronouncements on "Christian freedom" were readily interpreted by others as having secular implications; and the very fact that he provided a preface to the visitations of 1527-1528 lent the proceedings the authority of his name, whatever the reservations expressed in the preface itself.

The older Luther was a man who saw the world engaged in a metaphysical struggle between good and evil. He was a man gripped by apocalyptic hopes and fears; a man who had given his name to a movement that had taken, for him, a painful and frustrating direction. He was a man deeply involved in the politics of his time, as an advisor to his prince and coreligionists, as an indirect participant in colloquies between Protestants and Catholics, as a worried observer of wars and threats of war, and as the most influential publicist within Protestantism. Through compromise and accommodation to political realities, he tried to maintain his influence in order to preserve his central insights into Christian faith. But opponents and circumstances, and even the action of allies and friends, disappointed his hopes and marred his efforts. Not infrequently, he found himself mired in petty disputes that brought neither him nor the movement any credit. He found himself misunderstood and held reponsible for actions that he himself deplored. So as his own death neared, bringing with it both promised relief and fear for the fate of the movement after his death, he became ever more pessimistic, praying not only for his own release but for the end of the world.

Still, he remained involved and productive to his death. Sustained by his faith, his trust in God as the author of history, and by his robust sense of humor, he continued to learn and grow, especially in his study of history. He was vulgar and abusive when he wished to be, moderate and calmly persuasive when it suited his purposes. And all the treatises of his old age, even the most crude and abusive, contained some exposition of the Protestant faith. Luther could never just attack. He always had to profess and confess as well.

# Appendix

Historians would certainly like to know how influential Martin Luther's publications were and whether his influence varied over time. Unfortunately, we may never be able to determine this. We may, however, reduce this broad question to a more narrow but also more manageable one: where, when, and how many treatises, and of what sorts, were printed and how did this vary over time? The link between this narrow question and the broader one rests on several assumptions.

First, it seems reasonable that the printing of a work, and especially the reprinting of a work, may be taken as an indirect measure of public demand. Printers in the sixteenth century were presumably in the business to make money. They might also publish out of conviction and altruism, but they still had to make a profit over time or they would be forced out of business. At the very least, then, we should be able to assume that the *printer* expected that there would be a market for product. If he were correct in his expectation, then the printing of a work is a valid although indirect measure of public demand. If the printer reprints the work several times, we may safely assume that he does so to meet the demands of his customers.

Second, the locations where a work is printed and reprinted may offer a clue to the work's geographical influence. In an age well before copyright and with shipping over land expensive and printing relatively cheap, a work generally spread through reprinting. If, for example, there was interest in Saxony for a work first published in Basel, it was more common for a printer in Saxony to reprint the work than it was for the printer in Basel to ship a large number of copies to Saxony. Since, as already noted, works were printed with the expectation of sale, the printing or reprinting of a particular work in a particular place may also be an indirect measure of *local* or *regional* demand, and not merely demand in general.

To be sure, a moment's reflection will suggest problems with this approach. The fact that a work is printed or reprinted says nothing about the *size* of the printing. The number could easily vary from 200 to 2000 copies. Yet if one is only counting printings this considerable possible variance is disguised, and the results may be seriously misleading. If, for example, sermons are normally produced in much larger editions than, say, lectures, then the statistics for sermons will understate the relative demand for sermons and overstate the relative demand for lectures. This is a major source of potential error, yet all I can do is alert the reader to its possible presence.

Other objections may also be raised. Books are not consumed in one reading, so that publication dates may only reflect intial demand and thus suggest only the *beginning* of a work's influence. A work may circulate through many hands and exercise influence for years after its publication. Some of the decline in publication that I present may be due more to saturation of the market than decline in demand or interest. A further difficulty: some types of printed material may circulate more widely than others. For example, there may be more centralized production and wider distribution of particularly expensive items such as Bibles. Such objections, and the reader will surely think of others, demand a certain tentativeness about the graphs and tables I present.

The descriptive statistics in this book were based on computer tabulation done in 1980. Kurt Aland, *Hilfsbuch zum Lutherstudium*, 3rd ed. (Witten: Luther-Verlag, 1970), served as the source for individual works. Joseph Benzing, *Lutherbibliographie: Verzeichnis der gedruckten Schriften Martin Luthers bis zu dessen Tod* (Baden-Baden: Verlag Librairie Heitz, 1966) was used to determine date and place of publication of all printings. Using the introduction in the Weimar Ausgabe to each work, the works themselves, and Benzing, I classified each work according to

type:       first edition, reprint, translation, part of a collection, excerpts, etc.

language:   New High German, Latin, Low German (editions in other languages were not tabulated)

literary:   treatise, sermon, foreword, lecture, open letter, exposition of Scripture, woodcuts, glosses or commentary on the work of another

| character: | nonpolemical, polemical, mixed |
|---|---|
| audience: | general population, Lutherans, Jews, etc. |
| instigator: | Luther himself, his prince, a colleague, a layperson, etc. |
| opponent(s): | Catholics, other Protestants, peasants, nobles, etc. |
| tone: | nonpolemical, moderately polemical but with little or no *ad hominem* abuse, harshly polemical and abusive |

Obviously, some of the measures were more subjective than others. Type of edition, language, and literary type can be fairly objectively determined by the coder. In contrast, character, audience, and tone require the coder to make qualitative judgments. Somewhere between these two categories lies the determination of opponents. The question of who instigated a particular work is often unanswerable; we simply lack evidence. Because of this problem of coding, I have preferred to rest most of my argument on the more objective measures.

The tabulation and cross-tabulation was done by a program I wrote in PASCAL for this specific purpose.

Computers, like photocopy machines, encourage the collection of paper. The statistics presented in this book are the distillation of pages and pages of printouts. I am willing to share detailed printouts with any interested scholars.

# Notes

## Abbreviations

*ARG*    *Archiv für Reformationsgeschichte.*

*CR*    *Corpus Reformatorum.* Halle/Saale, 1835-60; 1905- .

W2    *Martin Luthers sämmtliche Schriften.* Edited by Johan Georg Walch, 2nd ed. published in modern German. 23 vols. St. Louis, 1880-1910.

WA    *D. Martin Luthers Werke. Kritische Gesamtausgabe.* 58 vols. Weimar, 1883- .

WABr    *D. Martin Luthers Werke. Briefwechsel.* 15 vols. Weimar, 1930- .

WADB    *D. Martin Luthers Werke. Deutsche Bibel.* 12 vols. Weimar, 1906-61.

WATR    *D. Martin Luthers Werke. Tischreden.* 6 vols. Weimar, 1912-21.

*ZKG*    *Zeitschrift für Kirchengeschichte.*

## Introduction

1. For extended comments on this phenomenon, see Heinrich Bornkamm, "Probleme der Lutherbiographie," in *Lutherforschung Heute*, edited by Vilmos Vajta (Berlin, 1958), pp. 15-23, and Bernd Moeller, "Probleme der Reformationsgeschichtsforschung," *Zeitschrift für Kirchengeschichte* 76(1965):246-57; translated in Bernd Moeller, *Imperial Cities and the Reformation*, edited and trans. by H. C. Erik Midelfort and Mark U. Edwards, Jr. (Philadelphia, 1972), pp. 3-16.

2. The most thorough and authoritative study of the older Luther remains the venerable study by Julius Köstlin, revised in 1903 by Gustav Kawerau (*Martin Luther, Sein Leben und Seine Schriften*, 5th ed. rev. [Berlin, 1903]; volume 2 deals with the older Luther). H. G. Haile, *Luther: An Experiment in Biography* (New York, 1980) offers a fine, sprightly overview that focuses on the older Luther.

3. A notable exception to this generalization, and a study to which I owe a great deal, is Eike Wolgast, *Die Wittenberger Theologie und die Politik der evangelischen Stände: Studien zu Luthers Gutachten in politischen Fragen* (Gütersloh, 1977).

## Chapter One

1. WATR 1:87 (no. 197).

2. Ibid.

3. WATR 2:455 (no. 2410a).

4. WABr 2:168. Luther added, "but I feel as you [Wenceslaus Link] do that perhaps in this way God is revealing the fictions of men. For I see that that which is treated quietly in our age soon passes into oblivion, no one caring about it." Cf. WABr 2:163-64, where Luther also observed, "If every chiding word [*increpatio*] is a slander [*conuitium*], then no one is more slanderous [*criminantior*] than the prophets." For a recent overview of Luther's "cursing," see Martin Brecht, "Der 'Schimpfer' Martin Luther," *Luther* 52(1981):97-113.

5. WA 7:834.

6. E.g., WABr 6:73-75; WA 30/3:470; WABr 11:71.

7. WA 30/2:68.

8. CR 11:729-30.

9. See the Appendix.

10. There is considerable literature on Luther's physical and mental health. Among the best is Annemarie Halder, *Das Harnsteinleiden Martin Luthers* (Munich, 1969). See also Friedrich Küchenmeister, *Dr. Martin Luthers Krankengeschichte* (Leipzig, 1881); Wilhelm Ebstein, *D. Martin Luthers Krankheiten und deren Einfluss auf seinen Körperlichen und geistigen Zustand* (Stuttgart, 1908); Erwin Mülhaupt, "Luthers Kampf mit der Krankheit," *Luther* 29(1958):115-23; and Ethel Bacchus and H. Kenneth Scatliff, eds., "Martin Luther: A Panel Postmortem," *Chicago Medicine* 69(1966):107-16.

11. Four of the more prominent, and notorious, diagnoses are Heinrich Deinifle, *Luther und Luthertum in der ersten Entwicklung* (Mainz, 1904); Albert Maria Weiss, *Lutherpsychologie als Schlüssel zur Lutherlegende: Ergänzungen zu Denifles Luther und Lutherthum* (Mainz, 1906); Hartmann Grisar, *Luther*, 3 vols. (Freiburg, 1911-12); and Paul J. Reiter, *Martin Luthers Umwelt, Character und Psychose*, vol. 2 (Copenhagen, 1941). Drawing heavily on these Catholic works is Erik Erikson, *Young Man Luther* (New York, 1958). Erikson's book, in turn, has generated a considerable secondary literature. For a bibliography and several of the best articles on the subject, see Roger Johnson, ed., *Psychohistory and Religion: The Case of Young Man Luther* (Philadelphia, 1977).

12. For several replies to the works cited in the previous note, see Gustav Kawerau, *Luther in Katholischer Beleuchtung: Glossen zu H. Grisars Luther* (Leipzig, 1911); Heinrich Boehmer, *Luther im Lichte der neueren Forschung*, 5th ed. (Leipzig, 1918); and Eberhard Grossmann, *Beiträge zur psychologischen Analyse der Reformatoren Luther und Calvin* (Basel, 1958).

13. This is suggested by H. G. Haile, *Luther: An Experiment in Biography* (New York, 1980), pp. 220-21.

14. On Luther's productivity, see Alfred Dieck, "Luthers Schaffenskraft," *Luther* 27(1956):35-39, for a year-by-year summary of Luther's productivity. In the Appendix I discuss my own statistical survey of Luther's publications.

15. The older Marxist argument that the Peasants' War marked the end of the popular Reformation was challenged by Franz Lau's classic article

"Der Bauernkrieg und das angebliche Ende der lutherischen Reformation als spontaner Volksbewegung," *Luther-Jahrbuch* 26(1959):109-34. The debate is far from over, however. (The best recent work on the Peasants' War, now translated into English, is Peter Blickle, *The Revolution of 1525: The German Peasants' War from a New Perspective*, trans. by Thomas A. Brady, Jr. and H. C. Erik Midelfort [Baltimore, 1981]. The editors have provided a useful bibliography of relevant English publications.) On the face of it, this decline in publication would appear to support those who see an end to the popular Reformation in these years. Miriam Chrisman, however, has shown for the case of Strasbourg that all types of printing declined at this time, and not merely religious materials. So this decline may reflect economic changes rather than a waning of interest in Luther's works (see Miriam Chrisman, *Lay Culture, Learned Culture: Books and Social Change in Strasbourg, 1480-1599* [New Haven, 1982]).

16. See note 11 preceding.

17. E.g., WATR 3:123-24; 4:7-8; 4:16; 4:200-2 (cf. 4:489-91); 4:321.

18. E.g., WATR 1:506; 4:8; 4:201; 4:329-30; 4:416-17; 4:687; 5:201; 5:222; 5:491.

19. WATR 5:201 (no. 5506). Cf. CR 4:882.

20. The literature on these issues is immense. See, among others, Mark U. Edwards Jr., *Luther and the False Brethren* (Stanford, 1975), especially chapter 5; Bornkamm, *Luther und das alte Testament*; Scott Hendrix, *Ecclesia in Via: Ecclesiological Developments in the Medieval Psalms Exegesis and the Dictata super Psalterium (1513-1515) of Martin Luther* (Leiden, 1974); Ernst Schäfer, *Luther als Kirchenhistoriker* (Gütersloh, 1897); John M. Headley, *Luther's View of Church History* (New Haven, 1963); Hans von Campenhausen, "Reformatorisches Selbstbewusstsein und reformatorisches Geschichtsbewusstsein bei Luther, 1517-1522," *ARG* 37(1940):128-49; Wolfgang Günter, "Die geschichtstheologischen Voraussetzungen von Luthers Selbstverständnis," in *Von Konstanz nach Trient. Beiträge zur Kirchengeschichte von den Reformkonzilien bis zum Tridentinum. Festgabe für August Franzen*, ed. R. Bäumer (Paderborn, 1972), pp. 379-94; Wolfgang Höhne, *Luthers Anschauungen über die Kontinuität der Kirche* (Berlin/Hamburg, 1963), pp. 124-56; and Ulrich Asendorf, *Eschatologie bei Luther* (Göttingen, 1967), pp. 214-21.

21. The history of the origin, original purpose, and status of these articles has been the subject of research and controversy. See, among others, H. Virck, "Zu den Beratungen der Protestaten über die Konzilsbulle vom 4. Juni 1536," *ZKG* 13(1892-93):487-512; Hans Volz, *Luthers Schmalkaldische Artikel und Melanchthons Tractatus de potestate papa* (Gotha, 1931); Ernst Bizer, "Die Wittenberger Theologen und das Konzil 1537: Ein ungedrucktes Gutachten," *ARG* 47(1956):77-101; idem, "Zum geschichtlichen Verständnis von Luthers Schmalkaldischen Artikeln," *ZKG* 67(1955-56):61-92; Hans Volz, "Luthers Schmalkaldische Artikel," *ZKG* 68(1957):259-86; Ernst Bizer, "Noch einmal: Die Schmalkaldischen Artikel," *ZKG* 68(1957):287-94; and Hans Volz, ed., *Urkunden und Aktenstücke zur Geschichte von Martin Luthers Schmalkaldischen Artikeln (1536-1574)* (Berlin, 1957). On Elector Johann Friedrich's

intentions, see Volz, *Urkunden*, pp. 23, 83-91.

22. *On the Ineffable Name and On Christ's Lineage* (WA 53:579-648) and *On the Last Words of David* (WA 54:28-100) are more addenda to *On the Jews and Their Lies* (WA 53:417-552) than independent treatises in their own right. On Luther's intentions in writing against the Jews, see his introductory and concluding remarks (WA 53:417 and 552). Luther wished to be absolved of responsibility for any untoward consequences stemming from a lax policy toward the Jews (see, e.g., WA 53:605-6). On his motivation for writing the *Short Confession* (WA 54:141-67), see WA 54:141. In *Against the Papacy at Rome* (WA 54:206-99), he announced his intention to write a second book (WA 54:299). Unable to carry out these plans, he issued the cartoons instead (see the next note).

23. WA 54:353. See also WA 54:356-58, and especially the discussion of WABr 11:115 and 120, which refer not to these cartoons but to a different antipapal cartoon by Cranach.

24. Hosea 1-3; Ezekiel 16 and 23. See, e.g., WA 51:502-4, where Luther makes his source explicit.

25. See Edwards, *Luther and the False Brethren*, chapter 5.

26. See, e.g., Helmut Appel, *Anfechtung und Trost in Spätmittelalter und bei Luther* (Leipzig, 1938); Paul Bühler, *Die Anfechtung bei Martin Luther* (Zurich, 1942); and Gordon Rupp, *The Righteousness of God* (London, 1953), esp. pp. 102-57.

27. WATR 5:86-88.

28. These treatises are discussed in detail in chapter 7.


## Chapter Two


1. See Karl Trudinger, *Luthers Briefe und Gutachten an weltliche Obrigkeiten zur Durchführung der Reformation* (Munster, 1975), pp. 8-10.

2. For the source of the following statistics, see the appendix.

3. The literature on Luther and resistance is vast, especially if the many pieces on Luther's two kingdoms doctrine are considered. For a general overview of the recent literature, see Rudolf Ohlig, *Die Zwei-Reiche-Lehre Luthers in der Auslegung der deutschen lutherischen Theologie der Gegenwart seit 1945* (Bern, 1974), and the bibliography in Heinz Scheible, ed., *Das Widerstandsrecht als Problem der deutschen Protestanten* (Gütersloh, 1969). I have found most satisfactory the older work by Karl Müller, *Luthers Äusserungen über das Recht des bewaffneten Widerstands gegen den Kaiser* (Munich, 1915). Two recent works have also been very useful: Hermann Kunst, *Evangelischer Glaube und politische Verantwortung: Martin Luther als politischer Berater seiner Landesherrn und seine Teilnahme an den Fragen des öffentlichen Lebens* (Stuttgart,1976), and Eike Wolgast, *Die Wittenberger Theologie und die Politik der evangelischen Stände* (Gütersloh, 1977). Wolgast's discussion is by far the best recent consideration of the matter, and should be consulted by those interested in all the legal and theological details surrounding the discussions of 1529-1530 (Wolgast, *Die Wittenberger*

*Theologie*, pp. 125-200). As will become obvious, I do not agree with Cynthia Grant Shoenberger ("Luther and the Justifiability of Resistance to Legitimate Authority," *Journal of the History of Ideas* 40[1979]:3-20) that Luther "converted" in the early 1530s to an acceptance of the right of resistance against the emperor. Our disagreement may, however, be largely in emphasis (see her qualification on p. 19, among others). Other recent contributions include Richard R. Benert, *Inferior Magistrates in Sixteenth-Century Political and Legal Thought* (PhD Diss., University of Minnesota, 1967); idem, "Lutheran Resistance Theory and the Imperial Constitution," *Il Pensiero Politico* 6(1973):17-36; Hermann Dörries, "Luther und das Widerstandsrecht," in *Wort und Stunde*, vol. 3 (Göttingen, 1970); Quentin Skinner, *The Foundations of Modern Political Thought*, vol. 2 (Cambridge, 1978); W. D. J. Cargill Thompson, "Luther and the Right of Resistance to the Emperor," in C. W. Dugmore, ed., *Studies in the Reformation: Luther to Hooker* (London, 1980); Eike Wolgast, *Die Religionsfrage als Problem des Widerstandsrechts im 16. Jahrhundert* (Heidelberg, 1980).

4. Wolgast, *Die Wittenberger Theologie*, pp. 173-85, esp. p. 184.

5. Wolgast, *Die Wittenberger Theologie*, pp. 175-76; WABr 6:17, 6:16, 6:38; CR 2:469.

6. Wolgast, *Die Wittenberger Theologie*, pp. 177 and 177n32. WABr 6:16-17; 6:36-37.

7. WABr 6:16-16; 6:36-37.

8. WABr 6:36-37; 6:56-57.

9. WABr 5:651; 5:653-55.

10. WA 30/3:276-320.

11. WA 30/3:277.

12. WA 30/3:282.

13. WA 30/3:283.

14. WA 30/3:282-83.

15. This is a debatable matter; see the literature cited in note 5.

16. WA 30/3:276-77.

17. WA 30/3:280-81.

18. WA 30/3:311.

19. WA 30/3:277-78.

20. WA 30/3:279-80.

21. WA 30/3:282-83.

22. See the preceding, especially note 10.

23. WA 30/3:419-20. Johann Cochlaeus, *Hertzog Georgs zu Sachssen Ehrlich vnd grundtliche entschuldigung, wider Martin Luthers Auffrüerisch vnd verlogenne, Brieff vnd Verantwortung* (Dresden, 1533), pp. Cij-Ciij, Fi-[Fiv(v)], Hij-Hij(v).

24. Joseph Benzing, *Lutherbibliographie. Verzeichnis der gedruckten Schriften Martin Luthers bis zu dessen Tod* (Baden-Baden, 1966), nos. 2908-2924. Sixteen editions were published through 1546. In 1531 Hans Lufft issued five printings at Wittenberg, Georg Ulricher issued one printing at Strasbourg, and Michael Lotter and Hans Walther each issued one low German printing at Magdeburg. In 1546 Hans Lufft issued two printings at

Wittenberg, Vaentin Otmar issued one printing at Augsburg, Johann vom Berg, Hans Daubmann, and Ulrich Neuber each issued one printing at Nuremberg, Wendelin Rihel issued one printing at Strasbourg, and Ulrich Morhart issued one printing at Tübingen.

25. In early December, 1536, Luther, Jonas, Bugenhagen, Amsdorf, Cruciger, and Melanchthon committed to paper their opinion on the proper response to an invitation to a general council called by the pope, on the elector's suggestion of a "counter-council," and on the propriety of armed resistance in the case the council proceeded against them (for the following, see CR 3:126–31 and Scheible, *Das Widerstandsrecht* [Gütersloh, 1969], pp. 89–92. For its proper dating, see H. Virck, "Zu den Beratungen der Protestanten über die Konzilsbulle vom 4. Juni 1536," *ZKG* 13[1892–93]:496f.). The theologians explained that the gospel supported and glorified the "external bodily government [*regiment*]" and permitted defense ordained by natural or positive law. Hence the question of resistance belonged not to the preachers but to secular authority. Each prince was responsible for protecting "Christian and outwardly correct divine services" against all unjust force, just as he was in other respects responsible for protecting his subjects against unjust force. Also, the prince was responsible, the theologians contended on the basis of the second commandment, for planting and maintaining proper doctrine in his territory. It was clear, they continued, that each authority was responsible for protecting his Christians and Christian doctrine against princes of equal standing and against private individuals. As for the emperor, if he undertook anything in religious matters contrary to the appeal and to the Nuremberg Standstill before there was a council and while the appeal was still pending, he was to be considered a private person and his unjust action a "public notorious injustice" that could be resisted.

As will be seen, the one argument advanced here that Luther himself seems to have adopted as his own and elaborated upon is the argument that the emperor was to be considered a private person, or a soldier of the pope, if he attacked the Protestants while their appeal was still pending.

On 13 or 14 November 1538 Luther, Jonas, Bucer, and Melanchthon signed another opinion on this question of armed resistance to Catholic attack (on the dating, see Scheible, *Das Widerstandsrecht*, p. 92n447. For a very perceptive analysis of this opinion, the letter to Ludicke, and Luther's *Concerning the Three Hierarchies*, see Wolgast, *Die Wittenberger Theologie*, pp. 239–51). Like the opinion of December 1536 it relied heavily on arguments based on natural law, a strong indication its primary author was Melanchthon rather than Luther (Müller, *Luthers Äusserungen*, pp. 67–73).

It dealt with two questions. First, whether secular authority had the duty to defend itself and its subjects against unjust force used by princes of equal standing and by the emperor, especially in religious matters. The theologians replied that it was, explaining:

> And just as the gospel confirms the office of [secular] authority, natural and constitutional law also confirms it. . . . And there is no doubt [that] every father has the duty, according to his

ability, to protect his wife and child against public murder, and there is no difference between a private murderer and the emperor when he, outside of his office, engages in unjust force and especially public or notorious unjust force. For public violence cancels all obligation between subject and sovereign [*oberherr*] according to natural law.

The same is true in this case: if the sovereign wishes to force the subject into blasphemy of God and idolatry.

As the theologians themselves pointed out, this was the same argument made two years previously. The second question was whether the "defender" was obliged to wait until the enemy actually attacked. As Luther had advised in 1529, the theologians replied that once the princes were placed under the ban, which was equivalent of a declaration of war, they could engage in a preventative attack. But, as before, they added that it was not proper for them to decide whether such a course of action was appropriate; the princes should themselves consider whether this was necessary and whether some other action might not come first (Scheible, *Das Widerstandsrecht*, pp. 92-94).

In both this opinion and that of 1536 the theologians relied almost exclusively on *legal* rather than *theological* arguments. This is fully consistent with their declaration in Torgau in 1530 that the decision to resist the emperor was not one that they, in their capacity as theologians, were in the position to make.

The theologians also gave their opinion on what should be done if the council met and condemned the Protestants. If the Protestants presented their case properly and the council nonetheless proceeded unjustly, and even if the Catholics claimed that the canon law allowed them so to proceed, such proceedings would nonetheless be contrary to natural law and to the scriptural command that the church was to be judge [cf. Matthew 18:17]. Such proceedings would accordingly be null and void, the council would be no council, and the appeal would remain in force. Resistance would therefore be justified. Resistance would also be justified in the case where the pope proceeded honorably but still wished to sanction idolatry and obvious injustice, just as a prince might properly resist the attempt of the Turks to impose idolatry on his subjects. The Protestant princes could also resist attempts to invalidate and forbid clerical marriage because such marriages were a secular matter. Attempts to invalidate or forbid them would be acts of "notorious injustice" and should be resisted just as murder on the streets or adultery was resisted.

Eike Wolgast, *Die Wittenberger Theologie,* pp. 224-30, discusses this opinion in detail.

26. On this, see WABr 8:365.
27. WABr 8:366-68.
28. Müller, *Luthers Äusserungen*, pp. 72f.
29. WABr 8:383-84, 386-88, 389-90, 393-94, 401.
30. WA 39/2:34-51.

31. WA 39/2:42, theses 51-56 with the numbering omitted.

32. WA 39/2:39-43.

33. See Wolgast, *Die Wittenberger Theologie*, pp. 243-51.

34. A year after his return to Wittenberg the elector had been faced with a papal brief, prepared for the Nuremberg Diet, which requested that Luther and other Protestants be rendered harmless or turned over to Catholic authorities. Unsure of what was the proper thing to do, the elector had requested a formal opinion from Luther and various other Protestant theologians on whether he might for the sake of the gospel wage war or offer armed resistance to an imperial attempt to seize and persecute Protestants within Electoral Saxony (actually, there is some question whether Friedrich himself initiated this inquiry. See Wolgast, *Die Wittenberger Theologie*, p. 101n32). Luther had replied that, given the elector's "neutrality" in the matter to date—the elector had responded to Catholic challenges by arguing that he was a layman and could not judge the matter—he could not wage war in behalf of the Protestant cause since the emperor was the elector's lord by the consent of God and men. But if the elector wished to wage war for the sake of the gospel, he would have to, first, openly declare for the cause as a just cause, second, fight as if he were a foreign prince coming to the aid of foreigners and not because his own subjects were involved, and, third, be called to such resistance by a special faith or inspiration. None of these three conditions were likely of fulfillment, but they took into account—especially the third point—situations in the Old Testament where God had called men to resist secular authority, an action apparently forbidden by New Testament passages such as Romans 13. Unless these extraordinary circumstances were met, the elector should not, Luther had stated, resist an imperial attempt to capture Luther or other Protestants. Instead, he should yield to the emperor, his superior, and, if necessary, suffer and die for his faith with other Protestants (Scheible, *Das Widerstandsrecht*, p. 17). Luther had repeated this advice, with a similar exception for Old Testament "*wundermänner*" like Samson, in his 1523 *On Secular Authority, To What Extent It Should Be Obeyed* (WA 11:261-76. See Müller, *Luthers Äusserungen*, pp. 7-9). To be sure, this advice applied only to resistance to superior authority. If the elector were to be attacked by princes of equal authority such as Duke Georg of Albertine Saxony, he should behave as in any other war between princes of equal standing. First he should offer peace and justice as directed by Deuteronomy 20 and then, if necessary, repel force with force.

## Chapter Three

1. For other studies of Luther's relations with Duke Georg, see Hans Becker, "Herzog Georg von Sachsen als kirchlicher und theologischer Schriftsteller," *ARG* 24(1927):161-269. Hermann Kunst, *Evangelischer Glaube und politische Verantwortung: Martin Luther als politischer Berater seiner Landesherrn und seine Teilnahme an den Fragen des öffentlichen Lebens* (Stuttgart, 1977), pp. 217-24, 288-316. Ingetraut Ludolphy, "Die

Ursachen der Gegnerschaft zwischen Luther und Herzog Georg von Sachsen," *Luther-Jahrbuch* 32(1965):28-44. O. A. Hecker, *Religion und Politik in den letzten Lebensjahren Herzog Georgs des Bärtigen von Sachsen* (Leipzig, 1912). Otto Vossler, "Herzog Georg der Bärtige und sein Ablehnung Luthers," *Historische Zeitschrift* 184(1957):272-91. Heinrich von Welck, *Georg der Bärtige, Herzog von Sachsen: Sein Leben und Wirken* (Brunswick, 1900). W2 19:9-25.

    2. E.g., Felican Gess, *Akten und Briefe zur Kirchenpolitik Hertzog Georgs von Sachsen* (Leipzig, 1905/1917), no. 819, p. 56, cited in Ludolphy, "Luther und Herzog Georg," p. 38n61.

    3. See Ludolphy, "Luther und Herzog Georg," pp. 33-37.

    4. Gess, *Akten und Briefe*, no. 146, cited in Ludolphy, "Luther und Herzog Georg," p. 34. W2 19:450-51.

    5. See Becker, "Herzog Georg von Sachsen."

    6. For the following, see von Welck, *Georg der Bärtige*, pp. 63-86.

    7. See Vossler, "Herzog Georg," pp. 274-77.

    8. See Gess, *Akten und Briefe*.

    9. von Welck, *Georg der Bärtige*, p. 80.

    10. For the duke's letter, see W2 19:450-51.

    11. WA 10/2:53-60.

    12. WABr 3:954- .

    13. W2 19:494ff.

    14. W2 19:494.

    15. For the edification of the reader the duke then described at length the teachings of the Lutheran and the other, subsequently arisen, fanatics and the fruits of their teachings. For example, the duke charged that this "godless teaching" had produced the following fruits: "Not only a carnal but also a bestial and devilish freedom, willfulness, wantonness, disobedience, and bloody rebellion of the poor misled subjects, contempt, insult, and abuse of all spiritual and secular authority, apostasy and pitiful fall of the clergy, the laying down of their habit along with all decency, modesty and fear of God, a forgetting of their vows and oaths, illegitimate matrimony and marriage of monks, priests, and nuns, alienation of their goods, destruction of their cloisters and churches, from which the vestments, chalice, monstrance, gold and silver censer and other holy treasures, likewise stone, iron, glass windows and other things that were given for the service and honor of God are sold on the free, open market [and] used for secular vainglory and enjoyment, and from the houses of God are made horse stalls and other unseemly buildings, all divine service and human devotion to God and his saints is extinguished and our holy Christian faith is completely wiped out in many places. We do not mention [the] many spiritual, pious virgins, who were removed from their cloisters by force and robbed of their virginal status and honor contrary to God, honor, and justice—although that too is of little moment in the face of the lamentable murder, killing and bloodshed of the poor misled subjects and so many wretched widows and orphans, to which they maliciously forced the authorities by their obdurate wantonness and disobedience. But of what account is even that in the face of the damage to and loss of so many Christian souls which Christ has purchased with his precious blood and [which]

Luther along with the false Protestant preachers, enthusiasts, and fanatics, who adhere to and follow him, have again alienated from him [Christ] through their misleading teaching and, as it is unfortunately to be feared, have consigned to eternal damnation" (W2 19:498-99).

16. W2 19:500-1.

17. See, e.g., WABr 4:294.

18. WABr 4:413-16. W2 16:373-80, esp. p. 375. On the Pack Affair in general, see Kurt Dülfer, *Die Packschen Händel* (Marburg, 1958).

19. WABr 4:449.

20. WABr 4:424-25, WABr 4:421-24, WABr 4:425-29, WABr 4:431-33, WABr 4:433-35, WABr 4:447-50, WABr 4:457, WABr 4:463-65.

21. W2 16:380-84.

22. WABr 4:479, 480, 483-84.

23. WABr 4:483-84.

24. WABr 4:481.

25. WABr 4:594, 596, 482f., Becker, "Herzog Georg von Sachsen," pp. 221f., WABr 4:620, WABr 4:611-12, WABr 4:619, WABr 4:620, WABr 4:613, etc.

26. W2 16:422-33.

27. WA 30/2:25-48.

28. WABr 5:7.

29. WABr 5:7-9. For the other reactions to this treatise, see WABr 5:9-10, 5:17, 5:28, 5:11.

30. WABr 6:69.

31. WABr 6:70-71.

32. WABr 6:71-72.

33. WABr 6:73.

34. WABr 6:73. See W2 16:1747n4.

35. WABr 6:73-74.

36. WABr 6:74.

37. WABr 6:74-75.

38. WABr 6:72.

39. On the question of authorship, see Becker, "Herzog Georg von Sachsen," pp. 251-53.

40. WA 30/3:416, 438f.

41. WA 30/3:416.

42. WA 30/3:416-17.

43. WA 30/3:418.

44. WA 30/3:417-18.

45. WA 30/3:418-19.

46. WA 30/3:417-18.

47. WA 30/3:319. Duke Georg has added "that works by love."

48. WA 30/3:418-19.

49. WA 30/3:419-20.

50. WA 30/3:422.

51. WA 30/3:422-23. In an appended paragraph Francis Arnoldi, pastor at Cölln, stated that he had published this treatise by an impartial layman in

order to further peace and obedience (WA 30/3:423).

52. See WA 30/3:439, and Becker, "Herzog Georg von Sachsen," pp. 260-66.

53. WABr 6:91.

54. WA 30/3:447-48.

55. WA 30/3:447.

56. WA 30/3:448.

57. WA 30/3:449-66.

58. WA 30/3:469.

59. WA 30/3:470.

60. WA 30/3:470.

61. See Kunst, *Evangelischer Glaube* pp. 263-87, and Georg Mentz, *Johann Friedrich der Grossmütige* (Jena, 1908), volume 2.

62. WABr 2:237, 238. Cited in Kunst, *Evangelischer Glaube*, p. 268.

63. To accomplish this the Council prepared lead tokens which the clergy were to present to those who confessed and communed. Possession of the token would be taken as proof that the individual was an obedient Catholic.

64. See WABr 6:444, WA 38:86-88.

65. WATR 5, 6046. On 5 April he dictated a possible appeal that the Leipzig Protestants might make to the duke. It does not appear, however, that the appeal was ever used (WABr 6:444f.).

66. The meaning is unclear. See WABr 6:450n2.

67. WABr 6:449f.

68. For details, see WABr 6:448f.

69. Reproduced in WABr 6:45.

70. See above.

71. For the full letter, see WABr:450f.

72. WABr 6:451f.

73. WABr 6:456f.

74. WABr 6:456f.

75. WABr 6:458.

76. WABr 6:452.

77. WABr 6:464.

78. WABr 6:465.

79. WA 38:96-107.

80. WA 38:99.

81. WA 38:101.

82. WA 38:102-3.

83. Ibid.

84. WA 38:104-6.

85. WA 38:108ff.

86. WA 38:119.

87. WA 38:121f.

88. For the following, see WA 38:135-38, and the cited literature.

89. WA 38:135-36.

90. The following points are taken from Johann Cochlaeus, *Hertzog Georgs zu Sachssen Ehrlich vnd grundtliche entschuldigung, wider Martin*

*Luthers Auffrüerisch vnd verlogenne, Brieff vnd Verantwortung* (Dresden, 1533).

91. Cochlaeus, *Ehrlich vnd grundtliche entschuldigung*, pp. Cij-Ciij, Fi-[Fiv(v)].

92. First, he mentioned Luther's teachings on both kinds (Cochlaeus, *Ehrlich vnd grundtliche entschuldigung*, pp. Ciij-Ciij(v)). He also related how in negotiations with Melanchthon at the Diet of Augsburg the Protestants had rejected a position on penance drawn directly from Luther's 1520 *Assertion of All the Articles*, arguing that the treatise was ten or twelve years old and, in any case, irrelevant since they were there to defend their Confession, not Luther's writings (Cochlaeus, *Ehrlich vnd grundtliche entschuldigung*, pp. Ciij(v)-[Civ(v)]). On several grounds Cochlaeus rejected as untenable Luther's argument in his 1533 *Catalogue* of his books that he had allowed too much to the papacy in his early books but that in his later books he had taught Christ alone and purely.

93. Cochlaeus, *Ehrlich vnd grundtliche entschuldigung*, pp. [Civ(v)]-Di.

94. Cochlaeus, *Ehrlich vnd grundtliche entschuldigung*, p. Dij(v).

95. Cochlaeus, *Ehrlich vnd grundtliche entschuldigung*, p. Gij.

96. Cochlaeus, *Ehrlich vnd grundtliche entschuldigung*, pp. Giij(v)-[Giv].

97. Cochlaeus, *Ehrlich vnd grundtliche entschuldigung*, pp. Iij-Li(v).

98. Cochlaeus, *Ehrlich vnd grundtliche entschuldigung*, pp. Gi-Gi(v)

99. Cochlaeus, *Ehrlich vnd grundtliche entschuldigung*, pp. Hij-Hij(v).

100. Cochlaeus, *Ehrlich vnd grundtliche entschuldigung*, pp. Eiij(v)-Fi.

101. WA 38:165-67.

102. WA 38:141.

103. "Denn es künde weder Hertzog Georg noch kein herr so from noch heilig sein, das er leiden möchte solche scherffe des greulichen rechts, wo er ein mal strauchelt odder feilete, das er darumb solt ein bösewicht odder ein verlogener man gescholten werden jnn allen andern stücken seines gantzen lebens und wesens, sonderlich, wo er solchen feyl selbs nicht ertichtet hette."

104. WA 38:143.

105. WA 38:161-65.

106. WA 38:168f.

107. WABr 6:72-73.

108. Maybe, see WABr 6:92n1.

109. The German reads: [Denn E. A. war zu] lange aussen, wie ich mich E.A. [Zukunft doch versehe]n hatte. The note to this sentence (WABr 6:92n2) suggests that Luther is referring to Brück's presence at the Diet of Grimma, 3 to 27 March. This, however, is *before* his meeting with Luther in Wittenberg on 16 April, when he conveyed to Luther the elector's prohibition of "sharp, hot-tempered" treatises. Moreover, Brück had been in Wittenberg several days before 16 August, since he refers in his letter to the elector of 18 August to a series of sermons that Luther preached from 2 to 16 April (WABr 6:72n6). If, then, Luther's *Assassin* was conceived or written after 16 [or 18] April, then Luther must be referring to some other trip of Brück's and WABr must be wrong. Another possibility is that *Assassin* was written before the 16 April meeting and before Brück arrived in Wittenberg. This seems highly unlikely

since this pushes the date of composition back into late March or early April and one would also expect some mention to be made of the treatise in the 16 April letter or the 18 April report.

110. See WABr 6:92n3.

111. WABr 6:91.

112. "Theologisch wolt ichs wol handeln, Aber historisch zu handeln wer mir seer nutze."

113. See WABr 6:91, lines 12-13.

114. WABr 6:154.

115. Cochlaeus, *Ehrlich vnd grundtliche entschuldigung*, pp. Nii-[Niv].

116. Wolgast, *Die Wittenberger Theologie*, p. 298.

117. See, especially, the excellent study by Peter Blickle, *Die Revolution von 1525* (Munich, 1975), now available in English as *The Revolution of 1525: The German Peasants' War from a New Perspective*, trans. by Thomas A. Brady, Jr. and H. C. Erik Midelfort (Baltimore, 1981).

## Chapter Four

1. See, for example, CR 3:99-104, Ernst Bizer, "Noch einmal: Die Schmalkaldischen Artikel," *ZKG* 68(1957):259-63, and CR 3:146-56.

2. See, for example, CR 3:119-25; CR 3:126-31; Ernst Bizer, "Die Wittenberger Theologen und das Konzil 1537: Ein ungedrucktes Gutachten," *ARG* 47(1956):77-101; WABr 8:35-38.

3. Elector Johann Friedrich thought of the task in just these terms. See, for example, WA 50:166f.

4. See Ernst Schäfer, *Luther als Kirchenhistoriker* (Gütersloh, 1897), esp. pp. 45-69. For Luther's view of history, see also John M. Headley, *Luther's View of Church History* (New Haven, 1963).

5. WA 2:36-40. In the following introductory pages, I relie heavily on Christa Tecklenburg Johns, *Luthers Konzilsidee in ihrer historischen Bedingtheit und ihrem reformatorischen Neuansatz* (Berlin, 1966), and Hubert Jedin, *A History of the Council of Trent*, vol. 1 (London, 1957).

6. WA 2:36-40; WABr 1:270.

7. WA 7:75-82, 85-90.

8. E.g., WA 2:279, 288, 298, 303.

9. E.g., *Resolutions* (WA 2:404), *Treatise on Good Works* (WA 6:258).

10. Johns, *Luthers Konzilsidee*, p. 117.

11. The following summary is drawn largely from Johns, *Luthers Konzilsidee*.

12. WA 6:404-69.

13. WA 6:406.

14. WA 6:413.

15. WA 6:415-68.

16. The following summary is drawn largely from Jedin, *Council of Trent*, 1:197-281. Jedin interprets all the Protestant calls for a "free Christian council" as insincere and mere tactic. While there was definitely the element

of "tactic" in the Protestant appeals to a council, there was also a sincere belief that a truly free Christian council which based its decisions solely on Scripture would sustain the Protestant teachings. The Protestants were sincerely appealing to a council as they defined it.

17. Quoted in Jedin, *Council of Trent*, 1:211.

18. Jedin, *Council of Trent*, 1:211-13.

19. Jedin, *Council of Trent*, 1:213-17.

20. Jedin, *Council of Trent*, 1:247f. Franz Lau and Ernst Bizer, *A History of the Reformation in Germany to 1555*, trans. by Brian A. Hardy (London, 1969), p. 77.

21. *Die Bekenntnisschriften der evangelisch-lutherischen Kirche*, 3d ed. (Göttingen, 1956), pp. 47-48.

22. Cited in WABr 6:480. For the following, see esp. Jedin, *Council of Trent*, 1:263-87.

23. WABr 6:480f.

24. WABr 6:483-87.

25. WABr 6:487f.

26. W2 16:1879-87.

27. Georg Mentz, *Johann Friedrich der Grossmütige* (Jena, 1908), 2:18.

28. CR 2, 667.

29. On Luther's authorship, see WABr 6:489 and H. Volz, "Eine Flugschrift aus dem Jahre 1533 mit einer Vorrede Martin Luthers," *Theologische Studien und Kritiken* (1933):78-96.

30. WABr 6:489-91.

31. For the following, see Jedin, *Council of Trent*, 1:283-87.

32. *Nuntiaturberichte aus Deutschland* (Gotha, 1892ff.), 1:266n1. Quoted in Jedin, *Council of Trent*, 1:285.

33. For the following, see Jedin, *Council of Trent*, 1:288-99.

34. For the following, see *Nuntiaturberichte*, 1:541-47; WABr 7:322; WATR 5,6384; W2 16:1888-92; Mentz, *Johann Friedrich*, 2:60-68, 2:72; CR 2:982-89, 992-95, 1018-22; W2 16:1892-1903.

35. See H. G. Haile, *Luther: An Experiment in Biography* (New York, 1980), pp. 19-29.

36. WA 39/1:13-38; WA 39/1:10.

37. WA 39/1:14.

38. WA 39/1:37f.

39. WA 50:3-5.

40. WA 50:1f.

41. WA 50:5.

42. On the problems of dating, see WA 39/1:181f.

43. WA 39/1:183 Ac.

44. The theses themselves provide such an excellent summary of Luther's view of a council that they are worth quoting almost in their entirety (numbering omitted and paragraphing changed): "No authority after Christ is equal to that of the apostles and prophets. All other of their successors should only be considered as their disciples. [For] the apostles had the certain promise of the Holy Spirit (not only in general but also as individuals). Therefore

they alone were called the foundation of the church who should hand down articles of faith. None of [their] successors had the promise of the Holy Spirit as individuals. Therefore it does not follow that the apostles were able [to do] this and this, therefore their successor can do the same. But rather in whatever they wish to teach or establish, they should follow and assert [*afferre*] the authority of the apostles. . . . For prophecy is not brought forward by the human will. . . . Rather the men of God are inspired by the Holy Spirit so that they might interpret the Scriptures, not according to their own interpretation. And if the successors do not follow or observe the foundation of the apostles, they are heretics or antichrists as [those] lost outside the foundation. Therefore an assembly of bishops or a council can err, just as other men, as well in [their] public [capacity] as in [their] private. If, however, they do not err, this occurs either by chance or by the merit of some saint among them or by merit of the church, not by the authority of their assembly. As for instance the Council of Nicaea avoided error by the strength [*virtute*] of the man Paphnutius. . . . For the Holy Spirit is not bound by any promise to the assembly of bishops or of the council, nor can they prove this. Therefore they boast arrogantly and falsely, not to mention blasphemously, that they are legitimately assembled in the Holy Spirit. What makes them or us certain that the Holy Spirit is necessarily bound to their assembly? It is easy to be assembled. But they cannot be assembled in the Holy Spirit unless, following the foundation of the apostles, they discuss not their [own] thoughts but rather the analogy [*analogiam*] of faith. This they rightly say, [namely], that they represent the church, then they are the church just as a painted man is a man, that is, only representatively. And if they are in some degree more (that is the true church) that occurs by chance (as has been said), not by virtue of representing the church. The histories testify [that] the councils were often the church only representatively, rarely [were they] the true church. Indeed, properly speaking, the council is always the church representatively but is the true church accidentally. Therefore no one is bound to believe the decrees of the representative church, that is, the council, unless they judge and speak according to the writings of the apostles. All the other [decrees] are mere [decrees] of the representative church or painted church which, if they are not impious, one may promote. And they themselves say that one man can contradict the whole council if he has a better reason or Scripture. This they say, but mendaciously, for they powerfully deny and condemn this in deeds. And not if an angel came from heaven would they allow themselves to be contradicted, nor would they listen to a thousand Paphnutiuses. In the Council of Nicaea one Paphnutius resisted the council. Nonetheless he was not burned but rather praised. In [the council of] Constance, two Paphnutiuses [Hus and Jerome of Prague], armed with Scripture, resisted. Nevertheless they were not praised but rather burned." (WA 39/1:184-87)

45. WA 50:23-34.
46. WA 50:21.
47. WA 50:37f.
48. WA 50:20.

49. WA 50:49, 52-64.
50. WA 50:51-61.
51. WA 50:50f.
52. WA 50:49f.
53. WABr 2:48f.
54. WA 50:73. Cf. WA 50:85.
55. WA 50:66f.
56. WA 50:339-43.
57. WA 50:255, text: WA 50:262-83.
58. Hubert Jedin, *A History of the Council of Trent* (London, 1957), 1:324-29, quote from p. 328.
59. WA 50:91f.
60. Quoted in Jedin, *Council of Trent*, 1:334.
61. See WA 50:126f., text: pp. 128-30.
62. On dating, see WA 50:96-98, text: pp. 98-105.
63. WA 50:46f.
64. WA 50:284-86. Jedin, *Council of Trent*, 1:423-26.
65. See WA 50:302 (marginalia). Jedin, *Council of Trent*, 1:427-33 describes the fate of these proposals.
66. See the marginalia on WA 50:308.
67. See previous chapter.
68. WA 50:353. *Deutsche Reichstagsakten, jüngere Reiche*, vol. 3, nos. 74, 75, 82, 83, 110. Or W2 15:374-81, 2125-87 (the estates' second reply is not included and W2 fails to note that no. 723 was also part of the treatise).
69. For Luther's preface and marginalia, see WA 50:355-63. For the documents themselves, see the previous note.
70. WA 50:361f. His Latin preface covered similar ground. His conclusion was different, however. He applauded the fact that the German princes had dared in their reply to the legate to tell the pope and the Roman curia "that which it could not, can not, and will not hear." And he noted that they had not allowed themselves to be swayed by the "splendid deceit and artifice of the curia which could be read in the Instructions of the legate. Had the devil not forestalled these happy developments through Müntzer's sedition and the "sects of the adversaries," Luther ventured, this papal confidence would have been conquered then and this insolence would have already fallen into the Jordan long ago (WA 50:356f.).
71. See, among others, H. Virck, "Zu den Beratungen der Protestaten über die Konzilsbulle vom 4. Juni 1536," *ZKG* 13(1892-93): 487-512; Hans Volz, *Luthers Schmalkaldische Artikel und Melanchthons Tractatus de postestate papae* (Gotha, 1931); Ernst Bizer, "Die Wittenberger Theologen und das Konzil 1537: Ein ungedrucktes Gutachten," *ARG* 47(1956):77-101; idem, "Zum geschichtlichen Verständnis von Luthers Schmalkaldischen Artikeln," *ZKG* 67(1955-56):61-92; Hans Volz, "Luthers Schmalkaldische Artikel," *ZKG* 68(1957):259-86; Ernst Bizer, "Noch einmal: Die Schmalkaldischen Artikel," *ZKG* 68(1957):287-94; and Hans Volz, ed., *Urkunden und Aktenstücke zur Geschichte von Martin Luthers Schmalkaldischen Artikeln (1536-1574)* (Berlin, 1957). For the history of the articles after Luther's death, see Volz,

*Luthers Schmalkaldische Artikel*, pp. 35-42.

72. WA 50:197f.

73. WA 50:198-200.

74. WA 50:200.

75. WA 50:211f.

76. In a late meeting convened in December, 1536, to discuss these articles, this article on the Lord's Supper also provoked some controversy. In February 1537 Melanchthon reportedly told Landgrave Philipp of Hesse that originally Luther had written in accordance with the formulation of the Wittenberg Concord "We hold that with the bread and wine . . . is the true body and blood of Christ" but had then struck the word "with" at the insistence of Bugenhagen "since he is a passionate man and a coarse Pomeranian" (Volz, *Urkunden und Aktenstücke*, p. 105). Many years later, in 1557, Melanchthon gave a different account, arguing that it was through the "vehemence" [*ungestimmikait*] of Amsdorf that the wording was changed and that when Melanchthon had asked Luther why he had not stayed with the synecdoche, Amsdorf had asked Melanchthon what a synecdoche was, saying that he did not understand the term (Volz, *Urkunden und Aktenstücke*, p. 105n10). These two accounts pose several difficulties (see Bizer, "Zum geschichtlichen Verständnis," pp. 73-80). For one thing, Luther never did use the formula of the Wittenberg Concord that specified that *with* the bread and wine was the body and blood. Rather, as we have seen, he first dictated that *under* the bread and wine was the body and blood, a formulation that was unacceptable to the South Germans since it suggested a spatial inclusion of Christ in the elements (see Bizer, "Zum geschichtlichen Verständnis," p. 74 and 74n46). He had then had his secretary strike the word "under," transforming the article into a form that was, as the historian Ernst Bizer puts it, "at least tolerable to the extent that he [Luther] had simply returned to the biblical 'is.' " Since this change occurred *before* the discussions of the articles by the theologians (see Volz, *Luthers Schmalkaldische Artikel*, p. 12. Bizer, "Zum geschichtlichen Verständnis," pp. 74f.), Melanchthon may have only known, perhaps through Bugenhagen (see Bizer's speculation (Bizer, "Zum geschichtlichen Verständnis," p. 75), that a change had been made but mistakenly thought that the change was from the formula of the Wittenberg Concord to this "somewhat harsh form [*etwas heftig gestalt*]" (Volz, *Urkunden und Aktenstücke*, p. 105). Since Bugenhagen was in fact a consistent supporter of the Wittenberg Concord, he may have actually been responsible for this change which brought the article at least closer to a form acceptable to the South Germans. Melanchthon, however, may have misunderstood this intervention of Bugenhagen's for the exact opposite of what it actually was. This is Bizer's suggestion (Bizer, "Zum geschichtlichen Verständnis," p. 75). Amsdorf, in contrast, was a vehement opponent of the Concord and refused on several occasions to sign it. The exchange reported by Melanchthon over the synecdoche would therefore have been completely consistent with Amsdorf's position.

77. WA 50:192-94.

78. See Annemarie Halder, *Das Harnsteinleiden Martin Luthers* (Munich, 1969).
79. WA 50:501.
80. WA 50:516 and 519.
81. WA 50:520 and 543.
82. WA 50:546f.
83. WA 50:501-4.
84. WA 50:606f.
85. WA 50:613f.
86. WA 50:615f.
87. Cf. WA 50:507 number 3a.
88. WA 50:624-26.
89. WA 50:628-29.
90. WA 50:630f.
91. WA 50:631-33. Excluded from this office are "women, children, and incompetent people" (WA 50:633).
92. WA 50:641.
93. WA 50:641f.


## Chapter Five

1. The 1530 Foreword to Daniel is found in WADB 11/2:2-48, 124-130. On the Turks and on Luther's writings against the Turks, see, among others, John W. Bohnstedt, *The Infidel Scourge of God: The Turkish Menace as Seen by German Pamphleteers of the Reformation Era*, Transactions of the American Philosophical Society 56, part 9 (Philadelphia, 1968). George W. Forell, "Luther and the War Against the Turks," *Church History* 14(1945):256-71. Stephen A. Fischer-Galati, *Ottoman Imperialism and German Protestantism, 1521-1555* (Cambridge, Mass., 1959). H. Lamparter, *Luthers Stellung zum Türkenkrieg* (Munich, 1940). Harvey Buchanan, "Luther and the Turks, 1519-1529," *ARG* 47(1956):145-59, Egil Grislis, "Luther and the Turks," *Muslim World* 64(1974):180-93, 275-91.
2. WA 1:233, 535.
3. Forell, "War Against the Turks," p. 257n4.
4. WA 7:140-41.
5. WA 30/2:107-48.
6. WA 30/2:149-51. The sermon itself is WA 30/2:160-97.
7. WA 30/2:198-208. The treatise appeared in early 1530 and was frequently reprinted in Latin as well as in German translations prepared by Sebastian Franck and Justus Jonas.
8. WA 30/2:143f.
9. Cf. his 1530 introduction to his German translation of Daniel (see note 1).
10. WA 30/2:181.
11. WA 30/2:181-97.

12. Fischer-Galati, *Ottoman Imperialism*, pp. 38-87. His treatment of the Protestants during this period is often inadequate and less than persuasive.

13. WA 50:478-87.

14. WABr 9:513f.

15. E.g., WABr 9:505.

16. WA 51:577-625.

17. WA 51:589.

18. WA 51:617.

19. WABr 10:17-22. He also revealed his inability to handle even simple calculations (see WABr 10:21f.).

20. WABr 10:23.

21. See Mark U. Edwards Jr., *Luther and the False Brethren* (Stanford, 1975), ch. 8.

22. WA 53:261-66.

23. WA 53:272.

24. WA 30/2:205.

25. WA 53:272.

26. WA 53:266-69.

27. WA 53:388-96.

28. WA 53:388f.

29. WA 53:391f.

30. WA 53:392-94.

31. WA 53:394.

32. WA 53:394-96.

33. WA 53:396.

34. CR 4:821. WABr 10:66f.

35. WABr 10:65.

36. WABr 10:169, 230, 252, 271-73.

37. WABr 10:161-63.

38. See WA 53:561-66 and WABr 10:161.

39. WA 53:569-72.

40. WA 53:558-60.

41. For an excellent comparative study, see John W. Bohnstedt, *The Infidel Scourge of God.*

42. WA 53:396.


## Chapter Six

1. The literature on Luther's relation to the Jews is so vast that a monograph recently appeared on the literature itself (Johannes Brosseder, *Luthers Stellung zu den Juden im Spiegel seiner Interpreten. Interpretation und Rezeption von Luthers Schriften und Äusserungen zum Judentum im 19. und 20. Jahrhundert vor allem im deutschsprachigen Raum* [Munich, 1972]. See also Kurt Meier, "Zur Interpretation von Luthers Judenschriften," in *Vierhundertfünfzig Jahre lutherische Reformation, 1517-1967* (Berlin/ Göttingen, 1967), pp. 233-52; C. Bernd Sucher, *Luthers Stellung zu den*

*Juden. Eine Interpretation aus germanistischer Sicht* [Nieuwkoop, 1977], pp. 125-99.). For reasons that will become apparent, I have found most useful the following works: Wilhelm Maurer, "Die Zeit der Reformation," in *Kirche und Synagoge*, edited by Karl-Heinrich Rengstorf and Siegfried von Kortzfleisch, (Stuttgart, 1968), 1:363-452; and C. Bernd Sucher, *Luthers Stellung zu den Juden.* During the final stages of revision before publication I received a copy of Heiko A. Oberman's *Wurzeln des Antisemitismus: Christenangst und Judenplage im Zeitalter von Humanismus und Reformation* (Severin und Siedler, 1981). Developing an analysis similar in some respects to my own but in considerably more detail, this fascinating monograph places Luther's writings back within their historic context and thus corrects many of the more exclusively theological studies.

2. Of the vast literature on the history of the Jews and of Jewish-Christian relations, I have found most useful Rosemary Radford Reuther, *Faith and Fratricide: The Theological Roots of Anti-Semitism* (New York, 1974); Alan Davies, ed., *Antisemitism and the Foundations of Christianity* (New York, 1979); Salo Baron, *A Social and Religious History of the Jews* (New York, 1957-73), vols. 2-15; Guido Kisch, *The Jews in Medieval Germany: A Study of Their Legal and Social Status* (Chicago, 1949).

3. See Kisch, *The Jews in Medieval Germany*, pp. 107-68.

4. Maurer, "Die Zeit der Reformation," pp. 367-69; Oberman, *Wurzeln*, pp. 52-55, 99-104.

5. *Ein grausame, erschrockenliche geschicht von einem vngotzförchtigem verrucktem vnnd verzweyfelten Christen man, der sein eigen fleiss vnd blüt, sein natürliches kind ein junges kneblin den Seellosen, Gottlosen, Gotts verretterschen Juden verkaufft vnd zü kauffen geben hatt* . . . (n.p.,n.d.), pp. Aii(v)-Ci(v). The copy of this tract found in the British Library [STC 4033.c.50(6)] has the date 1544 penned on the title page. I suspect that the treatise was originally published at an earlier date. The libel I am recounting occurred in 1503. Another murder treated in this account, to which the anonymous author claims to have been an eye-witness, apparently occurred in 1504 [see p. Dii(v)]. In any case, the verses appear to have been written before Emperor Maximilian's death in 1519 [see p. E(v)].

6. Johann Eck, *Ains Judenbüechlins verlegung: darin ain Christ, gantzer Christenhait zü schmach, will es geschehe den Juden vnrecht in bezichtigung der Kristen kinder mordt* (Ingolstadt: Alexander Weissenhorn, 1542), pp. Biii(v)-Biv(v).

7. Eck only says it sweated (p. Biv).

8. *Ein grausame, erschrockenliche geschicht*, p. Bii.

9. Ibid., p. C(v).

10. Since the treatise was written in German, I infer that Eck had a popular audience in mind. Most of his writings were in Latin (see "Verzeichnis der Schriften Ecks," in *Corpus Catholicorum* [Münster, 1930], 16:LXXII-CXXXII).

11. WA 11:316-25.

12. WA 11:325-36.

13. WA 11:336.

14. WATR 3, 3512b. WATR 4, 5026 and 4795. WA 53:461. Cf. WA 50:515. Cited in Maurer, "Die Zeit der Reformation," pp. 398-99.

15. E.g., WA 50:273-83.

16. C. A. H. Burckhardt, "Die Judenverfolgung in Kurfürstentum Sachsen von 1536 an," *Theologische Studien und Kritiken* 70(1897):593-98.

17. See the following discussion of his correspondence with Josel of Rosheim.

18. WATR 3:441-42.

19. See Selma Stern, *Josel of Rosheim in the Holy Roman Empire of the German Nation*, trans. by Gertrude Hirschler (Philadelphia, 1965).

20. WABr 8:76-78. For a discussion of these letters, see Stern, *Josel of Rosheim*, pp. 155-57, 303n7, 304n8.

21. WATR 3:441-42.

22. For the following, see WABr 8:89-91.

23. See Stern, *Josel of Rosheim*, p. 162.

24. WA 50:312-37.

25. WA 50:318.

26. WA 53:417-552, 53:579-648, 54:28-100.

27. WA 53:417.

28. For more on the background of these treatises and their sources, see WA 50:309-11, 53:412-14, 53:573-75, 54:16-24, as well as the literature cited in note 1 above.

29. WA 53:417.

30. WA 53:418-19.

31. WA 53:419-27.

32. WA 53:427-39.

33. WA 53:439-46.

34. WA 53:446-48.

35. WA 53:449.

36. WA 53:579-80.

37. WA 53:587-609, quote on pp. 605-6.

38. WA 54:28-100.

39. See WA 51:152-53, 166-67, 195ff.; WA 54:17-18.

40. Carl Cohen, "Martin Luther and His Jewish Contemporaries," *Jewish Social Studies* 25(1963):201. Benzing (Josef Benzing, *Lutherbibliographie: Verzeichnis der gedruckten Schriften Martin Luthers bis zu dessen Tod* [Baden-Baden, 1966]) does not list this Spanish translation, and I have been unable to verify its existence.

41. WA 54:24.

42. Stern, *Josel of Rosheim*, p. 95. See also Eck's *Verlegung*.

43. Stern, *Josel of Rosheim*, p. 307n6.

44. Stern, *Josel of Rosheim*, pp. 192-93, 196-99.

45. CR 5:21.

46. CR 5:76-77.

47. See, for example, his evaluation in his funeral oration for Luther (CR 11:727-28). See also Gustav Mix, "Luther und Melanchthon in ihrer

gegenseitigen Beurteilung," *Theologische Studien und Kritiken* 74(1901):458-521; and Wilhelm Pauck, "Luther und Melanchthon," in *Luther und Melanchthon*, ed. Vilmos Vajta (Göttingen, 1961), pp. 11-31.

48. CR 5:729; WA 53:574.

49. "So ist vorhanden Luthers Schwynins katigs Schemhamphoras, welches so es geschriben wäre von einem Schwynhirten, nit von einem berrümpten Seel hirten, etwas doch ouch wenig entschuldigung hette." *Wahrhaffte Bekanntnuss* (Zurich, 1545), p. 10r. For a brief discussion of this treatise, see my *Luther and the False Brethren* (Stanford, 1975), pp. 194-96.

50. Stern characterizes Eck's treatise as "the most abusive to have been written against the Jews even in that 'Age of Grobianism'." (Stern, *Josel of Rosheim*, p. 183). It certainly makes for grisly reading.

51. Martin Bucer *et al.*, *Ratschlag Ob Christlicher Obrigkeit gebüren müge, das sie die Jüden, vnter den Christen zu wonen gedulden, vnd wo sie zu gedulden, welcher gestalt vnd mais* (Erfurt, 1539). The pastors recommended that Jews be barred from all forms of employment except the most lowly and degrading, so that they would be constantly aware of their status.

52. See Oberman, *Wurzeln*, esp. parts I and II, for the linkage between anti-Jewish and reform sentiments held by Catholics and Protestants.

53. See the footnote on page 119.

54. Burkhardt, "Die Judenverfolgung," p. 597.

55. Stern, *Josel of Rosheim*, p. 195

56. Stern, *Josel of Rosheim*, pp. 199-200.

57. The following statistics are drawn from Benzing, *Lutherbibliographie*, numbers 1530-1542, 3293-3295, 3424-3426, 3436-3442, 3448-3449. One of the German editions of *Against the Sabbatarians* was printed in Augsburg by Alexander Weissenhorn, who, a year later in 1539, moved to Ingolstadt where he published much of the Catholic controversial literature issuing from that center including the only two editions of Eck's *Verlegung* ("Verzeichnis der Schriften Ecks," in *Corpus Catholicorum* [Münster, 1930], 16:CXXIX; Josef Benzing, *Buchdruckerlexikon des 16. Jahrhunderts (Deutsches Sprachgebiet)* [Frankfurt a.M., 1952], pp. 14, 81). Did he perhaps have a special animus toward Jews? Or is this just a coincidence?

58. As noted above, I have been unable to identify the Spanish edition mentioned by C. Cohen (see note 40).

59. There is some circumstantial evidence to support this suggestion. One of the two Frankfurt publishers of this treatise was Hermann Gülfferich, who generally specialized in popular literature for home and school (Benzing, *Buchdruckerlexikon*, p. 52).

60. Gordon Rupp has found some solace in *On the Jews and Their Lies* being a "worse seller" (Gordon Rupp, "Martin Luther and the Jews," *Nederlands Theologisch Tijdschrift* 31[1977]:130).

61. Benzing, *Lutherbibliographie*, numbers 3369-3372.

62. Benzing, *Lutherbibliographie*, numbers 3497-3502.

63. Benzing, *Lutherbibliographie*, numbers 3378-3387.

64. Benzing, *Lutherbibliographie*, numbers 3458-3463.

65. Maurer has published two major essays on Luther's attitude toward the Jews: Wilhlem Maurer, *Kirche und Synagoge. Motive und Formen der Auseinandersetzung der Kirche mit dem Judentum im Laufe der Geschichte. Franz Belitzsch-Vorlesungen 1951* (Stuttgart, 1953); and Maurer, "Die Zeit der Reformation" (see note 1). There are some significant differences between the two essays (see Brosseder, *Luthers Stellung zu den Juden*, pp. 270-75). In the later essay Maurer places less stress on the missionary aspects of the 1523 treatise and more on its Christological thrust. Brosseder, *Luthers Stellung zu den Juden*, follows Maurer on most points.

66. Maurer, "Die Zeit der Reformation," pp. 388-89, 407, 416, 427.

67. Maurer, "Die Zeit der Reformation," pp. 397-400.

68. Maurer, "Die Zeit der Reformation," pp. 421-22.

69. WA 53:522.

70. WA 53:525.

71. Maurer, "Die Zeit der Reformation," p. 426.

72. Maurer, "Die Zeit der Reformation," pp. 416, 407-15.

73. Ibid., pp. 428, 421.

74. Ibid., p. 427.

75. Maurer terms them *"unverlierbare."*

76. Maurer, "Die Zeit der Reformation," p. 421.

77. Maurer, "Die Zeit der Reformation," pp. 375-76.

78. Maurer, "Die Zeit der Reformation," p. 380, also makes this point.

79. See Hayim Hillel Ben-Sasson, "The Reformation in Contemporary Jewish Eyes," *Proceedings of the Israel Academy of Sciences and Humanities* 4(1971):239-326; and Cohen, "Martin Luther and His Jewish Contemporaries." I have not been able to consult E. Zivier, "Jüdische Bekehrungsversuche im 16. Jahrhundert," in *Beiträge zur Geschichte der deutschen Juden. Festschrift . . . Martin Philippson* (Leipzig, 1916), pp. 96-113.

80. See my *Luther and the False Brethren* for details.

81. See Maurer, "Die Zeit der Reformation," pp. 414-15, 436-38.

82. E.g., Oberman, *Wurzeln*, pp. 155-56.


## Chapter Seven

1. See, e.g., Bernhard Lohse, *Martin Luther: Eine Einführung in sein Leben und sein Werk* (Munich, 1981), pp. 91-96; Heinrich Böhmer, *Luther in Light of Recent Research*, trans. by Carl F. Huth, Jr. (New York, 1916), p. 193. For a recent examination of Luther's coarseness, see Martin Brecht, "Der 'Schimpfer' Martin Luther," *Luther* 52(1981):97-113.

2. See, e.g., Hartmann Grisar, *Luther* (Freiburg im Breisgau, 1911-12), esp. vols 2 and 3; and Böhmer, *Luther in Light of Recent Research*, pp. 188-204.

3. Böhmer, *Luther in Light of Recent Research*, p. 196.

4. *Luther's Works,* American Edition (Philadelphia, 1966), 41:183.

5. For the following, see Friedrich Koldewey, *Heinz von Wolfenbüttel* (Halle, 1883); Friedrich Bruns, *Die Vertreibung Herzog Heinrichs von Braunschweig durch den Schmalkaldischen Bund* (Marburg, 1889); Franz Petri, "Herzog Heinrich der Jüngere von Braunschweig-Wolfenbüttel: Ein niederdeutscher Teritorialfürst im Zeitalter Luthers und Karls V," *ARG* 72(1981):122-57. Also worth consulting are S. Issleib, "Philipp von Hessen, Heinrich von Braunschweig und Moritz von Sachsen 1541-1547," *Jahrbuch des Geschichtsvereins für das Herzogtum Braunschweig* 2(1903):1-80; Friedrich Koldewey, "Die Reformation des Herzogthums Braunschweig-Wolfenbüttel unter dem Regimente des Schmalkaldischen Bundes 1542-1547," *Historischer Verein für Niedersachsen* (1868):243-338; Hans-Walter Krumwiede, *Zur Entstehung des landesherrlichen Kirchenregimentes in Kursachsen und Braunschweig-Wolfenbüttel* (Göttingen, 1967); and WA 51:461-65.

Friedrich Hortleder, *Handlungen vnd Ausschreiben . . . von den Ursachen des deutschen Kriegs Kaiser Karls V . . . ,* 2nd ed. (Gotha, 1645), reproduces a majority of the documents and publications in this controversy. Unfortunately, Hortleder took it upon himself to bowdlerize the polemics, so that his collection is less useful than it might otherwise be.

To compile my bibliography of publications in this dispute I consulted, in addition to Hortleder, the following bibliographies: C. Borchling and B. Claussen, *Niederdeutsche Bibliographie. Gesamtverzeichnis der niederdeutschen Drucke bis zum Jahre 1800,* 3 vols. (Neumünster, 1931-1957); W. Brandes, *Bibliographie der niedersächsischen Frühdrucke bis zum Jahre 1600* (Baden-Baden, 1960); A. von Dommer, *Die ältesten Drucke aus Marburg in Hessen, 1527-1566* (Marburg, 1892); M. von Hase, *Bibliographie der Erfurter Drucke von 1501-1550* (Nieuwkoop, 1968); P. Hohenemser, *Flugschriftensammlung Gustav Freytag* (Frankfurt a.M., 1925); A. Kuczynski, *Thesaurus libellorum historiam Reformationis illustrantium. Verzeichnis einer Sammlung von nahezu 3000 Flugschriften Luthers und seiner Zeitgenossen* (Leipzig, 1870-74); M. Pegg, *A Catalogue of German Reformation Pamphlets (1516-1546) in Libraries of Great Britain and Ireland* (Baden-Baden, 1973); K. Schottenloher, *Bibliographie zur deutschen Geschichte im Zeitalter der Glaubensspaltung, 1517-1585,* 7 vols. (Stuttgart, 1956-66); O. Schade, *Satiren und Pasquille aus der Reformationszeit,* 3 vols. (Hannover, 1863; Hildesheim, 1966); *Short-Title Catalogue of Books Printed in the German-Speaking Countries and German Books Printed in Other Countries from 1455 to 1600 Now in the British Museum* (London, 1962); E. Weller, *Annalen der Poetischen National-Literatur der Deutschen im XVI. und XVII. Jahrhundert,* 2 vols. (Freiburg i. Br., 1862-64; Hildesheim, 1964); idem, *Die ersten deutschen Zeitungen* (Stuttgart, 1872; Hildesheim, 1962). See also the works cited in notes 39 and 40.

For a more extensive bibliography of bibliographies, see Pegg, *A Catalogue of German Reformation Pamphlets,* pp. xiii-xviii.

6. Heinrich, der Jüngere, duke of Braunschweig-Wolfenbüttel, *Erste, bestände, ergründete vnd warhafftige Antwort . . . Auff ein vermeynt nichtig vnd unwarhafftig Schreiben, des Churfürsten zu Sachsen vnd Landgraffen zu*

*Hessen, welchs sie erstlich an die Churfürsten, Pfaltz vnd Brandenburg ausgehen lassen . . .* (Wolfenbüttel, 1540).

7. Johann Friedrich, elector of Saxony, and Philipp, landgrave of Hesse, *Warhafftiger vnd gründlicher Bericht, auch glaubwürdige Abschrifften aller Brieff, Entschuldigung vnd Handlung, so sich verruckter Tage zwischen dem . . . Herrn Johanis Friederichen Herzog zu Sachsen . . . Und Herrn Philipsen Landgraffen zu Hessen . . . an einem. Und Hertzog Heinrichen von Braunschweig andern Theils. Eines vffgehaltenen Secretarien, auch Passes vnd Geleyts halber zugetragen haben* (Marburg, 1539).

8. Johann Friedrich, elector of Saxony, and Philipp, landgrave of Hesse, *Widerschreiben, auff das vnerfindlich Hertzog Heinrichs zu Braunschweig Antwortschreiben also derselbe zu ihrer Chur- vnd Fürstlichẽ Gn. Verunglimpffung, an etliche Chur- vnd Fürsten des Reichs, vnd hochgemeldte beyde Churfürst vnd Fürsten wiederumb gethan haben* (Wittenberg, 1539).

9. See note 6.

10. Heinrich, der Jüngere, duke of Braunschweig-Wolfenbüttel, *Andere beständige, ergründte vnd warhafftige Antwort . . . Auff des Churfürsten zu Sachsen, vnd Landgraffen zu Hessen, jüngst aussgangen lester, ehrenrürig, famos, erdicht, vnwarhafftig, vnd falsche Libel, an beide Churfürsten, Pfaltz vnd Brandenburg, geschrieben, Darinn der Leser zubefinden, wie bösslich, falschlich, erdichtiglich, vnd neben aller warheit, sein F.G. von Sachsen vnd Hessen, sein angeben, geschmecht, vnd ausgebreitet worden* (Wolfenbüttel, 1540).

11. Philipp, landgrave of Hesse, *Apologia oder andere warhafftige, ehrliche, beständige, Christliche Verantwortung . . . Aller erdichten, falschen Zumessung, seinen Fürstlichen Gnaden von Hertzog Heinrichen dem Jüngern von Braunschweig, in seinem letzten erdichteten, bösen, vnadeligen Ausschreiben auffgelegt. Darneben ein beständige, ehrliche, rechtmässige Assertion, Erklärung vnd Beweisung aller der Dinge, so hochgemeldter Landgraff Phillips von Hertzog Heinrichen, aus höchster gemeines Nutzes, vnd seiner Fürstlichen Gnaden Nothturfft, geklagt, geschrieben vnd gesagt hat* (Marburg, 1540); and *Contra scurriles, sycophanticas et parum principe viro dignas calumnias ducis Henrici a Braunsuig proxime aeditas, apologia Latinitate donata* (Marburg, 1540).

12. Johann Friedrich, elector of Saxony, *Anderer Abdruck . . . warhafftigen, beständigen vnd ergründeten Verantwortungen auff Hertzog Heinrichs von Braunschweig, der sich den Jüngern nennet, ehrenrühriges, erdichtetes vnd vnwahrhaftes famos Libell, Schandschrifften, vnd Abdruck an beyde Churfürsten, Pfaltz vnd Brandenburg geschrieben* (Wittenberg, 1540).

13. Heinrich, der Jüngere, duke of Braunschweig-Wolfenbüttel, *Dritte, bestendige, warhafftige, redliche, Göttliche, vnd ergründte, vnablegliche Antwort . . . Auff des Landgraffen wider S.F.G. neher aussgangene vngöttliche, vnchristliche, vnehrliche, vnwarhafftige erdichte vnd vnbestendige Lesterschrift. Vnd beständige, erhabliche, ergründte vnd rechtmässige Ableinung des Landgraffen berühmbter nichtigen Assertion. Item, Erklärung vnd Beweisung aller der Ding, so der Landgraff vmb eigne Nutz willen, vnd ohne Grundt E.F.G. auffgelegt hat* (Wolfenbüttel, 1540).

14. Heinrich, der Jüngere, duke of Braunschweig-Wolfenbüttel, *Ergrundte, beständige, erhebliche, warhafftige, Göttliche, Christliche, Fürsten vnd Adelliebende Duplicae . . . Wider des Churfürsten von Sachsen andern ehrnrührigen, vngegrünten, vnbestendigen, erdichten, vngöttlichen, vnchristlichen, truncknen, Gotteshessigen Abdruck* (Wolfenbüttel, 1540) [hereafter referred to as *Duplicae*].

15. Heinrich, der Jüngere, duke of Braunschweig-Wolfenbüttel, *An S.F.Gn. gemeine Landschafft aussgegangen warhafftige, Summarien Anzeige, vnd Beweisung, dass es nicht an S. Fürstl. Gn. sondern S. Fürstl. Gn. vngetrewen, vngehorsamen Vnterthanen, Bürgermeistern vnd Rathe der Stadt Braunschweig, vnd jhrem Anhang, als den muthwilligen Landfriedbrechern erwunden hat . . .* (Wolfenbüttel, 1540) [Hortleder, 1:1335, states that this was published in 1541, while Schottenloher, no. 29774, gives 1540 as the date]; Stechau, Balthasar von, *Ein vermeint vngegründ, vnerfindlich schreiben, so der Rath zu Braunschweig, wider den Ehrbarn vnd vesten Balthasern von Stechaw, grosse Vogt zu Wulffenbüttel, an die heimuerorodenten Hoffrethe daselbst ausgehen lassen, vnd sein des Vogts gegründter, erfindlicher vnd warhafftiger, den jtzt bemelten Hoffrethen gethaner gegenbericht, vier Bawrn aus Ampleuen, die mit urteil vnd recht Veruestet worden sein, vnd anders belangend* (Wolfenbüttel, 1540); *Ergangene schrifften zwischen Heinrichs des Jüngern, Hertzogen zu Braunschweig, Hoffrethen vnd Ernsten, Hertzogen zu Braunschweig, Der Stadt Braunschweig, der dar an vnd inliggenden Stifft vnd Closter vnd anderer gerechtigkeit halber, darinn zubefinden, Mit was vngrunde der Churfürst zu Sachsen vnd Landgrafe zu Hessen von wegen der Stadt Braunschweig inn irem vnerfindlichen offnem ausschreiben, an beide Churfürsten Pfaltz vnd Brandenburg ausgangen, bericht gethan haben* (Wolfenbüttel, 1540).

16. Ernst, duke of Braunschweig and Lüneburg, *Warhafftiger, beständiger Gegenbericht, wider Hertzog Heinrichs zu Braunschweig vnd Lüneburg, vnd seiner Hof-Räthe zu Wulffenbüttel, vermeynten vngegründten Bericht, als er in seinem schmählichen Ausschreiben, wider den Churfürsten zu Sachsen, u. vnd den Landgraffen zu Hessen, u. vnd die Hofräthe in ihren aussgegangenen Sendbrieffen, der Fürstlichen, Hoch- Ober- vnd Gerechtigkeit halben an der Stadt Braunschweig gethan haben . . .* (n.p., 1540); Braunschweig, City council of, *Wahrhafftige Verantwortung vnd Ablehnung eines Erbarn Raths der Stadt Braunschweig, wider Hertzog Heinrichs zu Branschweig vnnd Lüneburgk, u. vngnädig, vnerfindtlich Ausschreiben, vnd vermeynte berühmte Summarien Anzeige, als solte es an gemeldtem Raht erwunden seyn, dass die Gefangene gegen einander nicht ledig gelassen, noch sonst die Gebrechen, als sich zwischen gemeldtem Hertzogen vnd jhnen erhalten, durch die Landschafft, in der Güte mögen fürgenommen werden . . .* (n.p. [1540]); Koch, Hans, *An den Durchleuchtigen, Hochgebornen Fürsten vnd Herrn, Herrn Philipsen Landgraffen zu Hessen . . . Hansen Kochs wahrhafftige, gründliche Verantwortung vnd Ableinung aller Ehrenrührigen Anziehungen, Injurien, Schmähe- vnd Schelt-Wort, wider jhn durch Hertzog Heinrichen von Braunschweig den Jüngern, in seinem jüngsten Buch, in offenem Truck aussgangen . . .* (n.p., 1540).

17. See Wilhelm Maurer, "Luther und die Doppelehe Landgraf Philippus von Hessen," *Luther* (1953):49-120; William Walker Rockwell, *Die Doppelehe des Landgrafen Philipp von Hessen* (Marburg, 1904); and Walther Köhler, *Luther und die Lüge* (Leipzig, 1912), pp. 109-53.

18. See Hilmar von Strombeck, "Eva von Trott, des Herzogs Heinrich des jüngern von Braunschweig-Wolfenbüttel Geliebte, und ihre Nachkommenschaft," *Harz-Verein für Geschichte vnd Alterthumskunde* 2(1869):11-53; and Rockwell, *Die Doppelehe*, p. 102n4.

19. Georg Mentz, *Johann Friedrich der Grossmütige* (Jena, 1903-8), 2:305-6.

20. WA 51:463.

21. But see Mentz, *Johann Friedrich*, 2:306n3.

22. Johann Friedrich, elector of Saxony, *Warhafftige, Beständige, Wolgegründte, Christliche, vnnd auffrichtige Verantwortung wider des verstockten, Gottlosen, vormaledeieten, verfluchten Ehrenschänders, böstätigen Barrabas, auch hurensüchtigen Holofernes von Braunschweig, so sich Hertzog Heinrichen den Jüngern nennet, vnverschämtes, Calphurnisch Schand- vnd Lügenbuch* (Wittenberg, 1541) [hereafter referred to as *Verantwortung*].

23. Mentz, *Johann Friedrich*, 2:306.

24. Koldewey, *Heinz von Wolfenbüttel*, p. 33; WABr 9:360; WA 51:465f.

25. Georg Spalatin, *Chronica vnd Herkommen der Churfürst, vnnd Fürsten, des löblichen Hauss zu Sachsen, Gegen Hertzog Heinrichs zu Braunschweig, welcher sich den Jüngern nennet, herkommen. Daraus ein jeder Leser befinden wird, mit was offentlich Vngrundt, derselbe von Braunschweig, sich älters Herkommens gerühmbt, auch Mannlicher Handelung vnd Thaten, seinen Voreltern vnd Anherren, in seiner nähern Duplicenschrifft so er wider den Churfürsten zu Sachsen, u. hat aussgehen lassen, zulegen thut* (Wittenberg, 1541).

26. Mentz, *Johann Friedrich*, 2:306

27. *Supplication an kaiserliche Mayestat, der Mordbrenner halben, auf dem Reichstag zu Regensburg, Käyserlicher Mayestat vberantwortet, u.* (Wittenberg, 1541).

28. Heinrich, der Jüngere, duke of Braunschweig-Wolfenbüttel, *Antwort, der Key. May. auff die vbergebene Supplication, der Mordbrenner halben, gegeben* (Wolfenbüttel, 1541); *Anderweit Schrifft, So Römischer Käyserlichen Mayest. von Churfürst, Fürsten vnd Ständen, der Christlichen Religion, jüngst aufm Reichstage zu Regenspurg, gegen Hertzog Heinrichs von Braunschweig, der sich den Jüngern nennet, vermeynten Verantwortung, des Vnmenschlichen eingerissenen Mordbrennens halben, weiter vbergeben ist worden* (n.p., 1541).

29. *Copey des Vertrags, den Hertzog Heinrich von Braunschweig, mit seinem Brudern, Hertzog Wilhelm, auffgerichtet, eines vnfreundlichen vnd vnbrüderlichen Innhalts* (Wittenberg, 1541).

30. Philipp, landgrave of Hesse, *Dritte warhafftige Verantwortung, aller deren Dinge, so S.F.G. von Hertzog Heinrichen, der sich nennet den Jüngern von Braunschweig, zugelegt worden seyn, Es betreffe den auffgehaltenen Secretarien, oder anders . . .* (Marburg, 1541); idem, *Tertia adversus Ducis*

*Henrici sycophanticum scriptum, de novo aeditum, responsio* (n.p., n.d. [probably 1541]).

31. Ernst, duke of Braunschweig and Lüneburg, *Andere warhafftige, beständige, erwiesene vnnd bestettigte Verantwortung vnnd Schutzschrifft, wider Hertzog Heinrichs zu Braunschweig vnd Lüneburg vngegründte, blosse, vnerweissliche Ausschreiben, die er in seinem Namen, vnd vnter Titul seiner Hoffräthe zu Wolffenbüttel, von wegen der Fürstlichen Ober- vnd Gerechtigkeiten, an vnnd in der Stadt Braunschweig, hat aussgehen lassen* . . . (Wittenberg, 1541); Hans Koch, *An den Durchleuchtigenn Herrn Philipsen Lanndtgrafen zu Hessenn H. Kochs Ableynung aller der Schandtlichen Auflag, so jm durch des Meisters aller Lügen (Iustin von Warheytspruñ) zugemessen worden* (n.p. [1541]); Braunschweig, City council of, *Andere warhafftige, beständige, vnd vnverneinliche Verantwortung vnnd Gegenberich, wider Hertzog Heinrichs zu Braunschweig vnd Lüneburg, vermeynt vnerfindtlich Gedichte, das er wider gemelten Rath hat im Druck aussgegossen* . . . (Braunschweig, 1541); idem, *Warhafftiger bestendiger, gegrünter gegenbericht, des Erbarn Raths, der stad Braunschweig, an die Prelaten, Ritterschafft, Stete vnd Stende, des fürstentumbs zu Braunschweig, vnd die heimvorordente Hoffrethe zu Wulffenbüttel, Wieder das vnerfintlich, vormeint, vngegründt schreiben, so Baltasar von Stechaw, Grossevogt zu Wulffenbüttel, an die heimvorordente Hoffrethe daselbst vnlengest gestellet, vnd im abdruck ausgehen hat lassen* (Braunschweig, 1541).

32. *Gegründte, warhafftige, vnd vnwiderlegliche Supplication, einer ehrlichen Freundschafft, deren Schwester, Base, vnd Freundin, Hertzog Heinrich von Braunschweig, in seinem Frawenzimmer geunehret gehabt vnd anderer Gestalt mit ihr geparet, Vff jetzigem Reichstag zu Regenspurg der Römischen Keyserl. May. vbergeben. Auch was Hertzog Heinrich darauff geantwortet, wie er in derselben Sach tergiversiert. Vnd was die bemeldte Freundschafft desshalben weiter an die Keys. May. repliciret vnd gebeten hat* (n.p., 1541).

33. Heinrich, der Jüngere, duke of Braunschweig-Wolfenbüttel, *Vierte bestendige, warhafftige, ergründte, Christliche antwort Auff des Landgrauen zu Hessen (wie er sich nennet) vermeinte, nichtige, vnbestendige, erdicht vnd vngegründte verantwortung der ding, die S.F.G. demselben Landgrauen zu Hessen mit bestandt, grundt vnd warheit zugemessen* (Wolfenbüttel, 1541); and idem, *Erhebliche, ergrünte, warhafftige, Göttliche vnd Christliche Quadruplicae, wider des gottlosen, verruchten, verstockten, abtrinnigen Kirchenraubers, vnd vormaledeiten boshafftigen Antiochi, Nouatiani, Seueriani vnd Hurnwirts von Sachssen, der sich Hansen Friderichen, Hertzogen zu Sachssen nennt, erdicht, erlogen vnd vnverschempt Lesterbuch* (Wolfenbüttel, 1541) [hereafter referred to as *Quadruplicae*].

34. *Warhafftige, ergründte, vnwiderlegliche Antwort vnd Ableinung, wider H. Ernsts zu Braunschweig vnd Lüneburg, aussgangen vermeynten vnergründten Gegenbericht, Darum dass allein hochermelter Hertzog Heinrich der Stadt Braunschweig, Einiger, Rechter, Gehuldigter, Geschworner, Regierender Lands-fürst ist* . . . (Wolfenbüttel, 1541); Heinrich, der Jüngere, duke of Braunschweig-Wolfenbüttel, *Anderer bestendiger, warhafftiger, ergründeter Bericht . . . gegen S.F.G. vngetrewen Vnterthanen des Raths zu*

*Braunschweig erdichtete vermeinte Verantwortung vnd Ableinung* (Wolfen-büttel, 1541); for the third item, see note 28.

35. Heinrich, der Jüngere, duke of Braunschweig-Wolfenbüttel, *Fürtrag, Supplication, Bitt vnd Erbieten, so der Durchleuchtige, Hochgeborne Fürst vnd Herr, Herr Heinrich der Jünger, Hertzog zu Branschweig vnd Lüneburg u. vor der Röm. Keys. Maj. in Beyseyn vieler Churfürsten, Fürsten vnd Ständen des Heiligen Reichs zu Regenspurg, auff gehaltenem Reichs Tage, am zehenden Tag Junii, Anno u. 41. wider beyde Chur- vnd Fürsten, Sachsen vnd Hessen, gethan, vnd übergeben hat* (Wolfenbüttel, 1541); Johann Friedrich, elector of Saxony, *Antwort, Bitt, vnd Erbietung . . . an die Römische Keyserliche Majestat verfertiget, vnd seiner Churfürstlichen Gnaden Räthen, jhrer Keyserlichen Majest. zu Regenspurg, fürderlichen zu überantworten befohlen, Auff die vermeynte Supplication, welche Hertzog Heinrich von Braunschweig . . . Hochgemeldter Keyserlichen Majest. wider den Landgraffen zu Hessen, vnd Sein Churfürstliche Gnaden, doselbst überge-ben . . .* (Wittenberg, 1541); Philipp, landgrave of Hesse, *Fürstliche vnd ehrliche Verantwortung, an Römische Käyserliche Majestat, vnsern aller gnädigsten Herrn, nach seiner Fürstlicher Gnaden Abreisen von Regenspurg, dahin geschrieben, Auff Hertzog Heinrichs von Braunschweig . . . vermeynte Supplication-Schrifft . . .* (n.p., 1541); idem, *Warhafftiger, bestendiger, vnnd gegründter Gegenbericht, vnd verantwortung . . . So der Römischen Keyserli-chen Maiestat, auff yetzigem Reichstag zu Regenspurg, wider eynen truck den Hertzog Heinrich von Braunschweig, vnder eynem Titel, eynes fürtragens, Supplication vnd erbeitens, Welches er für der Römischen Keyserlichẽ Maies-tat, verschiener weil zu Regenspurg, wider die Chur vnd Fürsten, Sachsen vnnd Hessen, gethon zuhaben, vermeynlich für gibt, Vngeachtet des Keyserli-chen zwischen dem Landtgrafen zu Hessen, vnnd jme gebottenen still vnd fridstandts, hat auffgehn lassen, vberreycht, vnd zugestellt worden ist* (Mar-burg, 1541).

36. Anon., *Evangelische, Brüderliche, getrewe vnterrichtung, durch Meis-ter Justinum warsager Nachrichtern zu Warheitsbrun, jnn einem Sendbrieffe, dem Landgrafen von Hessen beschen, belangendt, enthaltung des viertelmessi-gen Verreterischen fleisch Böswichts, Hansen Kochs, vnd andere vnthaten, damit derselbig Landgrafe beschreiet vnd berüchtigt ist* (n.p., 1541).

37. [Johann Lening], *Expostulation vnd strafschriffe Satane des Fürsten diser welt mit hertzog Heintzen von Braunschweig, seinem geschworen diener vnd lieben getrewen, dass er sich vnbillicher weise, in der person eins diebhenckers wider den Landtgrauen, nicht one mercklich nachteil seins reichs mit vngeschicktem liegen eingelassen habe* (Utopia, 1541); Anon., *DIALOGVS, Oder gesprech wider ein vermeinte, vngeschichte Expostulation oder Straffschrifft Satane des Fürsten dieser welt mit Hertzogen Heinrichen zu Braunschweig, aus beuelch des Landgrauen zu Hessen gehalten* (n.p., 1541).

38. Anon., *Newe Zeitung. Zween Sendbrieff, An Hansen Worst, zu Wol-fenbuttel geschrieben. Der Erste. Vom Lucifer. Der Ander. Vom Diebhencker zu Wolffenbuttel* (n.p. 1541); Anon., *Drey newe vnd lustige Gespreche. Wie der Wolff, so etwan, doch nicht lang, ein mensch, Heintz*

*Wolfenbüttel genant, jnn abrund der Hellen verdampt say. Rheimweis, aus dem Latein inns Deutsch geben* (n.p., 1541) [reproduced in Schade, *Satiren und Pasquille*, 1:99-144]; and Anon., *Newe zeittung von Rom, Woher das Mordbrennen kome?* (n.p., 1541) [reproduced in Schade, *Satiren und Pasquille*, 1:210-14].

39. [Nicholas von Amsdorf], *Ein Getichte darin angezeigt wird, Wie from Hertzog Heinrich von Braunschweig, Vnd wie böse die Luterischen sein* (n.p., n.d.); Anon., *Contrarium wider ein erlogen schandgedicht welchs newlich im Druck wider Hertzog Heinrichen zu Braunschweig . . . vnd die Römischen Katholischen Kirchen ausgegossen ist* (n.p., n.d.). Rochus von Liliencron, ed., *Die historischen Volkslieder der Deutschen vom 13. bis 16. Jahrhundert* (Leipzig, 1869; Hildesheim, 1966), 4:176n2, argues for a publication date of 1541. Weller, *Annalen der Poetischen National-Literatur,* 1, nos. 156 and 160, give 1542 as a date without further explanation.

40. A number of the songs and poems have been republished. See Oskar L.B. Wolff, ed., *Sammlung historischer Volkslieder und Gedichte der Deutschen* (Stuttgart-Tübingen, 1830), pp. 115-37; Karl Gödeke, ed., "Gedichte auf Heinrich den Jüngern," *Zeitschrift des historischen Vereins für Niedersachsen* (1850):1-116, (1852):154-64; Liliencron, *Die historischen Volkslieder*, 4:170-200, 264-90. For other similar publications, see the bibliographies cited in note 5.

41. WA 51:466.

42. *Duplicae*, p. Aij(v).

43. *Duplicae*, p. Aiij.

44. E.g., *Duplicae*, pp. Riij and B.

45. *Duplicae*, p. D(v). See also p. Liv(v).

46. *Duplicae*, p. Aiv(v).

47. WA 51:471.

48. WA 51:471f.

49. WA 51:552.

50. *Duplicae*, p. Nij(v).

51. *Duplicae*, p. Kiij.

52. *Duplicae*, p. Zij(v).

53. WA 51:476-98.

54. WA 51:503f.

55. See, e.g., WA 51:553.

56. *Duplicae*, p. Tiv.

57. *Duplicae*, p. Jiv(v).

58. Heinrich, duke of Braunschweig-Wolfenbüttel, *Dritte . . . Antwort*, p. X(v).

59. *Duplicae*, p. K(v).

60. *Duplicae*, pp. K(v)-Kij.

61. WA 51:547-49.

62. WA 51:550.

63. Ibid.

64. WA 51:548.

65. See note 47.
66. WA 51:499.
67. See notes 49, 54, and 68.
68. WA 51:561f.
69. See Mark U. Edwards, Jr., *Luther and the False Brethren* (Stanford, 1975), p. 202.
70. WABr 9:366.
71. WABr 9:330.
72. Mentz, *Johann Friedrich*, 2:306.
73. Rockwell, *Die Doppelehe*, p. 106n1.
74. E.g., *Verantwortung*, pp. B(v), Biv(v), Cij, Dij, Jiij, Nij.
75. E.g., *Verantwortung*, pp. Biij(v), Jiv, Miij(v), Nij.
76. *Verantwortung*, pp. Biv, C, Cij(v), G, E(v)-Eij.
77. See notes 18 and 32.
78. See *Verantwortung*, p. Bij.
79. *Quadruplicae*, pp. Aij-Aiv(v).
80. *Quadruplicae*, pp. B(v), Cij(v), Diij, Gij(v), K, Kiij(v).
81. *Quadruplicae*, pp. Niij-Niij(v).
82. *Quadruplicae*, pp. Miv-Miv(v).
83. See notes 37 and 39.
84. Schade, *Satiren und Pasquille*, 1:139.
85. See Koldewey, *Heinz von Wolfenbüttel*, pp. 36-42.
86. See notes 39 and 40. Graffiti are mentioned and reproduced in *Verantwortung*, p. Niij, and *Quadruplicae*, p. Kiv(v).
87. I am currently engaged in a study of official propaganda, 1521-1555. I will be using this dispute as one of my case studies. Another study of this controversy is under way at the University of Göttingen; see Petri, "Herzog Heinrich," p. 123.
88. WABr 10:88-91.
89. WABr 10:124f. Cf. WABr 10:97f., 135f., 138, 156.
90. WABr 10:135f.
91. For the following, see Koldewey, *Heinz von Wolfenbüttel*, pp. 54-58.
92. WABr 10:141.
93. WABr 10:454-56.
94. WABr 10:469-73.
95. WABr 10:473-76.
96. For the following, see Friedrich Koldewey, *Heinz von Wolfenbüttel*, pp. 58-66, Hermann Kunst, *Evangelischer Glaube und politische Verantwortung: Martin Luther als politischer Berater seiner Landesherrn und seine Teilnahme an den Fragen des öffentlichen Lebens* (Stuttgart, 1977), pp. 375-97, and WA 54:374-82.
97. See WA 54:374-75.
98. WABr 11:223-25, and 234n4.
99. For the following, see WA 54:379-82. WABr 11:232-34.
100. WA 54:389-91.
101. WA 54:391.

102. WA 54:391.
103. WA 54:391-93.
104. WA 54:393-98.
105. WA 54:399-402.
106. WA 54:403-6.
107. WA 54:406-8.
108. WA 54:409-11.

## Chapter Eight

1. WA 54:206-99.
2. W2 17:956-98. Franz Lau and Ernst Bizer, *A History of the Reformation in Germany to 1555*, trans. by Brian A. Hardy (London,1969), pp. 184-86. Hubert Jedin, *A History of the Council of Trent* (London, 1957), 1:495-97.
3. WA 54:198; CR 5:655-66.
4. WA 54:198f.; CR 5:660-63.
5. For much of the following see WA 54:200-2.
6. WA 54:201; Georg Mentz, *Johann Friedrich der Grossmütige* (Jena, 1908), 3:594.
7. For example, his *Against the Bishop of Magdeburg, Cardinal Albrecht* (WA 50:395-431) caused some Protestant princes embarrassment, but see below. On this dispute see Hermann Kunst, *Evangelischer Glaube und politische Verantwortung: Martin Luther als politischer Berater seiner Landesherrn und seine Teilnahme an den Fragen des öffentlichen Lebens* (Stuttgart, 1977), pp. 329-49; H. G. Haile, *Luther: An Experiment in Biography* (New York, 1980), pp. 175-84; and my discussion below.
8. WABr 1:110-12. Kunst, *Evangelischer Glaube*, pp. 329-49.
9. WABr 2:421.
10. WA 18:408-11.
11. The treatise is in WA 23:402-31.
12. WA 30/2:397-412.
13. WA 30/3:400.
14. WA 30/3:402f. See above, ch. 3.
15. WA 50:429.
16. Ibid.
17. WABr 7:219, 368-71. See esp. WABr 7:370 lines 50-55.
18. Kunst, *Evangelischer Glaube*, esp. pp. 338 and 346. See also Haile, *Luther*, p. 181.
19. Georg Mentz, *Johann Friedrich der Grossmütige, 1503-1554* (1903-08), 2:508ff.; Eike Wolgast, *Die Wittenberger Theologie und die Politik der evangelischen Stände* (Gütersloh, 1977), pp. 253-62.
20. WABr 7:68-69.
21. Mentz, *Johann Friedrich,* 2:509.
22. For the following, see WA 50:387-92.

23. WABr 7:202f.
24. WA 50:389.
25. WABr 7:216-9.
26. WABr 7:219.
27. WABr 7:368-71.
28. Mentz, *Johann Friedrich,* 2:511.
29. WABr 7:457, 464f., 511-13, 513f., 526, 553f. Cf. WABr 7:351.
30. WABr 7:612n3.
31. WABr 8:20f., 254f., 299f.
32. WABr 8:255.
33. Mentz, *Johann Friedrich,* 2:512; WABr 7:610-11.
34. Mentz, *Johann Friedrich,* 2:510-13.
35. WABr 7:610-11.
36. Mentz, *Johann Friedrich,* 2:514-16.
37. WA 50:348-51, esp. 351.
38. WA 50:349.
39. Mentz, *Johann Friedrich,* 2:515 and 515n1.
40. Ibid.
41. Mentz, *Johann Friedrich,* 2:516-17.
42. WA 50:393f.
43. WA 50:426f.
44. WATR 4:414.
45. On the whole Naumburg issue, see Peter Brunner, *Nikolaus von Amsdorf als Bischof von Naumburg* (Gütersloh, 1961).
46. For the following, see WABr 9:310-20.
47. I am following the order of documents suggested by Brunner, *Nikolaus von Amsdorf,* pp. 24-31.
48. CR 4:683-89, line 14. For a much fuller analysis of this and the following documents, see Brunner, *Nikolaus von Amsdorf,* pp. 31-50.
49. WABr 9:539f.
50. Enders 14:101-5.
51. CR 4:689, line 15-694.
52. See Enders 14:105-8.
53. CR 4:697-99.
54. See Brunner, *Nikolaus von Amsdorf,* pp. 43-50.
55. See WABr 9:599-601, esp. 601 bottom.
56. WABr 9:597-99.
57. WABr 9:598f.
58. Brunner, *Nikolaus von Amsdorf,* p. 60.
59. See chapter 2, preceding.
60. For the following, see WA 53:224-29.
61. WABr 9:605f., WABr 10:16.
62. WA 53:231-60.
63. WA 53:232.
64. WA 53:233f.
65. WA 53:234-242.

66. WA 53:248-51.
67. WA 53:256-59. In the concluding paragraphs of the treatise Luther took brief notice of several of Pflug's recent treatises attacking the proceedings in Naumburg. He reserved the right, however, to issue later a longer reply once he saw what else the Catholics produced (WA 53:259f.). Bibliography on WA 53:259n3 cites several of Pflug's treatises.
68. See Brunner, *Nikolaus von Amsdorf*, pp. 54f.
69. Brunner, *Nikolaus von Amsdorf*, p. 94.
70. Ibid.
71. See note 2.
72. W2 16:999-1012. *Concilium Tridentinum: Diariorum, actorum, epistolarum, tractatuum nova collectio* (Freiburg, 1901ff.), 4:364-73.
73. WA 54:197f.
74. WABr 11:12. Cf. WABr 11:30.
75. W2 16:1012-19.
76. See notes 3 and 4.
77. WA 54:198f. CR 5:660-63.
78. WABr 11:58. WA 54:200.
79. WA 54:206-28.
80. WA 54:228-31.
81. WA 54:235-39.
82. WA 54:244.
83. WA 54:245-49.
84. WA 54:260-73.
85. WA 54:273-82.
86. WA 54:285-95.
87. WA 54:243.
88. WA 54:242f.
89. WA 54:260, 288.
90. WABr 11:71. WA 54:200-2 examines the reaction.
91. WA 54:353. See also WA 54:356-58, and especially the discussion of WABr 11:115 and 120, which refer not to these cartoons but to a different antipapal cartoon by Cranach.
92. WA 54:200.
93. WABr 11:71.
94. WABr 11:58. WABr 11:54 describes the landgrave's letter of transmittal but, for some reason, does not reproduce the actual text!
95. WA 54:188-94.
96. On the whole question of the treatise's translator and the history of its publication, see WA 54:300-7.
97. WA 54:307-9, 310-45.
98. For the following, see WA 54:412-25.
99. CR 5:758. Cited in WA 54:415.
100. WA 54:425-30.
101. WABr 11:177.
102. WABr 11:265f.

103. WA 54:444-58.

## Epilogue

1. Eike Wolgast, *Die Wittenberger Theologie und die Politik der evangelischen Stände* (Gütersloh, 1977), p. 298.

# Index

# Index

Braunschweig, city of, 144–46, 153, 158–59; city council of, 146, 148
Braunschweig-Wolfenbüttel, and League of Schmalkalden, 158–62
*Brief Reply to Duke Georg's Next Book* (1533), 60–63
Brück, Gregor, 166; and Duke Georg, 44, 53, 57, 63–64; and Braunschweig-Wolfenbüttel, 160–61; and Luther's later polemics, 160–61, 163, 168–69, 185; and the bishopric of Naumburg, 173, 175
Bucer, Martin, 60, 155; in Frankfurt, 33; and the Jews, 135
Buda, 98, 102
Bugenhagen, Johann, 2, 53, 111, 159, 173
Bullinger, Heinrich: his *True Confession*, 135; on Luther's polemics, 135, 154–55
Burgos, Paul of, 124, 128, 130

Cajetan, Thomas, cardinal, 70
Capito, Wolfgang, 124
Carafa, John (later Pope Paul IV), 88n
Catholic League, 144, 161
Chalcedon, Council of, 94
Charlemagne, 87
Charles V, emperor: and the League of Schmalkalden, 25, 33–34, 34n, 90, 163, 183; and a council, 73–76, 183–86; and Francis I of France, 93, 102, 160, 183; and the Turks, 102, 163, 183; and Braunschweig-Wolfenbüttel, 144, 160; and Naumburg, 174

Chrosner, Alexius, 65n
Chrysostom, John, 81–83
Church, territorial, 207
Clement VII, pope, 74–76
Cölln, 46, 54, 57
Cochlaeus, Johann: on Luther's language, 30, 58–60, 66; his *Honorable and Thorough Apology* (1533), 38–39, 57–61, 65; replying to Luther's polemics, 38–39, 57–61, 65, 79, 81, 83, 143; Luther on, 45–46, 61–63; his *True History of Master John Hus* (1537), 81
Cologne, 73
*Concerning the Captured Heinrich* (1545), 18, 160–62, 201
*Concerning the Three Hierarchies* (1539), 4, 33–34, 179
*Confession Concerning the Lord's Supper* (1528), 58
Constance, 159
Constance, Council of, 68–69, 75–81, 88
Constantine, Donation of, 83–84
Constantinople, Council of, 94
Contarini, Caspar, 88n

*Contrarium Against a Lying Poem*, 149
Cordatus, Cornelius, 160
Cortese, Gregory, 88n, 183
Council: Luther on, 4, 68–96, 185n, 185–86, 206; Duke Georg on, 40; Luther on power of, 70–73, 94–95; definitions of, 71–72, 74; in Germany, 73–75
Crabbe, Peter, 94
Cranach, Lucas, woodcuts by, 4, 189–99
Crepy, Peace of (1544), 160
Crescenzio, cardinal, 183
Cronberg, Hartmuth von, 41
Crusade, Luther on, 99, 112

Daniel, book of, Luther on, 97, 100–101, 112
*Dialogus* (1541), 148
Dietrich, Veit, 201
Dolschtz, Hans, 150
Döring, Matthew, 124
Dresden, 39, 49, 53, 63–64
Düring, Christian, 52–53

Eck, Johann, 86, 143; his *Refutation of a Jew-Book* (1542), 119–20, 135
Eichstätt, bishop of, 120n
Eisleben, 202
Emser, Hieronymus, 45–46, 143; his version of Luther's New Testament, 41–42
Ephesus, Council of, 94
Erasmus, 40
Erfurt, printing in, 21
Erikson, Erik, 8
Ernst, duke of Braunschweig and Lüneburg, 146, 148
Ernst, duke of Saxony, 181
Ernst, elector of Saxony, 39
Eusebius, *Ecclesiastical History*, 94
Eustathius, bishop of Sebaste, 88
*Example How to Consecrate a Proper Bishop, An* (1542), 164, 180–82
*Explanation of the Ninety-Five Theses* (1518), 98
*Exsurge, Domine* (1520), 70–71, 98

Faber, Johann, 45
Farnese, Alessandro. See Paul III, pope.
Ferdinand, archduke of Austria, king of Hungary, 42, 121, 144, 158, 199; and the Turks, 98, 101–2
Ferrara-Florence, Council of, 75
Fifth Lateran Council, 89
France, 75–76, 85–86
Francis I, king of France, and Charles V, 93, 102, 160; and a council, 75–76, 85–86, 93

# Index

# Index

Library of Congress Cataloging in Publication Data

Edwards, Mark U., Jr.
   Luther's last battles.

   Includes bibliographical references and index.
   1. Luther, Martin, 1483–1546. I. Title.
BR326.8.E38   1983        284.1'092'4        82–72363
ISBN 0–08014–1564–0